4 —

Ancient Egyptian Hieroglyphs

A Practical Guide

Janice Kamrin

illustrations by Gustavo Camps

Harry N. Abrams, Inc., Publishers

To my husband

PROJECT MANAGER: Eric Himmel
DESIGNER: Gustavo Camps
PRODUCTION MANAGER: Maria Pia Gramaglia

Library of Congress Cataloging-in-Publication Data

Kamrin, Janice, 1966-
Ancient Egyptian hieroglyphs : a practical guide / Janice Kamrin ; illustrations by Gustavo Camps.
p. cm.
Includes bibliographical references and index.
ISBN 0-8109-4961-X
1. Egyptian language--Writing, Hieroglyphic. I. Title.

PJ1097.K28 2004
493'.182421--dc22

Published in 2004 by Harry N. Abrams, Incorporated, New York

Printed and bound in China
10 9 8 7 6 5 4 3 2 1

ABRAMS
Harry N. Abrams, Inc.
100 Fifth Avenue
New York, N.Y. 10011
www.abramsbooks.com

Abrams is a subsidiary of

LA MARTINIÈRE GROUPE

Table of Contents

ACKNOWLEDGMENTS

The majority of this book has been written in Egypt, with the help and support of friends and colleagues both here and back in the States. I would like to thank Zahi Hawass, who taught me my first hieroglyphs, and who has encouraged and supported me from the very beginning. I honor his passion for and dedication to Egyptology and Egypt, and appreciate his constant generosity and friendship enormously. I wish also to thank Bruni Ridgway, whose enthusiasm and energy for archaeology is always infectious, and David O'Connor, whose wisdom and guidance have been of inestimable value. I apologize to my language professor, David Silverman for neglecting, for the practical purposes of this book, some of the important grammatical precepts he taught me.

Salima Ikram has helped and encouraged me in every way throughout the writing of this book; her friendship and support are jewels beyond price. I could not have managed without the generous advice of Lisa Sabbahy, whose experience and expertise have been critical in shaping this book into its present form. Janet Richards, whose friendship has seen me through every major life crisis since our graduate school days, has once again come through with flying colors, arriving in Egypt at a crucial moment and spending much of her precious time here reading and editing this manuscript. Jennifer Wegner has graciously taken time from her own work and her adorable baby to do a final check of my work, and Dr. Holeil Ghaly has taken the time from his busy schedule to get the manuscript to Jennifer (not an easy feat). Any errors or misrepresentations are entirely my responsibility.

Thanks also to my "book party" crowd, whose input, from feedback to proofreading, to major suggestions for improvement, came at a critical juncture: Kenneth Garrett; Kelly and Michael Zaug; Christine End; Ian Brier; and Peter Fiske. Additional and heartfelt thanks go also to Ken for allowing us to use one of his exquisite photographs on the cover of the book, and as the basis for one of the illustrations. Mom and Audrey, thank you for slogging through an early version of my manuscript, and also thanks to Dad for the much-needed and greatly enjoyed vacation. Phyllis, Elijah, and Michael, I hope you can come and visit next time!

Eric Himmel at Harry N. Abrams has believed in this book from the beginning; it would not exist without him. Thank you, Eric. Thanks also to Samantha Topol and Deborah Aaronson, who have helped to steer us through the publishing rapids.

Last, but very far from least, my eternal gratitude to my family: to my husband Gustavo, who illustrated and designed this entire book and made me my very own hieroglyphic font; and to Omar, who put up with Mommy working on her "blah, blah, slowpoke thing" instead of playing with him. Thank you both for your patience and understanding.

Introduction

The ancient Egyptian hieroglyphic script is one of the most elegant writing systems ever created. Hieroglyphs were used primarily for monumental inscriptions, carved carefully and with exquisite detail onto the walls of tombs and temples and then painted in vibrant colors, or inscribed on artifacts such as statues, offering tables, stelae (slabs of stone or wood), and coffins. Birds, fish, people, plants, baskets, architectural elements—all these and more adorn Egyptian objects and monuments, creating beauty and conveying clear messages to those who can read them. The ability to understand these inscriptions as you tour a great museum collection, or even better, visit Egypt, will enhance your experience enormously.

In this book, I will give you the information you need to decipher a wide range of inscriptions, including the sort of inscription you see on the facing page, which comes from a coffin in the Egyptian Museum, Cairo. Once you have finished this volume, you will be able to enter a tomb and decipher the names of the people buried inside, and even know something about what they did for a living. You will be able to read some of the captions on the scenes that cover the walls—brief descriptions of the activities that are represented, as well as the jokes or warnings the workers call out to one another while they butcher a cow, fish in the marshes, or build a boat. By the time you have finished this book, you will be able to decipher parts of the autobiographies—fascinating tales that informed the literate passer-by of the most important events of a well-lived life—that adorn some elite tombs. In temples, you will be able to identify the gods successfully, study a long list of ancient monarchs, and read some of the dialogue between kings and deities.

The Egyptians were fond of word play, and their artistic creations are full of symbolism linked to the written language. Many of the additional levels of meaning embedded within Egyptian art will be illuminated by your understanding of hieroglyphs. It has been said that language provides a window into the soul, and with a basic mastery of the hieroglyphic script, you will increase your understanding a hundredfold of the extraordinary men and women who built one of the world's oldest civilizations.

Egyptian hieroglyphs first appeared in around 3250 B.C. They were originally used to write names and label various commodities, but soon developed to the point where they could be used to commemorate historical events. The first complex hieroglyphic texts appeared in the early Old Kingdom, around 2600 B.C. There are three phases of the language: Old Egyptian (around 2600 to 2100 B.C.); Middle Egyptian (around 2100 to 1300 B.C.); and Late Egyptian (around 1500 to 600 B.C.). Although Late Egyptian appeared as a spoken language early in the New Kingdom (around 1500 B.C.), it was rarely used for monumental hieroglyphic texts, and Middle Egyptian continued to be used in many contexts until the end of pharaonic history.

This book focuses on common signs, words, names, and phrases—the ones you are most likely to encounter as you tour a museum or an Egyptian site. An important part of what you will be learning here is pattern recognition—recognizing certain formulaic expressions, and using your more detailed knowledge of hieroglyphs to translate the specific vocabulary, including names and titles, which vary from text to text. You will learn some basic Middle Egyptian grammar as you go, but I will keep it simple, and teach you only what you need to know. You do not need to worry too much about the differences between the phases of the Egyptian language, as most of the material you will see here will work, on a practical level, for a large corpus of monumental texts.

A word to the wise: The more you memorize, the more successful you will be, but do not let this scare you off; you will have lots of help. Buy yourself a stack of 3 x 5 index cards, and make flash cards; this will help with memorization—just the act of drawing the glyphs will help you to internalize them. (I suggest keeping them on your breakfast table, by your bed, or wherever you spend bits of downtime here and there.) There are many exercises in the book, designed to reinforce what you have learned; doing these exercises will help you memorize signs and vocabulary, give you practice with recognizing patterns, and build your familiarity with the language. As you advance through this book, you will work with monuments often visited by tourists or key pieces found in major museums (primarily the Egyptian Museum in Cairo).

In the process of learning to read the language of the ancient Egyptians, you will also learn something about their lives. You will learn what each sign is meant to represent, apart from its phonetic (sound) value, which will provide you with general information about ancient Egypt. Study of frequently seen royal names leads you through a brief history of Egypt, while private titles provide you with a window onto social structure and administrative organization. Through the study of the basic offering prayer, you will gain some understanding of funerary and religious beliefs; and reading scene labels and captions will give you glimpses into the daily lives of these ancient people. Your understanding of hieroglyphs will open a door into the magic and mystery of ancient Egypt, and you will astonish your friends and traveling companions with what you learn along the way.

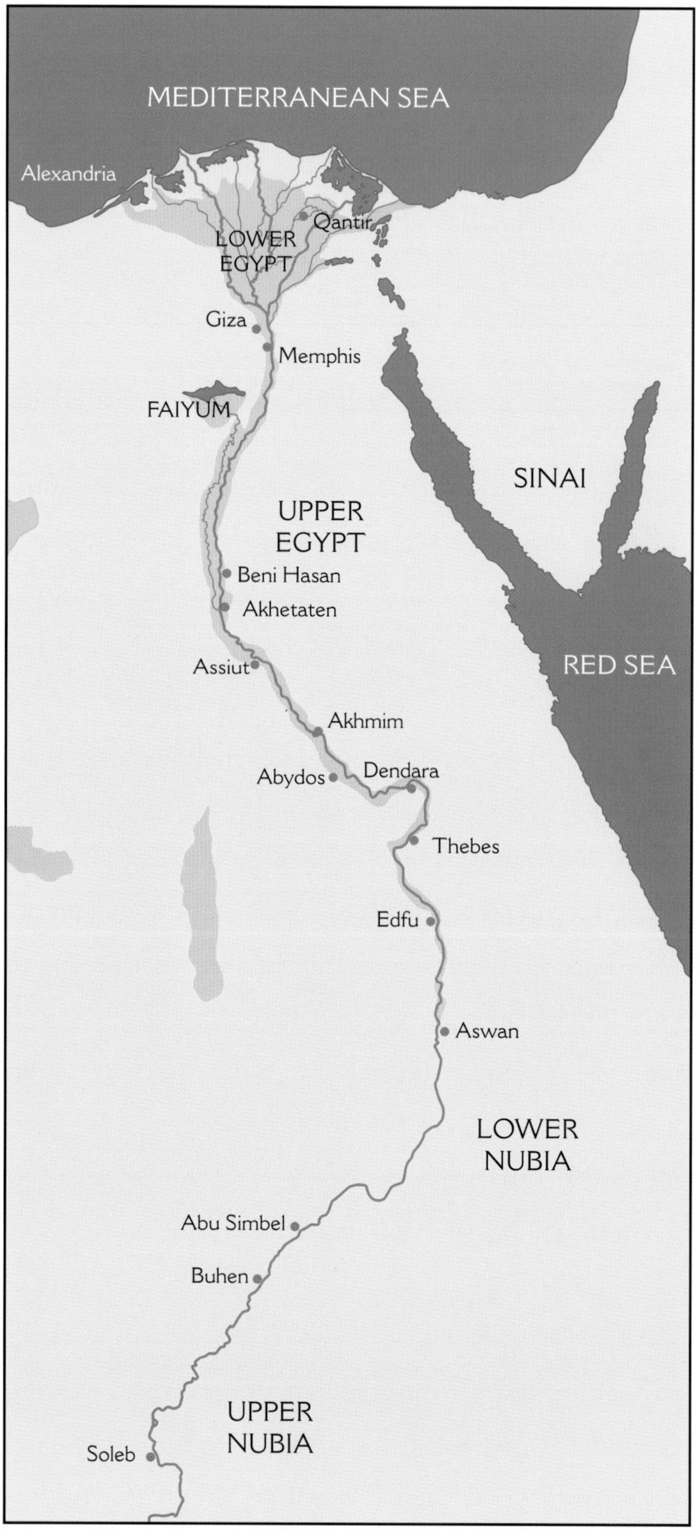
MEDITERRANEAN SEA
Alexandria
Qantir
LOWER EGYPT
Giza
Memphis
FAIYUM
SINAI
UPPER EGYPT
Beni Hasan
Akhetaten
Assiut
RED SEA
Akhmim
Abydos
Dendara
Thebes
Edfu
Aswan
LOWER NUBIA
Abu Simbel
Buhen
UPPER NUBIA
Soleb

Chapter I
The Egyptian Alphabet

In this chapter, you will learn the Egyptian alphabet. Memorizing these signs will give you a firm foundation on which to build your knowledge of hieroglyphs. As you progress through this chapter, you will begin to be able to read Egyptian names and will become familiar with some basic vocabulary words. You will also be introduced to some very basic grammar. Armed with this foundation, you will be able to interpret some commonly seen phrases and even translate some short sentences. Take your time with this chapter; really learning the alphabet, some additional hieroglyphs that act as labeling signs, and some basic vocabulary will get you off to an excellent start.

Lesson 1: Categories of Signs

Egyptian hieroglyphs fall into three basic categories: they can be sound signs ("phonograms"); they can be labeling signs ("determinatives"), which serve as clues to the meaning of the words they follow; and they can stand for entire words ("ideograms" or "logograms"). You do not need to memorize this information now, it is meant simply to orient you and prepare you for the material that follows. There are no exercises with this lesson.

Sound signs (phonograms) form the basis of the language. The most fundamental are the "uniliterals," signs that stand for one sound. These function like the letters of our alphabet. For example, the owl, 𓅓, is the equivalent of *m* in English. "Biliteral" signs stand for two sounds. An example of this is the sign, 𓉐, which represents the plan of a simple house as seen from above and stands for the two-sound combination *pr*. There are also "triliterals," such as 𓄤, *nfr*, and signs which stand for even more sounds.

Labeling signs, or determinatives, are silent, but give the reader clues to the meanings of the words they follow. For example, the sign  tells the reader that the word preceding it is a verb of motion. Thus the house plan, 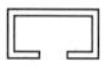, *pr*, by itself means simply "house"; with the walking legs after it, , it becomes a verb meaning "go forth."

Word signs (logograms or ideograms) can be (but do not have to be) distinguished by a single vertical stroke, which tells you that the sign is to be read as an entire word. Some of the same hieroglyphs used as sound signs are also used as word signs, and labeling signs can also stand alone as abbreviations for the words they normally follow. A good example of a word sign is the house plan, *pr*. If it is written like this: , you will know to translate it as a complete word, "house." If there is no stroke, and no determinative, you will usually read the sign as part of some other word, for example 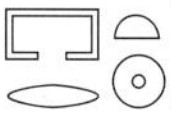, *prt,* one of the seasons of the Egyptian year. In both cases, the phonetic value of the sign is *pr*. An example of a labeling sign being used as an abbreviation is the word for oil, properly spelled 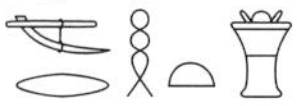, and having a phonetic value of *mrḥt* (the characters you see here in italics will be explained in Lesson 2) but often written just  (with the same phonetic value).

To review: There are three categories of signs in the ancient Egyptian hieroglyphic script:

1. Sound signs (phonograms); e.g. , with a phonetic value of *m*.

2. Labeling signs (determinatives), which have no phonetic value but give you information about the word they follow. An example of this is the walking legs, , which indicate a verb of motion.

3. Word signs (logograms or ideograms), such as , *pr,* meaning house, or  *mrḥt,* meaning "oil." Determinatives are often used alone as ideograms.

Lesson 2: Transliteration and Pronunciation

Twenty-four distinct sounds are represented by the signs of the Egyptian hieroglyphic system. Thirteen of these correspond to the sounds written by the English alphabet, such as "b," "p," and "m." Of the other eleven, seven are sounds that do not occur in English, and the other four must be represented in English by a combination of letters. For example, where English has one "h" sound, ancient Egyptian has four, each of which was pronounced slightly differently; where English must use two letters to represent the sound "sh," the ancient Egyptians could use a single sign, 𓈙. However, as you will see, you do not really need to worry about the actual sounds, as you will not be learning to speak ancient Egyptian.

Egyptologists use a special alphabet to transcribe the sounds represented by hieroglyphic signs. There are twenty-four characters used for transcribing texts (the technical name for this is transliteration), representing the twenty-four sounds known from ancient Egyptian, and they are for the most part exactly the same as our English alphabet: *b, p, f, m*, etc. There are nine special characters, such as *ꜣ, ḥ,* and *ṯ*. It is important, and it is not difficult, to learn these special characters.

When translating a text, you should first write down the sign in these special transliteration characters, and then translate the words they form. It is standard practice to use italics when printing transliteration characters, as this helps distinguish them from regular text.

Two more important points: First, the ancient Egyptians did not write vowels. This is not so unusual: some modern languages (such as Hebrew and Arabic) are written mostly without vowels. It would have been possible for a reader familiar with the language to figure out from the context which words were meant by which groups of signs. This is not as hard as it sounds: yw cn prbbly rd ths sntnc wtht trbl. It's even easier in ancient Egyptian, because of the labeling signs (determinatives). For example, in English the words "read" and "road" look the same if you write them without vowels. The Egyptians might have added this sign 𓏛 (representing a roll of papyrus, the material on which ancient Egyptian books were written) at the end of "rd = read" and 𓈐 (a depiction of a road flanked by bushes—they really do make it very easy sometimes) at the end of "rd = road" for clarification. The lack of vowels is not something that will affect your work here; it is just something of which you should be aware.

Second, we do not necessarily know exactly what sounds the written characters actually made. Ancient Egyptian is a "dead" language, not spoken today, so many of the consonant sounds have been reconstructed by comparing ancient Egyptian words and names to their Coptic (the liturgical language used by the Egyptian Christian church) descendents, and to Egyptian words found written in other ancient languages. In other words, being able to read and translate glyphs does not mean that we know exactly how the spoken language sounded. But again, since you are learning to read the language and not to speak it, this will not get in your way.

A distinguished Egyptologist named Dows Dunham, who worked at the Museum of Fine Arts in Boston, told the following story in his memoirs: One afternoon, he was in his office, working on the translation of a papyrus, when someone knocked on his door. "Come in," he called, and a man appeared and introduced himself as the god Amen-Re (king of the Egyptian pantheon). This was rather unusual, but you do get used to this sort of thing if you are an Egyptologist. Mr. Dunham invited Amen-Re to sit down, and they chatted for a while. Then Mr. Dunham picked up the papyrus he was translating (a copy, not the real thing, which would have been too delicate to handle) and said, "Well, you know we can read and understand these texts, but we don't know what they sounded like. Would you mind reading this out loud to me?" Amen-Re took the papyrus, stared at it, and then turned back to Mr. Dunham. He looked down at the papyrus again, hesitated a moment, and then handed it back, saying, "I'm sorry, but it's been a long time."

And on that note, it is time to start learning the basic signs and concepts that will enable you to read, if not speak, the language of the ancient Egyptians!

Lesson 3: The Egyptian Alphabet

There are twenty-four signs that comprise the basic hieroglyphic alphabet, plus five additional signs that are used as variations for certain of these basic signs. Once you have memorized the Egyptian alphabetic signs and their transliterations, you will have under your belt all the known Egyptian sounds. You will know all of the special characters you will need to transliterate inscriptions, and will also be able to write your friends' names in hieroglyphs (this is a great party trick). The basic sounds of Egyptian have been arranged in a standard order, which is how you will find them in hieroglyphic dictionaries. The word list at the back of this book is arranged in this order, and if you continue with your study of hieroglyphs, you will need to know it. The sequence of sounds will be repeated at the top of the pages of the word list at the back to help you if you need to look up words.

Egyptologists have adopted certain conventions in order to pronounce this unpronounceable language. The ancient Egyptian writing system does include sounds that are called "semi-vowels." These function something like English "y" and "w," and Egyptologists tend to use these as vowels for pronunciation. For example, the name of the king who built the Great Pyramid at Giza was . You can transliterate this as *ḫwfw*, and write or pronounce it in English as Khufu. (Note that the *ḫ* is a special transliteration character that gets turned into "kh" to put the name into English.) The other semi-vowels are treated similarly.

Another convention used to help us with the pronunciation of Egyptian words is the insertion of "e's" between consonants. For example, a royal name common during one period of Egyptian history can be transliterated as *snwsrt*. This can come out in English as Senwosret (e's between some of the consonants and the semi-vowel used as a "w") or as Senusert (e's between some consonants and the semi-vowel turned into a "u"). It is not that difficult, and you will see how this works as you go along. One note, however: Egyptologists like to disagree with one another, and there are many different systems used; for example, you might see the name of an important god written as Amon, Amun, or Amen. In this book, I will teach you some standard conventions, and then stick to these as closely as possible.

You are now ready to learn the Egyptian alphabet. Again, it is essential to memorize these signs and their transliterations. The proper transliteration for each sign is given, then a brief description of what the sign is thought to represent, and finally, the practical equivalent for the sign—the English letter or letters that can be used to write Egyptian words and especially names. Read the entries for all the signs, and then practice recognizing them, transliterating them, and using their functional equivalents in the exercises that follow.

The Egyptian Alphabet

Sign	Trans.	Equiv.	Sign	Trans.	Equiv.	Sign	Trans.	Equiv.
𓄿	ꜣ	a	𓅓 or 𓐝	*m*	m	𓈙	*š*	sh
𓇋	*ỉ*	i	𓈖 or 𓋔	*n*	n	𓈎	*ḳ*	q
𓇋𓇋 or 𓏭	*y*	y	𓂋	*r*	r	𓎡	*k*	k
𓂝	ꜥ	e	𓉔	*h*	h	𓎼	*g*	g
𓅱 or 𓏲	*w*	w,u,o	𓎛	*ḥ*	h	𓏏	*t*	t
𓃀	*b*	b	𓐍	*ḫ*	kh	𓍿	*ṯ*	tj
𓊪	*p*	p	𓄡	*ẖ*	kh	𓂧	*d*	d
𓆑	*f*	f	𓊃 or 𓋴	*s*	s	𓆓	*ḏ*	dj

List of Alphabetic Signs

Hieroglyph: 𓄿

Transliteration: ꜣ

What is it? This is an Egyptian vulture. This and the next six signs are all semi-vowels—you get the tricky ones first.

Practical Equivalent: Use here for "a" as in asp (the snake that bit Cleopatra). Remember that this is only a practical equivalent, not the way the Egyptians would have used it. This convention will simply help you create English versions of Egyptian names (and write English names in hieroglyphs!).

Hieroglyph: 𓇋

Transliteration: *ỉ* (a semi-vowel)

What is it? This is a reed leaf. Reeds grew in the marshes at the edges of the Nile Valley and in the Delta.

Practical Equivalent: For the purposes of this book, use as "i" as in Imhotep (the architect of the first pyramid, the Step Pyramid of Djoser).

Hieroglyph: 𓇌 or 𓏭

Transliteration: *y*

What is it? Two reed leaves, or two diagonal strokes.

Practical Equivalent: Use for "y" as in Pepy (an Egyptian king).

Hieroglyph: 𓂝

Transliteration: ꜥ

What is it? An outstretched arm and hand.

Practical Equivalent: For the purposes of this book, replace it in the English versions of words with "e."

Hieroglyph: 𓅱 or 𓏲

Transliteration: *w*

What is it? The first is a quail chick. Quails were a favorite game bird, and tomb scenes show them being trapped in the fields during the spring harvest. The alternative sign is a coiled rope.

Practical Equivalent: Use this in the English version of names as either a "w," an "o" or a "u."

Hieroglyph: 𓃀

Transliteration: *b*

What is it? A human foot and the attached lower leg (note that if you see a leg with the knee and thigh attached, it is a different sign).

Practical Equivalent: Use as a "b" as in bark (a special boat for gods).

Hieroglyph: □

Transliteration: *p*

What is it? This may look like a simple square, but it is actually the top of a stool, seen from above. Carved and painted examples of this hieroglyph can be quite beautiful, and the interior detail tells us that stools were often made with woven seats.

Practical Equivalent: "P" as in papyrus.

Hieroglyph: 

Transliteration: *f*

What is it? This is a horned viper, a dangerous snake still found in the Egyptian desert. Horned vipers travel in pairs, and can jump high enough to bite someone on horseback. Their venom is extraordinarily poisonous.

Practical Equivalent: Use for "f" as in felucca (you will still see these boats with trapezoidal sails on the Nile).

Hieroglyph:  or 

Transliteration: *m*

What is it? The first is an owl; no one really knows what the alternative represents.

Practical Equivalent: "M" as in Memphis (an ancient capital of Egypt).

.

Hieroglyph:  or 

Transliteration: *n*

What is it? The first sign is a wave of water. The use of zigzag lines to indicate water is seen in paintings and reliefs. The alternative is the red crown of Lower Egypt. Egypt was divided into two geographical regions: Upper Egypt—the Nile Valley south of Memphis (the Cairo area), and Lower Egypt—the delta area between Memphis and the Mediterranean (the Nile runs from south to north, so things get a bit topsy-turvy). According to the ancient Egyptian version of history (which does not exactly correspond with the archaeological evidence, but is based on reality to some extent), there were originally two kingdoms, one in Upper Egypt and one in Lower Egypt. An Upper Egyptian king named Menes united the two kingdoms and became the first king of the Two Lands, the first true ruler of Egypt. Throughout history, kings could wear the red crown (𓋔) or the white crown (𓋑) of Upper Egypt, or they could wear both combined (𓋖) as king of a united Egypt.

Practical Equivalent: "N" as in Nile.

Hieroglyph: 𓂋

Transliteration: *r*

What is it? This is a mouth. In some examples, the lips are drawn clearly, while in others, this sign is represented by a simple shape such as is used here.

Practical Equivalent: Use for "r" as in Re (the name of the sun god of the ancient Egyptians). When writing English names in hieroglyphs, it can also be used as an "l".

Hieroglyph: 𓉔

Transliteration: *h* (1st h)

What is it? The plan of a courtyard, seen from above.

Practical Equivalent: "H" as in house.

Hieroglyph: 𓎛

Transliteration: *ḥ* (referred to as 2nd h)

What is it? The "second h" is a twisted rope, probably of the sort that was used as the wick for a lamp.

Practical Equivalent: Use as "h" as in hawk. (In reality, this was probably an "h" sound made in the back of the throat. But remember, you do not really need to worry about the sounds, just recognize the sign and transliterate it correctly.)

Hieroglyph: 𓐍

Transliteration: *ḫ* (known as 3rd h)

What is it? This is a very mysterious sign, and no one is quite sure what it is supposed to represent. The best guess is that it is a placenta, although real placentas are not usually round.

Practical Equivalent: Use for "kh," as in Khufu. (This seems to have been some sort of a gentle, back-of-the throat "h" sound, like the Scottish "loch.")

Hieroglyph: 𓄡

Transliteration: *ẖ* (known as 4th h)

What is it? The "fourth h" represents the belly and udder of an animal, probably a cow or goat.

Practical Equivalent: Use this also as "kh," as in Khety, the name of several kings who ruled only part of Egypt. (This may be about the same as the third h, but followed by a "y" sound.)

Hieroglyph: 𓊃 or 𓋴

Transliteration: *s*

What is it? The first is the bolt of a door; the second is a folded bolt of cloth.

Practical Equivalent: Use for "s" as in sand.

Hieroglyph: 𓈙

Transliteration: *š*

What is it? This is a pool of water. In some really nice inscriptions, the Egyptians drew ripples across its surface.

Practical Equivalent: Use for "sh" as in *shawabti* (statuettes buried with the dead to do their work for them in the afterlife).

Hieroglyph: 𓈎

Transliteration: *ḳ*

What is it? This is a cutaway view of a hill.

Practical Equivalent: Use for "q" as in queen.

Hieroglyph: 𓎡

Transliteration: *k*

What is it? This is a wicker basket with a handle.

Practical Equivalent: Use for "k" as in king.

Hieroglyph: 𓎼

Transliteration: *g*

What is it? This represents a pottery stand in which a jar would have been set. (Many Egyptian jars had rounded or pointed bottoms, so had to be put into stands so that they would not tip over.)

Practical Equivalent: Use for "g" as in grave.

Hieroglyph: 𓏏

Transliteration: t

What is it? A loaf of bread. Bread was a major staple of the Egyptian diet. It came in many shapes and sizes, and was much denser than the light and fluffy bread we are used to today.

Practical Equivalent: "T" as in Tutankhamen.

Hieroglyph: 𓍿

Transliteration: *ṯ*

What is it? This is a hobble, made of rope, which would have been used to keep animals under control; similar ones are still used in Egypt today.

Practical Equivalent: Egyptologists use "tj" when turning this into English. (You will see "th" in some books; "tj" is the more current version.)

Hieroglyph: 𓂧

Transliteration: *d*

What is it? This is a human hand.

Practical Equivalent: Use this for "d" as in Delta.

Hieroglyph: 𓆓

Transliteration: *ḏ*

What is it? This is a cobra.

Practical Equivalent: Use for "dj" as in Djoser (an important early king of Egypt).

The Egyptian Alphabet (Repeated)

Sign	Trans.	Equiv.	Sign	Trans.	Equiv.	Sign	Trans.	Equiv.
𓄿	ꜣ	a	𓅓 or 𓐝	*m*	m	𓈙	*š*	sh
𓇋	*ỉ*	i	𓈖 or 𓋔	*n*	n	𓈎	*ḳ*	q
𓇌 or 𓏭	*y*	y	𓂋	*r*	r	𓎡	*k*	k
𓂝	ꜥ	e	𓉔	*h*	h	𓎼	*g*	g
𓅱 or 𓏲	*w*	w,u,o	𓎛	*ḥ*	h	𓏏	*t*	t
𓃀	*b*	b	𓐍	*ḫ*	kh	𓍿	*ṯ*	tj
𓊪	*p*	p	𓄡	*ẖ*	kh	𓂧	*d*	d
𓆑	*f*	f	𓊃 or 𓋴	*s*	s	𓆓	*ḏ*	dj

Special Transliteration Signs: Here is a brief review of the special signs used for transliteration, and how you should use them in the exercises.

ꜣ (𓄿) = English a

ỉ (𓇋) = English i

y (𓇌 OR 𓏭) = English y

ꜥ (𓂝) = English e

w (𓅱 or 𓏲) = English w, u, or o

ḥ (𓎛) = English h

ḫ (𓐍) = English kh

ẖ (𓄡) = English kh

š (𓈙) = English sh

ḳ (𓈎) = English q

ṯ (𓍿) = English tj

ḏ (𓆓) = English dj

Exercise 1: The Alphabet

This first exercise is a simple drill. Here are the alphabetic signs, in order; simply transliterate them and give their practical equivalent.

Example: 𓄿 . . ꜣ . . . . a

1. 𓇋 . . . .
2. 𓇋𓇋 . . . .
3. 𓏭 . . . .
4. 𓂝 . . . .
5. 𓅱 . . . .
6. 𓏲 . . . .
7. 𓃀 . . . .
8. 𓊪 . . . .
9. 𓆑 . . . .
10. 𓅓 . . . .
11. 𓐝 . . . .
12. 𓈖 . . . .
13. 𓋔 . . . .
14. 𓂋 . . . .
15. 𓉔 . . . .
16. 𓎛 . . . .
17. 𓐍 . . . .
18. 𓄡 . . . .
19. 𓊃 . . . .
20. 𓋴 . . . .
21. 𓈙 . . . .
22. 𓈎 . . . .
23. 𓎡 . . . .
24. 𓎼 . . . .
25. 𓏏 . . . .
26. 𓍿 . . . .
27. 𓂧 . . . .
28. 𓆓 . . . .

Lesson 4: Arrangement of Signs

Hieroglyphic texts are works of art that were planned and executed carefully for maximum aesthetic effect. They are often woven into the scenes that they are labeling or accompanying. They are therefore arranged very deliberately, with an eye to balance and symmetry.

Inscriptions could be written from right to left, from left to right, or from top to bottom. The preferred direction was from right to left. (However, most of the typeset glyphs in this book will be from left to right, to flow with the English text.) It will always be clear whether an inscription is to be read horizontally or vertically, but to figure out whether to move right or left, look at the animate creatures (birds, humans, fish, etc.) and read into their faces: if they are facing right, read right to left; if they are facing left, read left to right. I still remember my great amusement, early in my graduate school days, as I was watching an adventure movie that takes place in Egypt. The beautiful female archaeologist discovers an inscribed slab of stone, and carefully reads it out loud, pointing to the signs as she goes, absolutely backwards!

Here is an example of how this works, and how to figure it out: The English name Adam could be written in hieroglyphs in one of at least four ways:

1. Horizontally, left to right: 
2. Horizontally, right to left: 
3. Vertically, left to right: 
4. Vertically, right to left: 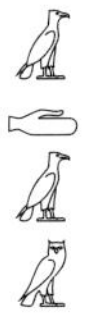

Within these four basic directions, signs are arranged carefully so that they fit the space in the most aesthetically pleasing fashion possible, based on regular rectangular groupings. For example, a tall vertical sign followed by two horizontal signs would be arranged like this: 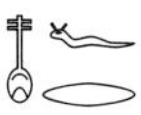, the tall sign followed by the first horizontal sign on top of the second. The size of particular signs can even be changed if it will help the arrangement. Adam might more likely be written, if working from left to right: 

Here are the two of the possible directions for another English name, Frank.

1. Horizontally from left to right: 
2. Horizontally from right to left: 

The vertical directions work similarly; the important concept to understand is that signs are arranged in rectangular groups. Typeset examples in this book will always be horizontal from left to right, and stacked within this orientation. When you get to the actual monuments, you will need to figure out which way to read the inscriptions.

Exercise 2: Names in English

This exercise, which consists of a series of English names, is designed to help you practice recognizing the alphabetic signs. After each name is a labeling sign: for each male name this is a seated man, ; for each female name this is a seated woman, . Transliterate each name accurately, and then turn it into English. Remember that, for the purposes of this exercise, the mouth, , *r*, can be rendered in English as "r" or "l."

Example:

 . . . . *mꜣry* . . . . Mary

1.  . . . .
2.  . . . .
3.  . . . .
4. 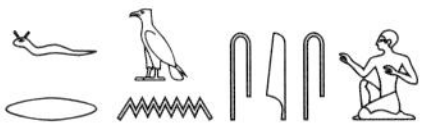 . . . .
5.  . . . .
6.  . . . .
7. 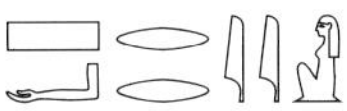 . . . .
8. 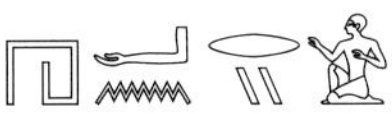 . . . .
9. 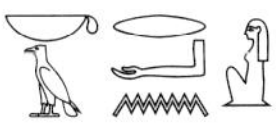 . . . .
10.  . . . .
11. 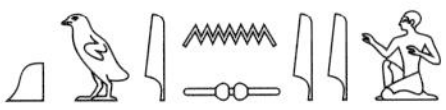 . . . .

12.  . . . .

13.  . . . .

14. 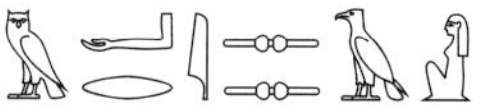 . . . .

15.  . . . .

16.  . . . .

17. 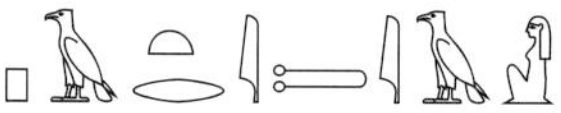 . . . .

Lesson 5: Egyptian Names of Humans and Gods

Now that you have learned the alphabet, you can start reading some real Egyptian names. The following exercise lists the names of some humans and gods that are spelled with alphabetic signs. This exercise uses , a seated god, or , a Horus falcon on a standard, as a labeling sign for male deities; and , a seated goddess, to distinguish female deities. As in the previous exercise,  will be used for human male names, and  for human female names.

Exercise 3: Egyptian Names

Transliterate each name, and then make up an English version. In order to do this, use the practical English versions of the transliterated letters, and insert e's between consonants that can't be pronounced together.

Example

 . . . . *dn* . . . . Den

1.  . . . .

2.  . . . .

3.  . . . .

4.  . . . .

5. 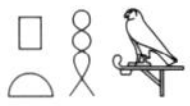 ....

6.  ....

7.  ....

8.  ....

9. ..

Lesson 6: Labeling Signs and Adjectives

The last two exercises have used labeling signs, known as determinatives (the seated man, woman, god, goddess, and falcon on a standard). These are very helpful signs, since they function as clues to the words they follow. Determinatives will help you memorize vocabulary, and aid you in distinguishing one similarly spelled word from another. They can also act as markers for the ends of words, so you will know that the first word has ended and the next will begin. Keep in mind, however, that determinatives could be omitted. This is usually because there are figures in the scenes that the texts accompany which act as labeling signs; you will see how this works later.

Here is a short list of several new labeling signs, or determinatives, that appear in the following vocabulary list. This will introduce you to a series of ancient Egyptian words, which you will then practice transliterating and translating in the next exercise. All of the words in this vocabulary list will be spelled with alphabetic (one-sound) signs.

Hieroglyph: 

What is it? A seated man with his hand to his mouth.

Use: This is a very common determinative, used for words that have to do with the mouth, such as speaking, eating, and drinking, and also for words connected with thinking and emotion.

Hieroglyph: 

What is it? A papyrus roll. Papyrus, made from beaten reeds, was the primary Egyptian medium for writing things like letters, stories, and administrative documents.

Use: This is a very common determinative, used for many abstract concepts and words that have to do with writing.

Hieroglyph: 

What is it? A penis.

Use: This indicates that the word it follows is male in some way. It is also, as you will see later, a word sign (ideogram/logogram) for bull.

Hieroglyph: 

What is it? This is a goose.

Use: This is used as a determinative for birds (and also insects).

Hieroglyph: 

What is it? An enemy of Egypt. Note that his elbows are tied behind his back in an extremely uncomfortable position: this was the standard posture for enemies.

Use: This follows words having to do with enemies and foreigners.

Hieroglyph: 

What is it? A swallow.

Use: This follows words that have to do with things that are small or bad in some way.

Hieroglyph: 

What is it? A folded bolt of cloth with a fringe.

Use: With words that have to do with cloth and clothing.

Hieroglyph: 

What is it? A throne.

Use: With words having to do with seats and thrones. It is also, as you will see later, a phonogram.

Hieroglyph: 

What is it? An older man.

Use: As a determinative for words concerned with age and seniority; also used as a word sign.

Vocabulary

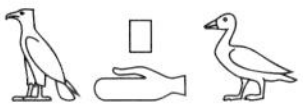	*ꜣpd*	bird; fowl
	*ỉḳr*	excellent
	*bỉn*	evil, bad
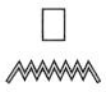	*pn*	this (masculine)
	*hꜣ*	naked
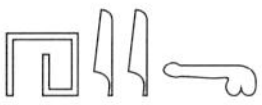	*hy*	husband
	*ḥḳr*	hungry
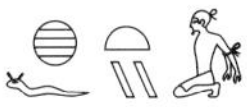	*ḫfty*	enemy
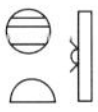	*ḫt*	thing
	*s*	man
	*st*	woman
	*st*	seat; throne
	*smsw*	elder, eldest
	*tn*	this (feminine)

Grammar Note: Gender

You will notice in the preceding vocabulary list that several of the nouns end with t (𓏏). This is an indication of gender. Egyptian nouns, like nouns in many modern languages, are either masculine or feminine. It is generally easy to tell which is which: feminine nouns end in *t* (𓏏); masculine nouns generally do not (although there are a few words ending in 𓏏 that are masculine). In this list, you see the words for man, 𓊃𓀀, *s,* and woman, 𓊃𓏏𓁐, *st,* which exemplify this concept. Masculine nouns can be rendered feminine by the addition of a 𓏏, *t.*

Introduction to Adjectives

There are several adjectives in the preceding vocabulary list. In general, the rule for Egyptian is that an adjective follows the noun it describes or modifies. For example, the adjective "this" (masculine 𓊪𓈖, *pn,* and feminine 𓏏𓈖, *tn*) comes after the noun it modifies: where an English speaker would say "this man," in Egyptian, it is "man this," 𓊃𓀀𓊪𓈖, *s pn.* Adjectives must correspond to the nouns they modify in gender and number. Thus, to say "an excellent man," the Egyptians would write, 𓊃𓀀𓇋𓈎𓂋𓏛, *s i͗ḳr*; to say "an excellent woman," they would write, 𓊃𓏏𓁐𓇋𓈎𓂋𓏏𓏛, *st i͗ḳrt.*

Important Note: There are no spaces between words in hieroglyphic texts, and no punctuation. Words and sentences flow continually from one to the next. It can sometimes be tricky to figure out where one word stops and the next starts, and to know where one phrase or sentence ends and the next begins. The more vocabulary you know, the easier it will be to figure this sort of thing out. Labeling signs (determinatives) will also give you clues. In this book, I will help you as much as possible, and teach you the sort of vocabulary you are likely to see frequently in monumental inscriptions.

Exercise 4: Practice with Vocabulary

Transliterate and translate the following phrases, all of which consist simply of noun plus adjective. Remember that there are no spaces between words; do put spaces in your transliterations, as you see in the examples above.

Example:

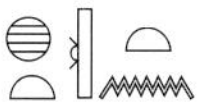 . . . . *ḫt tn* . . . . this thing

1.  . . . .
2.  . . . .
3.  . . . .
4. 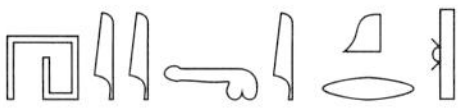 . . . .
5.  . . . .
6.  . . . .
7. 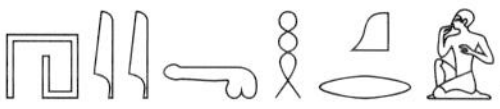 . . . .
8.  . . . .
9.  . . . .

Lesson 7: Suffix Pronouns

Egyptian had three types of pronouns. The most common is the suffix pronoun. Suffix pronouns come at the end of words and have two main uses: to indicate possession, and as the subject of a verb. For now, you will see these only as possessive adjectives—words that tell you to whom particular nouns belong. Like all adjectives, suffix pronouns follow the noun they modify. However, they agree with the noun to which they refer rather than the noun they follow. In other words, to say "your seat," when the person who owns the seat is a man, you will use the masculine form of the suffix pronoun for "your" (), even though the word for seat is feminine (, *st.k*).

Suffix pronouns are not considered freestanding words, but are, in fact, attached to the words they follow. When transliterating suffix pronouns, put a dot between the suffix pronoun and the word it follows.

SUFFIX PRONOUNS

	*ỉ*	I, my
	*k*	you, your(m.)
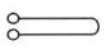 or 	*ṯ or t*	you, your (f.)
	*f*	he, his, it, its
	*s*	she, hers, it, its
	*n*	we, our
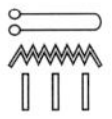 or 	*ṯn or tn*	you, your (pl.)
	*sn*	they, theirs

These examples will help you understand how suffix pronouns work:

 *ꜣpd.f* = his bird

 *ꜣpd.sn* = their bird

 *ꜣpd.ỉ* = my bird (when the speaker is masculine)

 *ꜣpd.ỉ* = my bird (when the speaker is feminine)

Since suffix pronouns are attached to the words they follow, they come before any other adjective:  *hy.ỉ ỉḳr* = my excellent husband.

Here are some more common determinatives, another vocabulary list, and some exercises.

HIEROGLYPH: 

WHAT IS IT? The sun.

USE: This sign labels words having to do with time or the sun and its activities.

HIEROGLYPH: 

WHAT IS IT? This represents the sky.

USE: This follows words that concern the sky.

HIEROGLYPH: 

WHAT IS IT? A loaf of bread.

USE: This is used as a determinative for bread.

HIEROGLYPH: 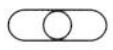

WHAT IS IT? Another type of bread.

USE: This is also used as a determinative for bread.

HIEROGLYPH: 

WHAT IS IT? A pustule.

USE: This follows words having to do with the body and bodily functions.

And one new determinative:

HIEROGLYPH:

WHAT IS IT? This is just a line, but it is an important one.

USE: This vertical stroke tells you that the sign it follows stands alone for a complete word. The technical term for this, as mentioned above, is ideogram or logogram.

IMPORTANT NOTE: It is crucial as you study hieroglyphs to remain flexible at all times. Ancient Egyptian spelling was not standardized, and determinatives could often be left out, or used as abbreviations for the words they usually followed. Endings, such as the feminine , *t*, could sometimes be excluded. There are also words, some of them very common, for which the standard transliteration does not match the hieroglyphic spelling. Two of these appear in the next vocabulary list: , *ỉt*, "father," and  *ḥnḳt*, beer. For , as you see, you do not transliterate the viper, so there is an extra letter in the hieroglyphic writing that does not appear in the transliteration. This is a very important and frequently occurring word, and can also be spelled without the reed leaf, as , or even without the determinative: . The word for beer, 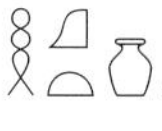, on the other hand, is missing a letter in the hieroglyphs that appears in the transliteration *(ḥnḳt)*. Do not worry about why these anomalies exist, just recognize the words.

Vocabulary

	*ỉt*	father (not *ỉtf)*
	ʿ	arm
	*wỉꜣ*	sacred bark
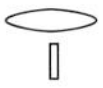	*r*	mouth
	*ḥnḳt*	beer (the *n* is not written)
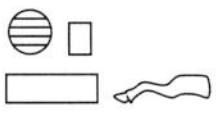	*ḫpš*	foreleg of ox
	*ẖt*	body
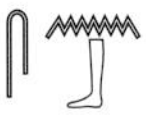	*snb*	health
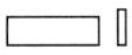	*š*	pool
	*t*	bread

Note on Lists: When creating lists, the ancient Egyptians generally put one word after the other, with no conjunction. Where we would say "bread and beer and meat," the Egyptians would say "bread beer meat." There are several lists in the next exercise; watch out for them.

Exercise 5: Suffix Pronouns

1. 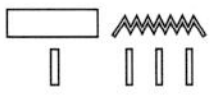 . . . .

2. 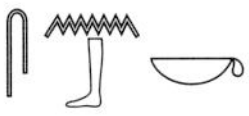 . . . .

3. 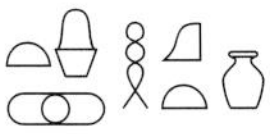 . . . .

4.  . . . .

5.  . . . .

6.  . . . .

7.  . . . .

8.  . . . .

9.  . . . .

Lesson 8: Dual (Two) and Plural

The Egyptians had two ways of indicating that a noun was plural. One way was to repeat the determinative (or the logogram, if the word was spelled with a single sign) three times, and another was to add an ending. For three or more of something, the ending was *w*, written as "plural strokes": or . The artist or scribe might also add a *w* in the form of  or . Whether or not the  or  is included, you should add a *w* to your transliteration. If the noun is feminine, the *t* still comes last in the transliteration.

The Egyptians also used a form called the dual to indicate that there were two of something. You know you are looking at the dual if there are two determinatives or logograms, or if you see the dual endings: *wy* for masculine nouns (often written without the *w*), and *ty* for feminine nouns. Here are some of the various ways that the dual and the plural could be written:

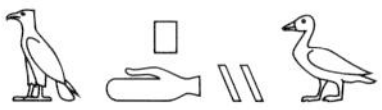	*ꜣpdy*	two birds
	*ꜣpdy*	two birds
	*ꜣpdw*	birds
	*sty*	two women
	*swt*	women
	*swt*	women

Exercise 6: Dual and Plural

1.  . . . .

2.  . . . .

3.  . . . .

4. 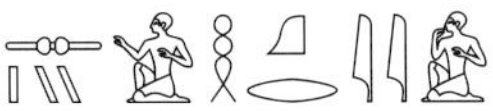 . . . .

5.  . . . .

6.  . . . .

Lesson 9: Sentences Without Verbs

Ancient Egyptians used two basic types of sentences: the non-verbal sentence; and the verbal sentence. In English, sentences have verbs. If there is no verb, there is no sentence. This is not the case in ancient Egyptian. "Non-verbal" sentences, which are, as their name indicates, sentences without verbs, are very common. These sentences, in general, are translated with some form of our verb "to be." Here is a short vocabulary list; some of these words appear in the examples, and are then used in an exercise. Note that one of the vocabulary words, the name of the sun god, Re, is followed by two determinatives. You will be able to tell which are the determinatives because they are not transliterated.

Vocabulary

	*ỉnpw*	Anubis (a god)
	*wt*	place of embalming
	*pt*	sky
	*ptḥ*	Ptah (a god)
	*m*	in, from
	*rʿ*	Re (the sun god)

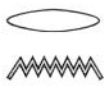	*rn*	name
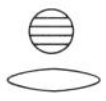	*ḫr*	before, in front of; with
	*skr*	Sokar (a god)

This lesson will deal with three types of sentences without verbs: a subject plus a noun (nominal); a subject plus an adjective (adjectival); or a subject plus an adverb (adverbial).

Nominal Sentences: Nominal sentences give the reader information about the identity of the subject. Where we would say: "Anne is my mother," or "My mother is Anne," the Egyptians would say "mother my Anne." Here are two examples:

, *ỉt.ỉ rꜥ* = My father is Re

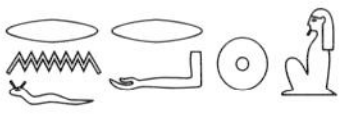 *rn.f rꜥ* = His name is Re.

Adjectival Sentences: As you have seen, the general rule for adjectives is that they follow the noun they modify. They also agree with it in number (singular, dual, or plural) and gender (masculine or feminine). However, if an adjective precedes a noun, it is usually part of an adjectival sentence. In this case, the adjective does not have to agree with the noun and is, in fact, usually in the masculine singular (default) form.

Noun with adjective:  *st ỉḳrt* = An excellent woman.

Adjectival sentence: 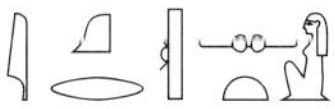 *ỉḳr st* = The woman is excellent.

Adverbial sentences: In this type of sentence, as in the adjectival and nominal sentences, the verb of existence is implied rather than written.

Example:  *rꜥ m pt* = Re is in the sky.

Exercise 7: Non-Verbal Sentences and Short Phrases

Here are just a few non-verbal sentences to try.

1. 

2. 

3. 

4. 

5. 

Lesson 10: Verbal Sentences

The Egyptian verbal system is complex, and scholars continue to argue about its intricacies. At this level, it is neither necessary nor advisable to try to learn all the verb forms and their standard translations, as the number of potential variations is somewhat overwhelming. The various forms are also very difficult to distinguish by their spelling alone. Therefore, this book will teach you only the most common and important forms and some of the ways in which they are used in texts.

There are a few common verbs that are spelled with alphabetic signs. Here is a vocabulary list of verbs that will be used in the examples and the exercise.

Vocabulary

ỉp	count; inspect
wbn	rise
rẖ	know
ḏd	speak

This lesson introduces you to two important verb forms, using the verb , *ḏd,* "speak," in the examples. These two forms can be used to express the present, past, and future tenses.

Word Order: In an English verbal sentence, the verb generally comes second, after the subject. In an ancient Egyptian verbal sentence, the verb comes first, followed by the subject. If this subject is a pronoun, the suffix pronouns are used, and are attached directly to the verb. If the subject is a noun, it also follows the verb. As long as both are nouns, the direct object will follow the subject.

Present or Future Tense: The basic form (the root) of the verb, in this case , *ḏd,* can be used to express present or future tense.

Example 1: *ḏd s* = The man speaks/The man will/may speak.

Example 2: *ḏd.ỉ* = I speak/I will/may speak.

Past Tense: If an , *n,* is attached to the verb: , *ḏd.n,* the verb is translated in the past tense (notice the dot between the verb stem and the *n* in the transliteration).

Example 1: *ḏd.n.f* = He spoke.

Example 2: *ḏd.n ptḥ* = Ptah spoke.

Exercise 8: Verbal Sentences and Short Phrases

1. 
2. 
3. 
4. 
5. 
6. 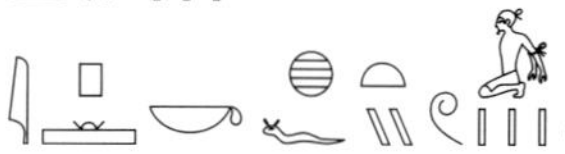
7. 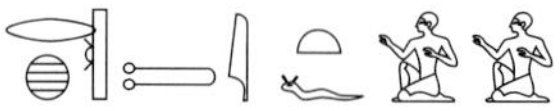

You have now learned all of the alphabetic signs, a great deal of vocabulary, and some fundamental grammar. Congratulations! You are on your way to reading hieroglyphs.

END OF CHAPTER I

Chapter II
Beyond the Alphabet

In order to expand your repertoire of words and phrases, it is necessary to move beyond the alphabet—the single-sound signs (uniliterals) you have been working with thus far. This chapter introduces over fifty of the seven hundred and fifty signs used regularly in hieroglyphic inscriptions, bringing your total repertoire of signs to nearly one hundred. This may sound like a lot, but it is far fewer than you would find, for example, in an ideographic (picture-sign) language like Chinese. Each lesson presents a few signs at a time, along with some information about what they represent. The exercises will give you the chance to practice with them and thus commit them to memory. As you learn these signs, you will also be building your vocabulary (using words and phrases you will see again later in this book and frequently on monuments), and learn a little more grammar. This is an important chapter, containing lots of material. Take your time; what you learn here will serve you in good stead throughout this book and in your travels.

Lesson 11: Two-Sound Signs

Most hieroglyphic signs stand for more than one sound. It is now time to learn some two-sound signs, which are called biliterals. Each biliteral sign is transliterated with two characters. When you need to look up a word that begins with a biliteral sign in the word list at the back of this book, or another dictionary, you will look under the alphabetic character that corresponds to the first sound.

Important note: From now on, all common transliterations will be given for sound signs. Assume that the first given is the one that you will use in the exercise that follows, but take note of all of options; you may see them later. (However, you will never be expected just to remember them without help).

Here is a list of ten common biliteral signs. Look them over, and then you will practice them in an exercise.

Hieroglyph:  **Transliteration:** *ꜣb* or *mr*
What is it? A chisel.

Hieroglyph:  **Transliteration:** *ỉr*
What is it? A human eye.

Hieroglyph:  **Transliteration:** *ỉb*
What is it? A heart.

Hieroglyph:  **Transliteration:** *wn*
What is it? A hare.

Hieroglyph: 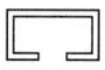 **Transliteration:** *pr*
What is it? The plan of a simple house.

Hieroglyph:  **Transliteration:** *mꜣ*
What is it? A sickle.

Hieroglyph:  **Transliteration:** *mỉ*
What is it? A jug of milk suspended on a loop.

Hieroglyph: 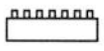 **Transliteration:** *mn*
What is it? A gameboard, used to play the sort of games that eventually became checkers and chess.

HIEROGLYPH: 𓌸 **TRANSLITERATION:** *mr*

WHAT IS IT? A hoe.

HIEROGLYPH: 𓏌 **TRANSLITERATION:** *nw*

WHAT IS IT? A pottery jar.

HIEROGLYPH: 𓈋 **TRANSLITERATION:** *ḏw*

WHAT IS IT? Two mountain peaks flanking a valley.

HIEROGLYPH: 𓊽 **TRANSLITERATION:** *ḏd*

WHAT IS IT? A column made of reeds.

And two new determinatives:

HIEROGLYPH: 𓈊

WHAT IS IT? Mountains.

USE: Used for foreign countries and desert areas.

HIEROGLYPH: 𓊖

WHAT IS IT? Crossroads.

USE: Used for the names of towns. (Also a phonogram).

PHONETIC COMPLEMENTS: A note on phonetic complements, which are extra signs added to words. These are your friends. After signs standing for more than one sound, the Egyptians would often add the sign for the second (and/or third or fourth) sound as an aid to the reader. These should NOT be transliterated separately.

Some examples: 𓊽𓂧𓅱𓊖 (the name of a town named Djedu, in Greek Busiris) should be transliterated *ḏdw*, not *ḏddw*, and 𓇋𓏠𓈖𓀭 (the name of the god Amen) is transliterated *ỉmn*, not *ỉmnn*.

Exercise 9: Names with Biliterals

The following exercise will help you practice the new signs you have just learned. Transliterate and give English versions for the following names. Some are the names of gods and kings; some are the names of towns (you can tell which is which by the determinative). You will see that one of the names here is in an oval ring; this is called a cartouche, and indicates that the name inside is the name of a king. You will learn more about royal names in the next chapter.

Example:  *mnṯw* = Mentju (the name of a god, usually written in English as Montu).

1. 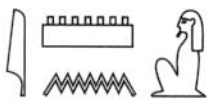

3. 

2. 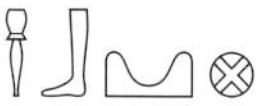

3. 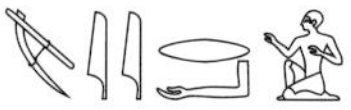

4. 

5. 

6. 

7. 

8. 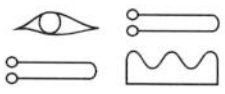

9. 

Lesson 12: Possession

Ancient Egyptian had two ways of expressing possession. One was simply to juxtapose two nouns: XY, which is translated "X of Y," or "Y's X." The technical word for the possessive is the genitive, so the correct term for this is the **direct genitive**.

Here is an example of the direct genitive: 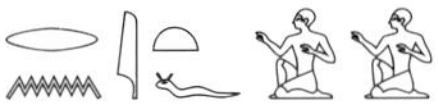 *rn ỉt.ỉ* = the name of my father/my father's name.

The second way to express possession is to use , *n*, meaning "of." This is called the **indirect genitive**.

Example of the indirect genitive:  *rn n ỉt.ỉ* = the name of my father.

The form of the indirect genitive will correspond to the noun it modifies (i.e. masculine, feminine, singular, plural). You now know the masculine singular; the feminine (both singular and plural) is 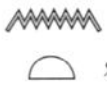, *nt*; the masculine plural is  *nw*. After a certain point in history, the masculine singular  could be used for any noun.

Here are some new signs, and then some vocabulary.

Hieroglyph: **Transliteration:** *ꜥꜣ*
What is it? A wooden column (?).

Hieroglyph:  **Transliteration:** *nb*
What is it? A basket without a handle.

Hieroglyph:  **Transliteration:** *ḫꜥ*
What is it? The rays of the sun shining from behind a hill.

Hieroglyph:  **Transliteration:** *sꜣ*
What is it? A duck.

Hieroglyph: 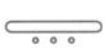 **Transliteration:** *tꜣ*
What is it? Land, with grains of sand underneath.

Hieroglyph:  **Transliteration:** *tp*
What is it? A human head in profile view.

One new determinative:

Hieroglyph:  **Transliteration:** ꜥꜣ

What is it? A donkey.

Vocabulary

	*ꜣbḏw*	Abdju (the town of Abydos)
	*ỉb*	heart
	*ꜥꜣ*	great
	*ꜥꜣ*	donkey
	*pr*	house
	*nb*	lord, master
	*nbt*	lady; mistress
	*sꜣ*	son
	*sꜣt*	daughter
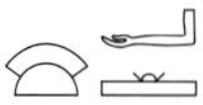	*ḫꜥ*	appearance
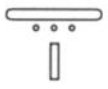	*tꜣ*	earth
	*ḏdw*	Djedu (the town of Busiris)

Exercise 10: Possession

Most of these sentences and phrases use the direct and the indirect genitive. Transliterate and translate.

1.  ....
2.  ....
3.  ....
4.  ....
5. 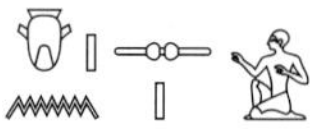 ....

6.  . . . .

7. 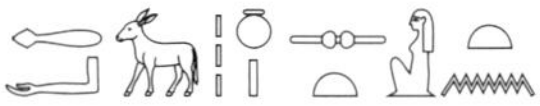 . . . .

8.  . . . .

9.  . . . .

Lesson 13: Honorific Transposition

Honorific transposition, which is changing the order of signs or words because of their relative importance, is an important concept to understand and recognize, and you will need to understand it to do the next exercise properly. Ancient Egypt was a very hierarchical society. The gods were a class apart, worshiped by humankind. The king, who was partly human and partly divine, stood alone at the top of the social pyramid, intermediary between gods and mortals. Below him were his queens and the other members of his immediate family, then the high nobles, then the scribal class, then a small middle class, and then the mass of farmers and laborers who tended the fields, carried out manual tasks, and generally provided the energy that kept the machinery of Egyptian civilization functioning.

Many personal names are compounded with the names of gods or kings. Because of the hierarchical structure of society and the respect accorded to the king and the gods, when the name of either a god or a king, or the word for either, appears within a name it comes first, even if it is transliterated and translated last. For example, the royal name Djedefre is written 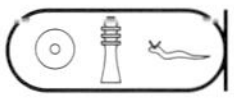, although it looks like "Redjedef." However, it should properly be transliterated *ḏd.f-rˁ* = Djedefre. (Notice the dots and dashes here, but don't worry about them yet. For now, just run your transliterations together.)

Here are three new signs:

Hieroglyph:  **Transliteration:** *ḥs*

What is it? A water jar, used especially for offerings and libations (rituals involving liquid).

HIEROGLYPH:  **TRANSLITERATION:** *ḥm*

WHAT IS IT? Probably a vulva.

HIEROGLYPH:  **TRANSLITERATION:** *kꜣ*

WHAT IS IT? Two arms reaching out in an embrace.

HIEROGLYPH:  **TRANSLITERATION:** *ms*

WHAT IS IT? Three fox-skins, tied together at the top.

HIEROGLYPH:  **TRANSLITERATION:** *sn*

WHAT IS IT? An arrow.

DETERMINATIVES AS WORD SIGNS (LOGOGRAMS): The names in the next exercise use one of the determinatives that you have learned to stand alone for one of the words with which it is commonly used. This is the sun disk, , which is used here to stand for the name of the god Re, more fully written: . (You just saw this, in Djedefre.) Since you are not expected to translate names, simply transliterate this sign as *rꜥ*.

Exercise 11: Names with Honorific Transposition

1.  . . . .
2. 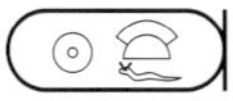 . . . .
3. 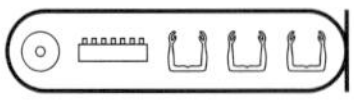 . . . .
4.  . . . .
5.  . . . .
6.  (note: do not use honorific transposition here) . . . .

. . . .

Lesson 14: Participles and Relative Forms

This lesson will briefly introduce you to participles and relative forms, which are special verbal forms that appear in some common patterns that you will encounter over the course of the following chapters. You do not need to understand these in detail, just learn to recognize the patterns in which they appear. Here are two new determinatives and a vocabulary list with signs and words you will need in the examples and then in the exercises.

Hieroglyph: 

What is it? The spine and spinal cord of an animal.

Use: As a determinative for , *ỉmꜣḫ*, "revere"; "honor."

Hieroglyph: 

What is it? A woman giving birth.

Use: As a determinative for words having to do with childbirth.

Here are some more vocabulary words to learn; these will be used in the discussion and then in an exercise. From now on, when a verb appears in the vocabulary, it will be labeled as such. Some of the verbs have an extra *ỉ* in the transliteration; this tells you to which category of verb they belong. (However, you do not need to worry about verb categories at this level.)

Vocabulary

	*ỉmꜣḫỉ*	revere; honor (verb)
	*ỉrỉ*	make; do (verb)
	*mrỉ*	love (verb)
	*msỉ*	bear; give birth
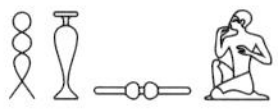	*ḥsỉ*	praise
	*ḥmt*	woman; wife
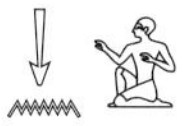	*sn*	brother, companion

Introduction to Participles and Relative Forms

Egyptian verbs can be used as nouns, adjectives, and what are known as relative clauses. (An example of this in English would be "The son **who listens** to his father." or "**One who was borne** by his mother." You do not really need to understand this, what is important is that you recognize the patterns described here and know their standard translations. One common construction you will see in this chapter and the chapters that follow uses a verb form known as a participle, which combines subject and verb in one word, and the genitive: "one beloved [participle] of [genitive] his father. **Participles** can be active (one who hears) or passive (one who is heard); they agree with the nouns they modify:

- The masculine versions of these forms tend to end with 𓇌, *y*, or 𓅱, *w*;
- The feminine versions end in 𓏏, *t*, or 𓇌𓏏, *yt*;
- Plural forms end most often with 𓅱, *w*, or 𓏏, *t*.

Here is an example in hieroglyphs: the verb 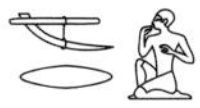, *mri,* "love," can be turned into a participle meaning "one beloved," or "who is beloved." It can then be used in a phrase with the genitive:

Example : 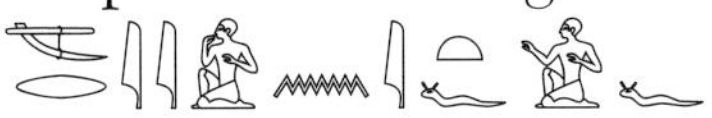

mry n it.f = one beloved of/by his father.

Another frequently seen phrase is:

Example: 

im3ḫt ḫr it.s = one revered before her father. (Notice the use of the feminizing 𓏏, since the participle refers to a woman.)

Relative forms are much like participles in that they create relative clauses and modify nouns. The main difference between participles and relative forms is that participles include the subject within the verb form, and relative forms do not. A very common construction using the relative form is:

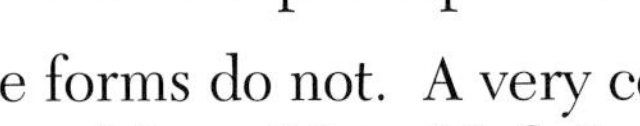 *hy.s mry.s* = her husband whom she loves

In this case, the suffix pronoun 𓋴, *s*, "she," serves as the subject of the relative form "whom she loves." Again, do not go crazy with this grammar, just recognize the pattern.

Exercise 12: More Sentences and Phrases

Transliterate and translate the following phrases, which use the participles and relative forms.

1.  ....
2. 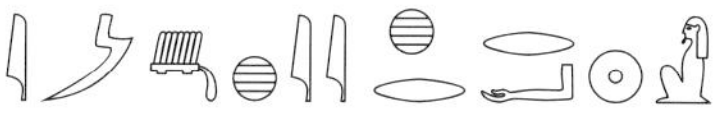 ....
3.  ....
4.  ....
5. 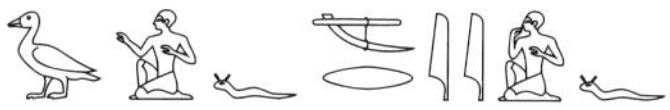 ....
6. 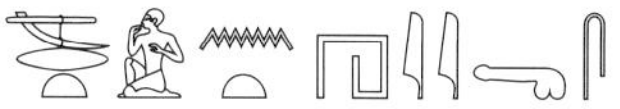 ....
7. 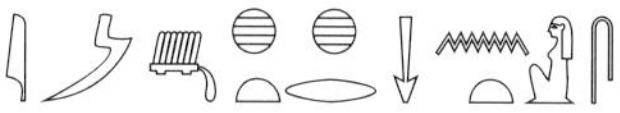 ....
8. 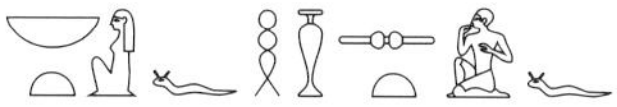 ....
9. 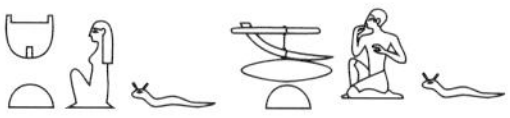 ....
10.  ....

Lesson 15: More Two-Sound Signs

Here are seven more biliterals to learn, followed by some vocabulary and an exercise.

Hieroglyph:  **Transliteration:** *ỉn*

What is it? A jar carried by walking legs.

Hieroglyph:  **Transliteration:** *wr*

What is it? A forktailed swallow.

Hieroglyph:  **Transliteration:** *bꜣ*

What is it? This is a bird called a *jabiru*.

HIEROGLYPH:  **TRANSLITERATION:** *ḥm*

WHAT IS IT? A club.

HIEROGLYPH:  **TRANSLITERATION:** *ḥr*

WHAT IS IT? A human face.

HIEROGLYPH:  **TRANSLITERATION:** *ḥḏ*

WHAT IS IT? A mace.

HIEROGLYPH:  **TRANSLITERATION:** *ḫt*

WHAT IS IT? A stick.

Exercise 13: More Names with Biliterals

Here are some names with which to practice these signs.

1.  . . . .
2.  . . . .
3.  . . . .
4.  . . . .
5.  . . . .
6.  . . . .
7.  . . . .

LESSON 16: A FEW MORE TWO-SOUND SIGNS

Here is another small group of biliterals. Look at this list, then learn the vocabulary that follows.

HIEROGLYPH:  **TRANSLITERATION:** *wp*

WHAT IS IT? Cow horns.

HIEROGLYPH:  **TRANSLITERATION:** *mw*
WHAT IS IT? Three waves of water (also a determinative).

HIEROGLYPH:  **TRANSLITERATION:** *ꜣw*
WHAT IS IT? The vertebral column and spine of an animal.

Starting with the next vocabulary list, you will no longer be given explanations for the new determinatives you might see. If a sign is not transliterated in the vocabulary list, assume that it is a determinative; if you are curious about it, you can look it up in the sign list at the back of the book.

VOCABULARY

	*ꜣw*	be long (verb)
	*ḥm*	servant; Majesty (for king)
	*ḥr*	upon
	*kꜣ*	bull
	*mi͗*	like (similar to)
	*mw*	water
	*nḫt*	strong; mighty
	*ḥḏ*	white; silver
	*tp*	head; upon
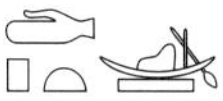	*dpt*	boat
	*ḏw*	mountain
	*ḏt*	forever

MORE ON HONORIFIC TRANSPOSITION: You have seen honorific transposition within names; it also appears within phrases. For example, a common phrase used to refer to the king is "like Re, forever," meaning that the king should be associated with the sun god for eternity. Since Re is a god, his name comes first in the phrase, so that you will see . Still transliterate this as *mi rꜥ ḏt*.

Exercise 14: Sentences and Common Phrases

This exercise uses a number of abbreviations and alternative spellings, of which you will see more and more as you work through the book. As you have seen, one common way of abbreviating words was by using the determinative alone; if you see a sign that has been used as a determinative standing alone, use the full transliteration. If you can't remember the entire word, look up the sign in the sign list in back.

Example:  . . *ꜣw ib.f* . . . . may his heart be long (may he be happy)

1.  . . . .
2. 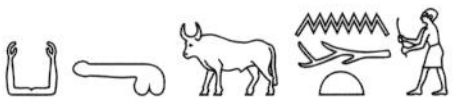 . . . .
3.  . . . .
4.  . . . .
5.  . . . .
6.  . . . .
7.  . . . .
8.  . . . .
9. 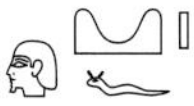 . . . .
10. 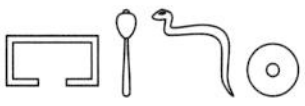 . . . .

Lesson 17: Three-, Four-, and More-Sound Signs

You have now been introduced to the alphabet and many of the most common biliteral signs. What you have learned so far will allow you to transliterate (and thus, with the aid of a dictionary, to translate) many of the words you will see. I will now start to bring in signs that represent more than two sounds. Some are fairly common, but even these tend to be used in a limited range of words. Here are fourteen multi-sound signs to learn.

HIEROGLYPH:  **TRANSLITERATION:** *ꜥnḫ*
WHAT IS IT? The strap of a sandal.

HIEROGLYPH: 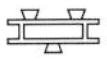 **TRANSLITERATION:** *wꜣt*
WHAT IS IT? A path bordered by shrubs.

HIEROGLYPH:  **TRANSLITERATION:** *wsr*
WHAT IS IT? The head of a jackal on a pole.

HIEROGLYPH:  **TRANSLITERATION:** *mꜣꜥ*
WHAT IS IT? A sickle and a throne base.

HIEROGLYPH:  **TRANSLITERATION:** *mꜣꜥt*
WHAT IS IT? A goddess with a feather on her head (the goddess Maat).

HIEROGLYPH:  **TRANSLITERATION:** *nfr*
WHAT IS IT? The heart and windpipe of an animal.

HIEROGLYPH:  **TRANSLITERATION:** *nṯr*
WHAT IS IT? A pole with a standard flying from the top.

HIEROGLYPH:  **TRANSLITERATION:** *ḥꜣt*
WHAT IS IT? The forepart of a lion.

HIEROGLYPH: 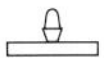 **TRANSLITERATION:** *ḥtp*
WHAT IS IT? A mat for offerings with a loaf of bread on top.

Hieroglyph:  **Transliteration:** *ḫpr*

What is it? A scarab beetle.

Hieroglyph:  **Transliteration:** *ẖnm*

What is it? A jar with a handle.

Hieroglyph:  **Transliteration:** *sꜣḥ*

What is it? These are supposedly very stylized toes.

Hieroglyph:  **Transliteration:** *špss*

What is it? A nobleman seated on a chair, holding a flail as a sign of office.

Hieroglyph:  **Transliteration:** *ḏḥwty*

What is it? An ibis bird on a standard.

Exercise 15: Names with Multi-sound Signs

Here is an exercise to help you practice some of these new signs in names, both royal and private. Watch out for honorific transposition.

1. 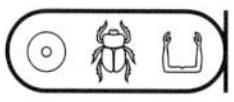 . . . .
2. 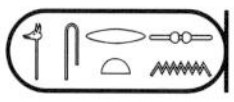 . . . .
3.  . . . .
4. 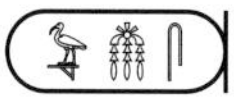 . . . .
5. 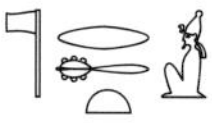 . . . .
6. 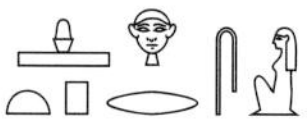 . . . .
7. 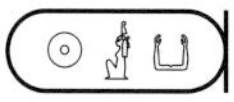 . . . .
8. 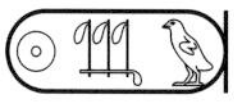 . . . .
9.  . . . .

10.  . . . .

11. 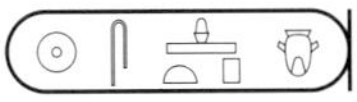 . . . .

12.  . . . .

13.  . . . .

14.  . . . .

Lesson 18: More Multi-Sound Signs

Here are another thirteen new signs to memorize. These will be followed by a short vocabulary list and some exercises that incorporate the material you have learned so far in this chapter.

Hieroglyph:  **Transliteration:** *wꜣs*

What is it? A scepter with the head of a canine on top.

Hieroglyph:  **Transliteration:** *ws* (or *ꜣs); st*

What is it? A throne.

Hieroglyph:  **Transliteration:** *mwt*

What is it? A vulture.

Hieroglyph:  **Transliteration:** *sw*

What is it? A sedge plant, heraldic plant of Upper Egypt.

Hieroglyph:  **Transliteration:** *ḥwt*

What is it? The plan of an enclosure.

Hieroglyph:  **Transliteration:** *ḥḳꜣ*

What is it? A shepherd's crook.

HIEROGLYPH:  **TRANSLITERATION:** *ḫrw*

WHAT IS IT? An oar.

HIEROGLYPH:  **TRANSLITERATION:** *stp*

WHAT IS IT? An adze.

The following exercise will help you practice reading these signs. For now, just transliterate these words and names; you will learn their meanings later.

Exercise 16: Transliteration Practice

1.  ....

2,  ....

4. 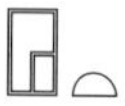 ....

5.  ....

7. 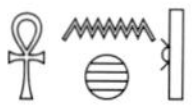 ....

9.  ....

10.  ....

11.  ....

12. 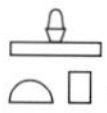 ....

13.  ....

14.  ....

15. 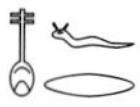 ....

LESSON 19: COMMON PHRASES

This lesson and the next are devoted to common phrases—groups of words that you will see frequently in monumental texts. Here are some new signs to learn, followed by some vocabulary. I will review some of the common phrases that use these words (and others you have already learned), then you can practice these, and others that you should be able to figure out based on what you know so far, in the exercises.

Hieroglyph:  **Transliteration:** *ỉwn*

What is it? A column with a tenon on the top.

Hieroglyph:  **Transliteration:** *wꜥ*

What is it? A harpoon.

Hieroglyph:  **Transliteration:** *wḥm*

What is it? The leg and hoof of an ox.

Hieroglyph:  **Transliteration:** *bỉty*

What is it? A bee.

Hieroglyph: 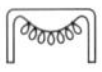 **Transliteration:** *nbw*

What is it? A collar made of beads.

Hieroglyph:  **Transliteration:** *nbty*

What is it? Two *neb* signs, one surmounted by a vulture, symbol of Nekhbet, goddess of Upper Egypt, and the other by a cobra, symbol of the goddess Wadjet of Lower Egypt.

Hieroglyph:  **Transliteration:** *ḥr*

What is it? A Horus falcon.

Hieroglyph:  **Transliteration:** *dỉ*

What is it? A loaf of bread.

Hieroglyph:  **Transliteration:** *ḫꜣst*

What is it? Mountains (Also a determinative).

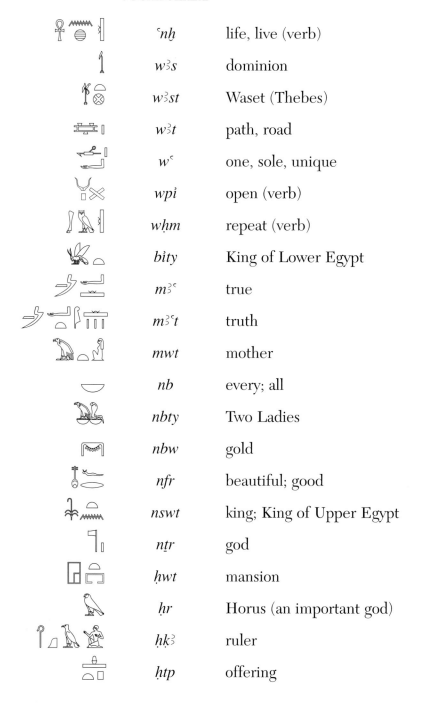

The following list includes the word for king, , *nswt*. It looks as though it should be transliterated *swtn*, but it is not. As you did with "father" and "beer," just memorize the correct transliteration.

VOCABULARY

	*ꜥnḫ*	life, live (verb)
	*wꜣs*	dominion
	*wꜣst*	Waset (Thebes)
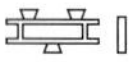	*wꜣt*	path, road
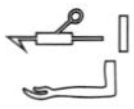	*wꜥ*	one, sole, unique
	*wpỉ*	open (verb)
	*wḥm*	repeat (verb)
	*bỉty*	King of Lower Egypt
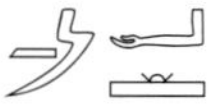	*mꜣꜥ*	true
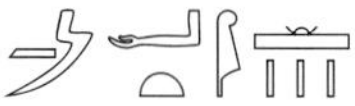	*mꜣꜥt*	truth
	*mwt*	mother
	*nb*	every; all
	*nbty*	Two Ladies
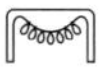	*nbw*	gold
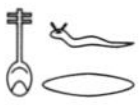	*nfr*	beautiful; good
	*nswt*	king; King of Upper Egypt
	*nṯr*	god
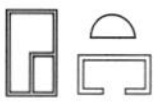	*ḥwt*	mansion
	*ḥr*	Horus (an important god)
	*ḥḳꜣ*	ruler
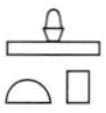	*ḥtp*	offering

	ḫꜣst	foreign land
	ḫrw	voice
	stp	choose (verb)
OR	*rdỉ, dỉ*	give; cause (verb)
	ḏd	stability

Common Phrases

, *nb ỉrt ḫt* = lord of doing things (lord of ritual). (You may notice that , *ḫt,* is transliterated without the plural *w*. This is standard practice.) This common royal epithet introduces you to another verbal construction, the infinitive. In English, we translate the infinitive as "to X," for example, "to do." In Egyptian, the infinitive can be translated like an English infinitive, "to do," or as what is called in English a gerund, "doing."

The form of the Egyptian infinitive depends on the category to which the verb belongs. The few infinitives you will be seeing in the next chapters will either look the same as the root (the form given in the vocabulary lists) or will add a , *t,* to the end. The infinitive for , *ỉr,* "do, make," has a , *t,* on the end: , *ỉrt*. The phrase here is translated as "lord of doing things," which is usually rendered as "lord of ritual." You can understand this as a direct genitive that uses an infinitive as the second noun in the pattern.

, *dỉ ʿnḫ* = (one) given life. There are several ways to understand this phrase; the easiest is to think of the first word as a participle (one given) followed by a direct object.

, *wḥm ʿnḫ* = repeating life/repeater of life. This can be understood either as a participle (one who repeats) or as an infinitive.

, *nb ḫꜣswt nbt* = lord of all foreign lands. This phrase uses two different words spelled with the *nb* sign, "lord," and "all." Both are very common words, and when, as is often the case, "lord" is spelled with no vertical stroke and no determinative, they are impossible to distinguish through their spellings. Context will give you the clue you need: "lord" will come first, as it does here, and "all" will, like most adjectives, follow the noun it modifies.

, *mꜣꜥ ḫrw* = true of voice; justified. This is a direct genitive, using an adjective plus a noun. It is a phrase used to refer to a deceased person, and makes reference to the ceremony of the weighing of the heart. In this mythological ritual, the heart of the dead person would be weighed against the feather of Maat, of truth and justice. If the two balanced, he or she would become an eternally blessed spirit. If not, the heart would be eaten by a dreadful monster, and the unfortunate soul would die again, this time forever. You will often see this in a very abbreviated form: 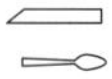.

Exercise 17: Common Phrases

Here are some common phrases that use the vocabulary you have learned in this chapter. You have seen some of these before; you will meet most of these again later in the book, and you will see them often on monuments. Remember to be flexible; this exercise includes words you know, but many of them are spelled differently or are missing their determinatives. This will be the case when you begin to work with monuments, so start getting used to it now! Watch out for honorific transposition.

1.  . . . .

2. 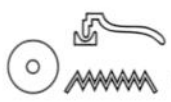 . . . .

. . . .

3.  . . . .

. . . .

4.  ....

....

5.  ....

....

6.  ....

....

7. 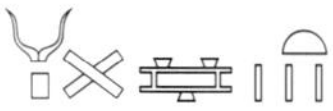 ....

....

8.  ....

....

9.  ....

....

10. 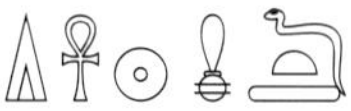 ....

....

11.  ....

....

12.  ....

....

13.  ....

....

14.  ....

....

15.  . . . .

. . . .

16.  . . . .

. . . .

Lesson 20: North, South, East, and West

Orientation was extremely important to the ancient Egyptians. Their world had two primary axes: north-south, the axis of the Nile; and east-west, the axis of the sun's journey through the sky. The west, where the sun set, was the land of the dead. In this lesson, you will be introduced to the words for the cardinal directions, which you will then practice in some exercises (along with some additional phrases).

Hieroglyph:  **Transliteration:** *ỉꜣb*
What is it? A standard with an emblem representing a spear on top.

Hieroglyph:  **Transliteration:** *ỉmn*
What is it? A standard with a feather on top.

Hieroglyph:  **Transliteration:** *mḥ*
What is it? A whip.

Hieroglyph:  **Transliteration:** *rs*
What is it? A sedge plant on top of a mouth.

Hieroglyph:  **Transliteration:** *ḫnt*
What is it? Three or four water jars in a rack.

Hieroglyph:  **Transliteration:** *šmꜥw*

What is it? A flowering sedge plant on top of a sign for land.

Hieroglyph:  **Transliteration:** *tỉw*

What is it? A vulture. (The aleph bird, , is often used instead of this sign.)

Hieroglyph:  **Transliteration:** *nḥḥ*

What is it? A guinea-fowl.

Vocabulary

	*ỉꜣbty*	eastern
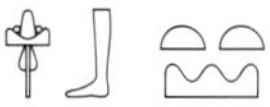	*ỉꜣbtt*	East
	*ỉwnw*	Iunu (Heliopolis)
	*ỉmnty*	western
	*ỉmntt*	West, western
	*ỉmntỉyw*	Westerners
	*wr*	great one
	*wsỉr*	Osiris
	*mḥt*	north
	*mḥty*	northern
	*nḥḥ*	eternity
	*r*	to; for
	*rsy*	southern
	*ḫnt*	before; in front of
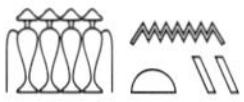	*ḫnty*	who is in front of; foremost
	*šmꜥw*	Upper Egypt

Exercise 18: More Common Phrases

1.  ....

2. 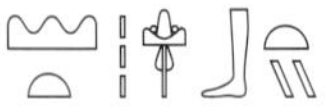 ....

3.  ....

3. 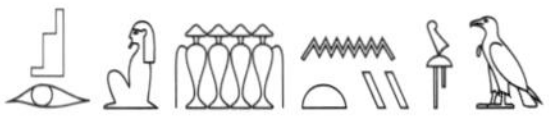 ....

4.  ....

5.  ....

6.  ....

7. 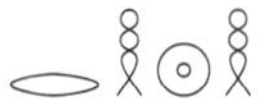 ....

Lesson 21: Scene Labels

People, animals, and objects depicted on the walls of tombs and temples are often labeled with their names or identifying information. With what you have learned in this chapter, you can already begin to interpret some of these inscriptions. With a little bit of vocabulary, you will be able to look at your first examples of actual monuments. Remember that the figures in the scenes themselves often serve as determinatives. Here are a few new signs to learn.

Hieroglyph:  **Transliteration:** *pḏt, stỉ*

What is it? A bow.

Hieroglyph:  **Transliteration:** *mr*

What is it? A canal. This sign is often used as a substitute for  (beloved). In this exercise, it functions as a determinative.

Hieroglyph:  **Transliteration:** *stỉ/sṯỉ*

What is it? A bow. (Also used as a determinative.)

Hieroglyph:  **Transliteration:** *sṯ*

What is it? A complicated knot.

Hieroglyph:  **Transliteration:** *ꜣḫ, šꜣ*

What is it? A marshy piece of land sprouting plants.

Hieroglyph:  **Transliteration:** *tỉ*

What is it? A pestle

Hieroglyph:  **Transliteration:** *ṯḥnw*

What is it? A throwstick. (Also a determinative.)

Vocabulary

	*pḏt*	bow; foreigner
	*mꜣ-ḥḏ*	oryx
	*nwḏw*	antelope
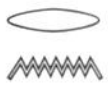	*rn*	young
	*gḥs*	gazelle

Exercise 19: Labels

Here are illustrations of two monuments with labels. In the first example there are no animate hieroglyphs to use for orientation; instead, the figures in the scene itself give you the clue that you need to decide which way to read the labels. This is also the first time that you are being confronted with the difference between typeset and actual hieroglyphs. No two actual hieroglyphs look exactly the same! They will vary from monument to monument. So remember to stay flexible; do not expect things to look exactly the same in actuality as they do on the printed page.

Object 1: Animal Offerings from the Old Kingdom

This is part of a procession of offering bearers. The animals shown here are being brought to the tomb owner to be sacrificed as part of his funerary meal. Work from top to bottom and right to left; transliterate first and then translate. Note that you will immediately run into a spelling "mistake."

Animal 1:. . . . .

Animal 2:. . . . .

Animal 3:. . . . .

Object 2: List of Enemies

The last exercise in this chapter is adapted from a throne base depicted in the tomb of a New Kingdom official named Anen. In the actual painting, nine enemies (the traditional number) are arranged in a horizontal band. The labels here are all the names of places and their inhabitants. Practice transliterating the hieroglyphs and producing an English version. I will do two of these for you; these are highlighted in green and are on the bottom right.

Examples:

Enemy 7: *ṯḥnw* = Tjehenu. This name was used to refer to the Libyans (the inhabitants of the Western desert).

Enemy 8: *tꜣ-nwt sṯt* = Ta-nut-setjet. This was somewhere to the south.

The signs  and  should be understood in the remainder of these names as determinatives, so do not transliterate them!

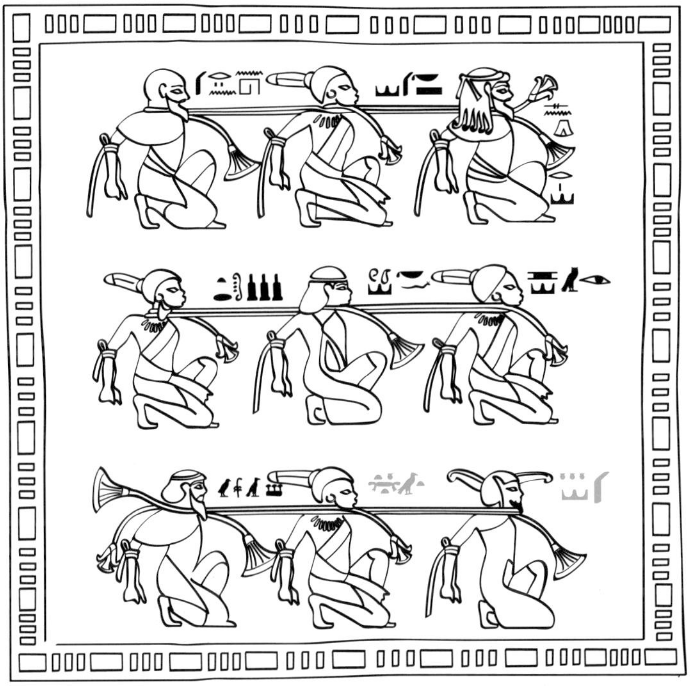

Enemy 1: . . . .

Enemy 2: . . . .

Enemy 3: . . . .

Enemy 4: . . . .

Enemy 5: . . . .

Enemy 6: . . . .

Enemy 9: . . . .

END OF CHAPTER II

Chapter III

ROYAL NAMES AND TITLES

This chapter introduces you to many of the important kings of Egypt, and exposes you to a bit of Egyptian history in the process. As you have already seen, kings' names are generally easy to recognize, as they are usually placed inside cartouches (oval rings of knotted rope which symbolized the circuit of the sun and protected the king). They can also be placed inside *serekhs* (rectangles bordered at the bottom by a row of vertical niches and surmounted by a falcon). In fact, royal names provided the key to the modern decipherment of hieroglyphs. At the very end of the eighteenth century, a member of Napoleon Bonaparte's expedition to Egypt discovered an inscribed slab of granite. The text on the slab was written in two languages: ancient Greek and ancient Egyptian. The Egyptian version was written in two scripts, hieroglyphic and a cursive script called demotic. Scholars at the time were able to read the Greek, but the Egyptian was, well, Greek to them.

In 1822 a young French scholar named Jean-François Champollion succeeded in cracking the hieroglyphic code. A major piece of the puzzle was solved when he focused his efforts on several oval rings that surrounded groups of hieroglyphs in the Egyptian text on the stone slab found by Napoleon's team. (This was called the Rosetta Stone because it had been discovered near the Rosetta branch of the Nile.) Noting that there were several royal names in the Greek version, he hypothesized that the rings, called cartouches after the French word for gun cartridge, held the same royal names. Working with this theory, he was able to assign alphabetic characters to each of the hieroglyphs in the cartouches, and he was on his way to successful decipherment.

This chapter will focus on the most famous, important, and often-seen kings of Egypt—the ones whom you are most likely to encounter on monuments. In addition, you will learn common royal titles and epithets, some of which you have encountered already. By the time you have finished this chapter, you will be able to interpret many royal monuments. The chapter is organized chronologically, and each lesson includes exercises, some typeset but most using illustrations of actual inscriptions, that will help you practice reading royal names and titles from throughout Egyptian history.

Lesson 22: Introduction to Royal Names

The history of ancient Egypt is traditionally divided into dynasties, which are then grouped into larger periods: kingdoms—when the country was strong and united; and intermediate periods—when the land was divided into two or more regions ruled by competing royal houses. The best-known kings come from the Old, Middle, and New Kingdoms: since the country was secure and wealthy during these periods, the kings had the resources with which to erect major monuments, including temple, tombs, statues and stelae. The lessons in this chapter will therefore focus on the kings from these periods.

Our understanding of the names of the kings and the order in which they ruled has been reconstructed from many different sources. The basic outlines are well-known, and most of the kings introduced here are securely placed within the standard chronology of ancient Egypt.

All dates given here are approximate, rounded up or down for ease of memorization. Due to uncertainties about the astronomical markers that anchor the ancient chronology, there is still some debate about exact dates before 664 B.C, so these are usually marked by circa (c.) or "about."

ROYAL NAMES: Beginning with Dynasty 5, kings had five names, each preceded by an epithet; these were standardized a bit later into:

- the Horus (, *ḥrw)* name (often placed in a serekh, a rectangle bordered by niched paneling);
- the Two Ladies name (*nbty*);
- the golden Horus *(* , *ḥr nbw)* name;
- the throne name, or prenomen; and
- the birth name, or nomen.

The throne and birth names, both written inside cartouches, are the names most commonly seen on monuments. The throne name is preceded by the title King of Upper and Lower Egypt (, *nswt bỉty*), and the birth name follows the epithet Son of Re (, *sꜣ rꜥ)*.

This chapter will focus on the birth and throne names, which are the names most often seen on monuments.

LESSON 23: ROYAL NAMES OF THE EARLY DYNASTIC PERIOD

Egyptian history proper starts in approximately 3100 B.C., the date which marks the beginning of the Early Dynastic Period (Dynasties 0, 1 and 2). During the millennium or so preceding this watershed, the material culture of ancient Egypt had been divided geographically into two areas: Lower Egypt—the delta formed by the branching of the Nile as it flows into the Mediterranean Sea; and Upper Egypt—the relatively narrow Nile Valley between Aswan, the traditional southern border of the country, and the apex of the Nile Delta. These two areas have distinctive characteristics: In Upper Egypt, the floodplain is for the most part narrow, surrounded on either side by low desert flanked in turn by the cliffs of the high desert. In Lower Egypt, the Nile has deposited a wide plain of fertile soil that stretches for miles and miles.

In the centuries immediately preceding 3100 B.C, the material culture of Upper Egypt spread throughout the country, through either trade or conquest. Evidence of a stratified society, where power and wealth become concentrated in fewer and fewer hands, begins to appear in the archaeological record. By 3100 B.C., Egypt was united under the rule of one king, and the technology of writing, which had appeared for the first time a century and a half earlier, was already developing rapidly. Egyptologists label this transitional period Dynasty 0, followed by Dynasty 1.

The kings of Dynasties 0 and 1 and several kings of Dynasty 2 were buried in Upper Egypt, at the site of Abydos, and ruled from a capital city called  *(ỉnb ḥḏ,* "White Wall"), traces of which have recently been uncovered near modern-day Cairo. Extremely impressive tombs generally thought to belong to high nobles (although I have my doubts) were built in the high desert overlooking the floodplain in which the city lay, at the site of Saqqara. Several kings of Dynasty 2 were buried here, in mazes of underground galleries.

From the earliest times, each king seems to have had two names: a birth name and a royal name adopted at his accession to the throne. In these dynasties, the second name, the name most frequently seen on monuments, was the Horus name. The row of niches that decorated the bottom of the serekh in which this name was placed imitated the paneling that adorned the outer walls of royal palaces. (Cartouches were not used until later.)

You will not be reading Early Dynastic texts here. This is a specialty, and very few people know how to interpret the earliest inscriptions. However, you can recognize a few important names. Here are a few new signs that you will need, and then an exercise, in which you will read the names of some Dynasty 1 and 2 kings on illustrations of actual monuments.

Here are two new signs to learn.

HIEROGLYPH:  **TRANSLITERATION:** *nꜥr*

WHAT IS IT? A catfish.

HIEROGLYPH:  **TRANSLITERATION:** *sḫm, ḫrp*

WHAT IS IT? A scepter.

Note on Transliteration of Royal Names: This note will hold for this chapter and the rest of the book. Most scholars put dots or dashes into names to separate the individual words within them. Since you are not expected to translate the names (which is difficult to do properly), you should feel free to run the transliteration together and use a standard English version for each name. You will be given the correct transliteration, complete with dots and dashes, in the text and in the keys to the exercises.

Exercise 20: Early Dynastic Monuments

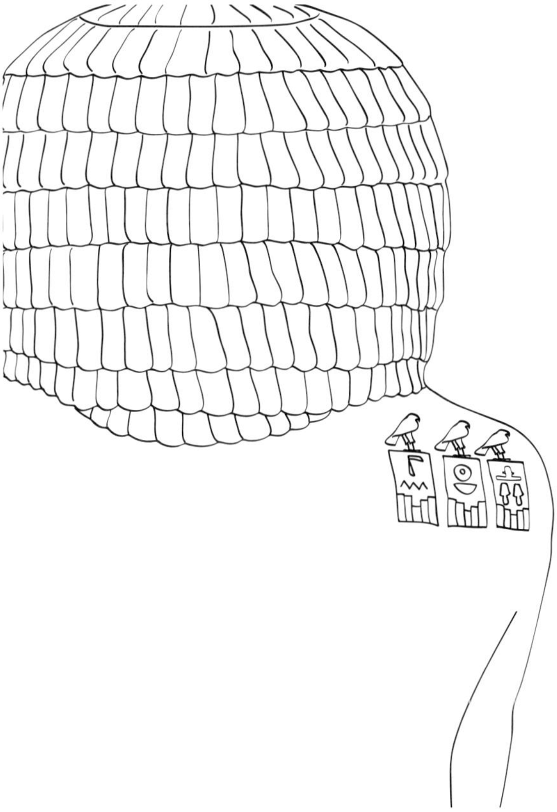

Object 1: Statue of Hetepdief

This is the back of a granite statue found somewhere in the vicinity of ancient Memphis. The statue as a whole shows a priest named Hetepdief. There are three serekhs here; they name three Dynasty 2 kings whose mortuary cults Hetepdief may have served. Transliterate the name in each serekh and give a standard English version. Work from right to left.

Serekh 1: . . . .

Serekh 2: . . . .

Serekh 3: . . . .

Object 2: Abydos Stela

This stela, on display at the Louvre in Paris, bears the name of a king of Dynasty 1. It was found at Abydos, one of a pair set up in front of the tomb of the king it names. You can add a "t" to the end of this name to make it pronounceable.

Transliterate: . . . .

Give an English version: . . . .

Object 3: Slate Palette

Although this palette, which stands twenty-five inches (sixty-four centimeters) high and once stood in a temple, bears little actual text, the images carved on its surface convey important narrative information to the informed viewer. It was once interpreted as a historical document; many scholars now believe that it depicts ritual activity of some sort rather than a specific event. Read only the royal name, which appears twice here; this is the name of the king thought to have completed the unification of the Two Lands.

King (in blue): . . . . English version: . . . .

Lesson 24: The Old Kingdom

The Old Kingdom, Dynasties 3 through 8, began in about 2700 B.C. and lasted for six hundred-odd years. The first king of Dynasty 3 is known to us now as Djoser, even though this name does not survive in any inscriptions or texts from his reign. His Horus name is Netjerikhet, , *nṯr-ḫt,* and it is this name that appears on contemporary monuments. Djoser's principal claim to fame is that he built an enormous step pyramid of stone to serve as his tomb. This was both the first pyramid and the first monumental stone building in the world.

Dynasty 4 was was the great age of pyramid building, a time of enormous power and wealth. The dynasty was founded by Sneferu, , *snfrw,* who built four pyramids, including the two earliest true (straight-sided) pyramids. His father was the first to put his name in a cartouche. Sneferu's son and successor was Khufu, , *ḫwfw (*known in Greek as Cheops); he built the largest pyramid the world has ever seen, the Great Pyramid at Giza. He was followed at Giza by his son, Khafre, , *ḫʿ.f-rʿ*, and his grandson, Menkaure, *mn-kꜣw-rʿ*.

The kings of Dynasty 5 built smaller pyramids at a different sites which were, like Giza, along the edge of the western desert in what is known as the "Memphite" region (close to modern Cairo). There were nine kings in this dynasty; here are the names of two: Sahure, , *sꜣḥw-rʿ*, and Wenis, , *wnỉs,* also known as Unas.

The Dynasty 6 court stayed in the Memphite region, building beautiful pyramid complexes decorated with exquisite reliefs. Following a tradition begun by Wenis, the Dynasty 6 kings and their most important queens inscribed spells known as Pyramid Texts inside the burial chambers of their pyramids. These were designed to help them reach the afterlife safely. Two kings of this dynasty bore the birth name Pepy , *ppy*. Pepy I was also known as Meryre, , *mry-rʿ*, and Pepy II's throne name was Neferkare , *nfr-kꜣ-rʿ*. Neferkare Pepy II came to the throne as a child, and is thought to have lived well into his nineties.

As you have seen, many Old Kingdom royal names are compounded with the name of the sun god, Re, which comes first because of honorific transposition. Also note that the use of Roman numerals following kings' names is an Egyptological construct, added to distinguish monarchs with the same birth name (nomen) from one another without having to add the throne name (prenomen) all the time.

Royal Titles: Royal inscriptions generally include, in addition to the king's name, special epithets and titles. You have already learned most of these (an example is , *nb tꜣwy,* "lord of the Two Lands") ; now you will have a chance to see how they are used on real monuments.

Exercise 21: Old Kingdom Monuments

Example: Lintel of Sahure

This lintel once stood in the pyramid complex of the king named here. It bears the cartouche of the king and his Horus name, in this case not inside a serekh. Here is how you would interpret this monument:

As the overlaid grid shows, you would approach this lintel in four sections, reading from left to right.

Red: First, transliterate the first title and its attached cartouche:

nswt bi͗ty sꜣḥw-rꜥ = King of Upper and Lower Egypt, Sahure.

Blue: Next, transliterate and give an English version of the Horus name:

ḥr ṯmꜣꜥ = the Horus, Tjemaa.

Green: Thirdly, transliterate and translate the next epithet:

nb i͗rt ḫt = lord of ritual (lord of doing things).

Yellow: Finally, transliterate and translate the last phrase:

ꜣw ib.f ḏt = may his heart be long (may he be happy) forever.

Object 1: Statue Base of Djoser

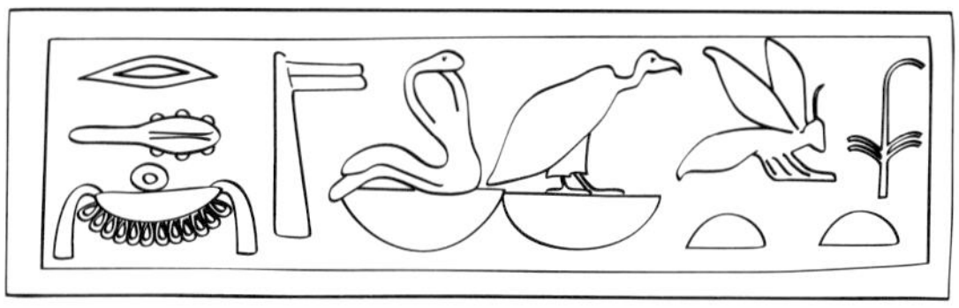

This is the base of a very famous statue of King Djoser, now in the Egyptian Museum, Cairo. Transliterate and translate; remember, first pay attention to which way the animals are facing to determine the direction in which to read.

. . . .

. . . .

Object 2: Lintel

The next illustration depicts a lintel originally erected in the pyramid complex of this Dynasty 4 king. This complex appears to have been destroyed in the First Intermediate Period; this lintel was discovered inside the 12th Dynasty pyramid of Amenemhat I at Lisht, where it had been taken and re-used. It is still inside this later pyramid; a cast is in the Metropolitan Museum of Art, New York. Transliterate and translate the name and titles inside the cartouche.

Transliteration: . . . .

Translation: . . . .

Object 3: Relief Fragment from Coptos

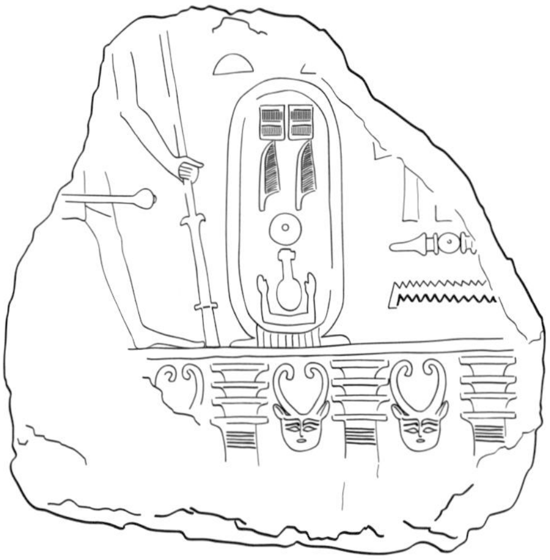

This bit of relief comes from a temple at the site of Coptos dedicated to the god of fertility, Min (you can see a bit of Min's name () to the right of the cartouche). Coptos was one of the main cult centers for this god. Notice that two of the names of the king have been placed inside one cartouche.

LESSON 25: FIRST INTERMEDIATE PERIOD AND MIDDLE KINGDOM

Towards the end of the Old Kingdom, the government became very decentralized, and the First Intermediate Period began. For the next century or so, powerful local rulers jockeyed for power. The strongest of these were based at Herakleopolis, in Middle Egypt, and Thebes, further to the south. There are few monuments from this period.

In about 2040 B.C., a king of the Theban Dynasty 11 succeeded in reuniting the country. This inaugurated the Middle Kingdom, another period of great wealth and centralized power. The prince who succeeded in uniting the Two Lands was Nebhepetre Mentuhotep (II) 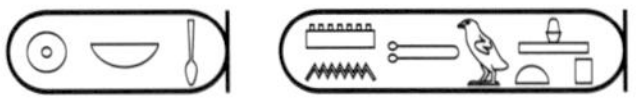, *nb-ḥpt-rꜥ mnṯw-ḥtp*. This line was replaced by the family that dominated Dynasty 12.

The first king of Dynasty 12 was Sehetepibre Amenemhat I , *sḥtp-ib-rꜥ imn-m-ḥꜣt*. He ruled for almost thirty years, and inaugurated what the ancient Egyptians themselves considered to be a golden age.

The Dynasty 12 rulers followed the example of their Old Kingdom predecessors, and had themselves buried in pyramids. Most of the kings were named either Amenemhat, after the founder of the dynasty, or Senwosret. The last ruler of Dynasty 12 was a queen named Sobekneferu. Kings whose monuments you are likely to see are: , *ḫpr-kꜣ-rꜥ snwsrt***,** Kheperkare Senwosret I; , *ḫꜥ-ḫpr-rꜥ snwsrt,* Khakheperre Senwosret II; , *ḫꜥ-kꜣw-rꜥ snwsrt***,** Khakaure Senwosret III**;** and , *n-mꜣꜥt-rꜥ ỉmn-m-ḥꜣt***,** Nimaatre Amenemhat III.

Exercise 22: Middle Kingdom Monuments

Here are three pieces of jewelry found with the burials of princesses named Mereret and Sithathor. These tombs were within the pyramid complex of Senwosret III at the site of Dahshur, not far from modern Cairo. All of these pieces are now in the Egyptian Museum, Cairo.

Object 1: Pectoral

This jewel depicts the cartouche of the king beneath the outstretched wings of the protective vulture; she holds the cartouche symbol in each claw. On each side, a hawk-headed griffin subdues a fallen enemy of Egypt.

Transliterate:. . . . .

Translate:. . . . .

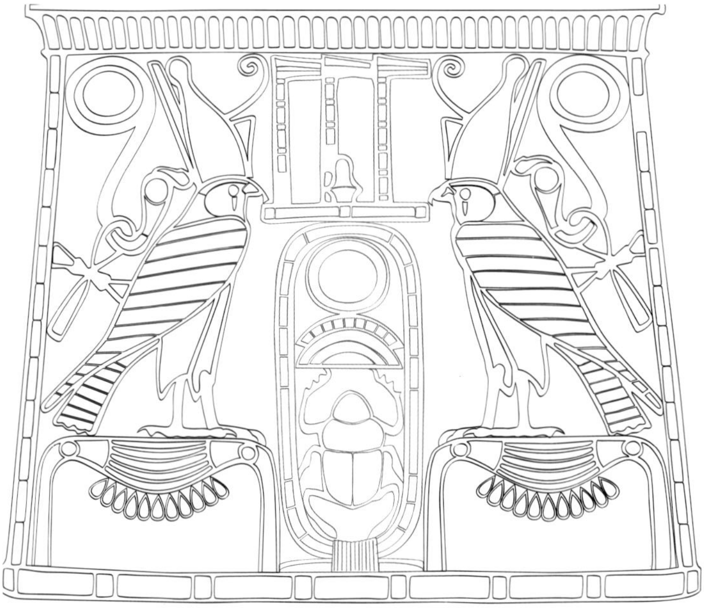

Object 2: Pectoral The name of the king is surrounded and protected by two figures of Horus in the double crown standing on the sign for gold. Transliterate and translate the colored text.

. . . .

. . . .

Object 3: Pectoral

This elaborate pectoral depicts the king in the traditional smiting position. An ankh stands behind each figure of the king, giving him air, and thus life. Transliterate and translate the signs above the vulture, the central inscription, and the repeated cartouche.

. . . .

. . . .

Object 4: Pyramidion

This pyramidion once topped the pyramid of the king named in the inscription. Begin in the center and go first to the right and then to the left. You do not need to translate the central inscription (the eyes, the nefer signs, and the sun disk).

. . . .

. . . .

Lesson 26: 2nd Intermediate Period & New Kingdom

You need to know three new signs in order to read the following section:

Hieroglyph:  **Transliteration:** *ꜣḫ*

What is it? A heron.

Hieroglyph:  **Transliteration:** *ỉʿḥ*

What is it? A crescent moon. Sometimes this is seen upside-down.

Hieroglyph:  **Transliteration:** *stḥ, sṯḥ*

What is it? An unidentifiable canine creature, the god Seth.

During the late Middle Kingdom, there was an influx of foreigners from the northeast into the Delta. By about 1630 B.C. these foreigners, known as the Hyksos (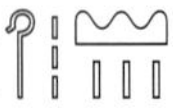 *ḥḳꜣw ḫꜣswt*, "Rulers of Foreign Lands"), had taken over rule of the Delta as Dynasty 15, sharing power with various vassal dynasties (16 and 17) in other regions of the country. Far to the south, the Nubian kingdom of Kush was on the rise, and the Egyptians were caught between the two emerging powers.

In about 1600 B.C., Dynasty 17, based at Thebes, began the struggle for independence under a king named Seqenenre Taa II. We know that he died in battle, because the skull of his mummy shows the marks of the Asiatic battle axes with which he was killed. He was succeeded by his son Kamose, who seems to have died young. The throne passed to Kamose's younger brother, Nebpehtyre Ahmose,  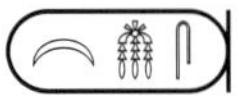, *nb-pḥty-rꜥ ỉꜥḥ-ms*; the Theban kingdom was held together during his childhood by their mother, Iahhotep (Ahhotep).

When Nebpehtyre Ahmose reached adulthood, he went back on the offensive, and succeeded in expelling the Hyksos in about 1550 B.C. He is considered the first king of Dynasty 18, a warrior pharaoh who reunited the country and ushered in the New Kingdom. Over the next two centuries, the native rulers of the Nile expanded their territory to include much of the land to the south, and also conquered many cities to the northeast, holding much of Syria-Palestine as vassal states. Great wealth poured into Egypt's coffers, and there was a blossoming of international trade. Most, but not all, of the kings of Dynasty 18 were named Amenhotep (sometimes rendered as Amenophis) or Djehutymes (usually seen as Tuthmosis).

The first pharaohs of the 18th Dynasty left relatively few monuments behind them. Two names you are likely to encounter are Maatkare Hatshepsut (united of/with Amen), 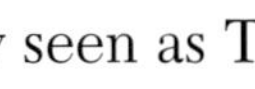 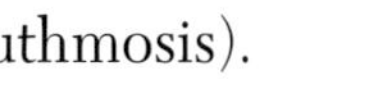, *mꜣꜥt-kꜣ-rꜥ ḥꜣt-špswt ẖnmt-ỉmn* , a queen who ruled as pharaoh for twenty years; and her stepson/nephew, 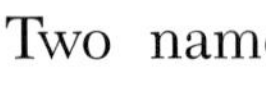 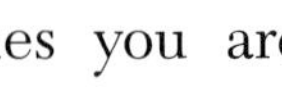, *mn-ḫpr-rꜥ ḏḥwty-ms*, who campaigned extensively and expanded the borders of the Egyptian empire to their greatest extent. You will notice inside the cartouche of Hatshepsut an extra epithet: *ẖnmt-ỉmn*, "united with Amen." Beginning in the 18th Dynasty, it became common for epithets to be included inside cartouches; in general, you do not need to memorize these epithets, but I include some of them here for the sake of completeness. Menkheperre Tuthmosis III was followed by his son, Aakheperure Amenhotep II (ruler of Iunu),  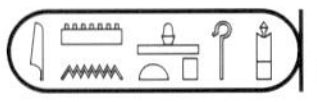, *ꜥꜣ-ḫprw-rꜥ ỉmn-Htp ḥḳꜣ-ỉwnw*, and then grandson, Menkheperure Tuthmosis IV, , *mn-ḫprw-rꜥ ḏḥwty-ms*.

The next king, Nebmaatre Amenhotep III (ruler of Thebes),  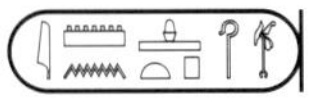, *nb-mꜣꜥt-rꜥ ỉmn-m-ḥꜣt ḥḳꜣ-wꜣst*, ruled during a period of enormous wealth, when Egypt held sway over much of the known world. The son of Amenhotep III began his reign as Amenhotep IV. However, in the 5th year of his reign, he changed his name to Neferkheperure Waenre Akhenaten, , *nfr-ḫprw-rꜥ wꜥ-n-rꜥ ꜣḫ-n-ỉtn*, so that he could compound it with the sun disk, Aten, rather than the Theban god state Amen. This king was married to the beautiful Nefertiti, and ruled the country from his new capital of Akhetaten. Akhenaten allegedly closed the temples of many other gods, worshipping only his chosen deity. The period he inaugurated is known as the Amarna Period. The best-known monarch of this era is Nebkheperure Tutankhamen (ruler of southern Iunu) , *nb-ḫprw-rꜥ twt-ꜥnḫ-ỉmn ḥḳꜣ-ỉwnw-šmꜥw*, who began life as Tutankhaten and ruled for only about ten years, dying before the age of twenty.

Dynasty 18 was followed by Dynasty 19, another era of warrior kings. The most famous king of this time was Usermaatre (chosen of Re), Ramesses II (beloved of Amen) , *wsr-mꜣꜥt-rꜥ stp-n-rꜥ rꜥ-ms-sw mry-ỉmn*.

Usermaatre Ramesses II was the son of a king named Menmaatre Sety I (beloved of Ptah), , *mn-mꜣꜥt-rꜥ sty mry-n-ptḥ*, whose cartouche includes the name of Seth, god of chaos and disorder. If Sety's name was inscribed someplace where chaos was not allowed, such as inside a temple or a tomb, the hieroglyph for Seth was often replaced by the image of his brother Osiris (). This name is still written as Sety (or, as many people do, Seti).

Dynasty 19 was followed by Dynasty 20, which comprised a series of ten kings; nine of these were named Ramesses. Only Usermaatre (beloved of Amen) Ramesses III (ruler of Iunu) , *wsr-mꜣꜥt-rꜥ mry-ỉmn rꜥ-mss ḥḳꜣ-ỉwnw* left significant monuments. (Here you see why learning the epithets is important; otherwise it could be hard to distinguish Ramesses II from Ramesses III.)

As time passed, the world changed, and by 1200 B.C. Egypt was struggling to confront powerful new rivals in the Near East (primarily the Hittites, and later the Assyrians, Nubians, and Persians). The wars that had once filled its treasure chests now emptied them, and the movements of displaced peoples around the Mediterranean challenged the stability of the empire. By 1100 B.C., the empire had been lost and the New Kingdom was over.

Exercise 23: New Kingdom Monuments

By the way, here is an interesting fact. The term pharaoh was not used before the New Kingdom, and comes from the word for palace, , *pr ꜥꜣ*, literally "Great House."

Part 1: Tiles

These are faience (a silicate-based ceramic) tiles from a royal palace. Transliterate, translate, and identify the king by birth name and Roman numeral.

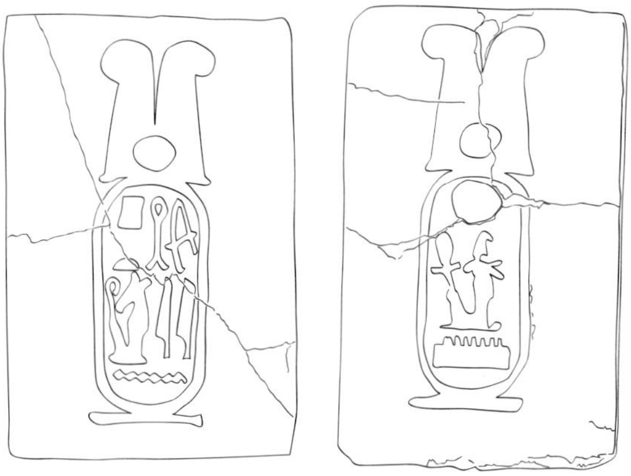

. . . .

. . . .

. . . .

Part 2: Box and Jewel

The two objects on the next page are examples of the way in which hieroglyphs can be used as miniature works of art. The first is a box in the shape of a cartouche; the second is a piece of jewelry in which the glyphs have been used to form both the name of the king and the jewel itself.

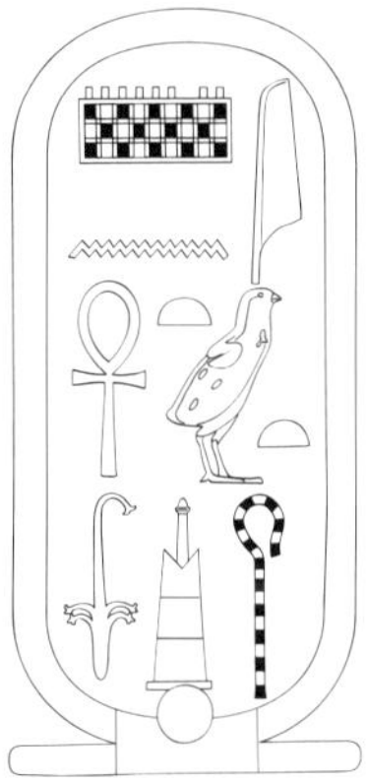

Box: . . . .

Jewel: . . . .

Part 3: Architrave

The next inscription is on the architrave (the beam that runs across the top of columns) of a temple, now set up in the Open Air Museum at Karnak temple in Luxor. Transliterate and translate.

. . . .

. . . .

. . . .

Part 4: Back pillar of statue of Amenhotep II

This is the back pillar of a statue that is currently in the Egyptian Museum, Cairo. You can just see the bottom of the tail of the king's nemes headdress above the pillar that bears the inscription. The bottom of the inscription is a bit worn, so you will have to depend on your knowledge of vocabulary and common formulas to make it out. Watch out for honorific transposition. Transliterate and translate.

. . . .

. . . .

. . . .

. . . .

. . . .

. . . .

. . . .

Lesson 27: After the New Kingdom

For the most part, this book will not deal with inscriptions from the periods after the New Kingdom, but you can still recognize some names. The history of the Third Intermediate Period, which lasted from about 1100 B.C. to about 700 B.C., is complex, with various kings ruling different parts of Egypt—either fighting with one another or co-existing more or less peacefully and even intermarrying. The era began with a theocracy based at Thebes sharing power with a series of Libyan dynasties centered in the Delta; it ended with a Nubian dynasty from Kush, far to the south, invading Egypt and making it part of their own empire.

During this period, the center of power in the eastern Mediterranean shifted to Assyria (in what is now Iraq). In 664 B.C., the mighty Assyrian army, with the help of a powerful family from the Delta city of Sais, swept into Egypt and defeated the Nubian kings, inaugurating what is known as the Late Period (664 to 332 B.C.). The Assyrians could not hold Egypt, as it was too far from their homeland; the family from Sais stepped into the power vacuum they left behind and ruled as the last great Egyptian dynasty.

The next century or so saw the balance of power in the larger region swinging between Assyria, Chaldea (in southern Iraq), and Egypt, with Libya and Nubia making an occasional play for dominance over the Egyptian Nile Valley. The late sixth century saw the rise of the Persian empire, which added Egypt to its vassals in 525 B.C. Apart from several more or less brief resurgences of native rule, Egypt remained an Assyrian province until 332 B.C., when the Egyptians voluntarily surrendered Memphis to Alexander the Great. After Alexander's death, Egypt was inherited by one of his generals, Ptolemy, and the Ptolemaic Period began. In 30 B.C., Egypt's last great queen, Cleopatra VII, committed suicide, and Egypt became a province of the Roman Empire.

Here are three new signs that you need to learn in order to do the next exercises.

HIEROGLYPH:  **TRANSLITERATION:** *wꜣḥ, sk*
WHAT IS IT? A twisted bit of fiber, evidently used for cleaning.

HIEROGLYPH:  **TRANSLITERATION:** *rw, l*
WHAT IS IT? A reclining lion. In the Ptolemaic Period, the lion could be used for the letter "l."

HIEROGLYPH:  **TRANSLITERATION:** *wꜣ*
WHAT IS IT? A lasso. In the Ptolemaic Period, this could be used as an "o."

Exercise 24: Post-New Kingdom Monuments

Here is some vocabulary you will need to do this exercise.

Vocabulary

	*nt*	Neith (a goddess)
	*sꜣw*	Saw (Sais,)
	*ꜣst*	Isis (a goddess)

Object 1: Column of Psametik I

This column, now in the Egyptian Museum, Cairo, is topped with the head of Hathor, goddess of music and love. The inscription bears the name of a king of Dynasty 26, the last significant native dynasty to control all of Egypt. The signs inside the serekh and the cartouche write the names of this king, so just transliterate and give an English version. Also, remember to be flexible: the determinative for the name of the goddess Neith is sideways, so that it fits better into the space. There is a good example of honorific transposition in the phrase that follows the name in the cartouche; the name and epithets of the deity will come before "beloved of" in the hieroglyphs, but should come afterwards in the transliteration and translation.

. . . .

. . . .

. . . .

Object 2: Relief from Dendera

The next illustration comes from the outer wall of a Ptolemaic temple to the goddess Hathor at Dendera in southern Egypt. This is an extraordinary monument, and is still in an excellent state of preservation. In the partial scene illustrated here, the king offers incense to the god, while the queen offers a necklace and shakes a musical rattle called a sistrum. Only try to read the first three cartouches (in purple). They are very crowded, but you should be able to make them out.

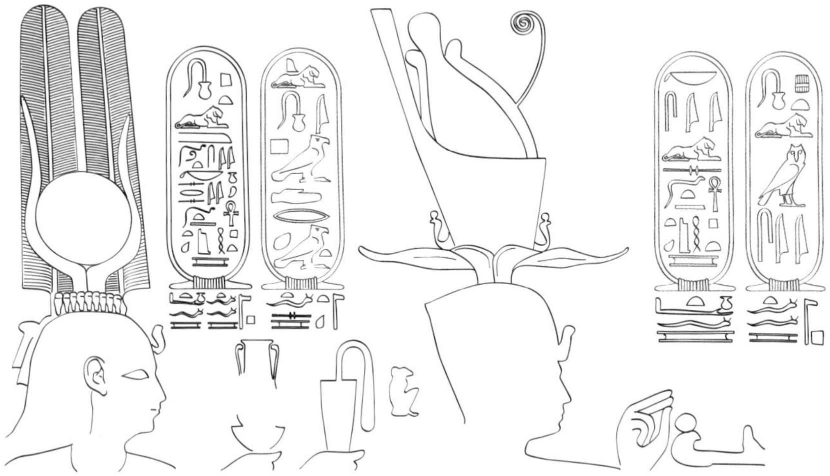

Cartouche 1: . . . .

Cartouche 2: . . . .

Cartouche 3: . . . .

Lesson 28: Royal Dating

Egyptian dates were calculated according to the number of years the king had been on the throne (this is known as regnal dating). In other words, instead of our 'absolute' dating, where we just keep counting the years in sequence from a fixed historical point, the Egyptians began over again with the accession of each new king.

Fortunately, the Egyptians were of necessity accomplished astronomers, a crucial skill as they were dependent on the agricultural cycle. Some astronomical observations have come down to us from ancient times, and a few of these are linked to regnal dates of specific kings, giving us relatively fixed points on which to hang Egyptian chronology (although, as mentioned earlier, there is still debate over where these observations were made, which makes a difference in the results).

Regnal dates usually include year, season, month and day. The Egyptian calendar was based on a year of 360 days, with five days, referred to as "epogomenal," inserted between the end of one year and the beginning of the next. There were ten days to a week, three weeks to a month, four months to a season, and three seasons to a year. After the date comes the phrase: , *ḫr ḥm n,* "under the Majesty of," and then the titulary and name of the king. Here are some new signs and vocabulary.

HIEROGLYPH:  **TRANSLITERATION:** *ꜣbd*
WHAT IS IT? A crescent moon.

HIEROGLYPH: 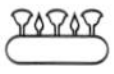 **TRANSLITERATION:** *ꜣḫ, šꜣ*
WHAT IS IT? A marshy piece of land sprouting plants.

HIEROGLYPH:  **TRANSLITERATION:** *ḥsbt; ḥꜣt, tr; rnpt*
WHAT IS IT? The rib of a palm branch, stripped of leaves and notched. Remember that many signs have several possible uses; the vocabulary list will tell you which to use for the next exercise.

HIEROGLYPH:  **TRANSLITERATION:** *sp*
WHAT IS IT? A threshing floor covered with grain.

HIEROGLYPH:  **TRANSLITERATION:** *ḫꜣ*
WHAT IS IT? A lotus plant.

Vocabulary

	*ꜣbd*	month (abbreviated 𓇹)
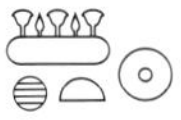	*ꜣḫt*	Akhet (inundation season)
	*prt*	Peret (season of emergence)
	*ḥsbt*	year (used for regnal dates)
	*ḫꜣ*	one thousand
	*sw*	day (in dates)
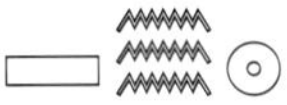	*šmw*	Shemu (season of summer)

Numbers

Regnal dates include numbers. Ones and tens are all you need for regnal dates; here are hundreds, one thousand, one hundred thousand, and a million for the sake of completeness.

Ones: The numbers from one to ten are simply indicated by strokes, similar to those used to indicate singular (𓏺), dual, (𓏭), and plural (𓏺𓏺𓏺). These are generally arranged artistically in a way that best fits the space.

Example: 𓏺𓏺𓏺𓏺 𓏺𓏺𓏺𓏺 = 8.

Tens: Ten is represented by a hobble for cattle: 𓎆, repeated as often as necessary.

Hundreds: A coiled rope represents one hundred: 𓍢.

Thousands: One thousand is represented by a lotus plant: 𓆼 (*ḫꜣ*).

One Hundred Thousand: A tadpole is used to represent 100,000: 𓆐.

One Million: The god Heh supporting the sky symbolizes 1,000,000 𓁨.

Exercise 25: Numbers

Here are some simple numbers to interpret.

Example: 𓆼𓍢𓍢𓎆𓎆𓎆𓏺𓏺𓏺𓏺 1,234

1. 𓎆𓎆𓎆𓏺𓏺𓏺 . . . .

2. 𓍢𓍢𓍢𓍢𓍢𓍢𓍢𓎆𓎆𓎆𓎆𓎆𓏺𓏺𓏺 . . . .

3.  . . . .

4.  . . . .

5.  . . . .

Exercise 26: Regnal Dates

Based on the following example, see if you can translate these imaginary regnal dates.

Example:

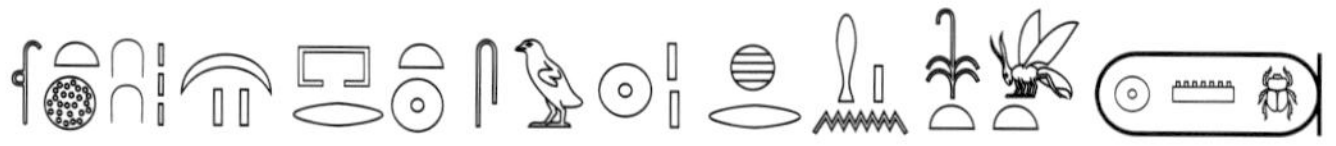

ḥsbt 23 ꜣbd 2 prt sw 2 ḫr ḥm n nswt bi͗ty mn-ḫpr-rꜥ Year 23, Month 2 of Peret, Day 2, under the Majesty of the King of Upper and Lower Egypt, Menkheperre (Thutmosis III).

1. 

. . . .

. . . .

2. 

. . . .

. . . .

3. 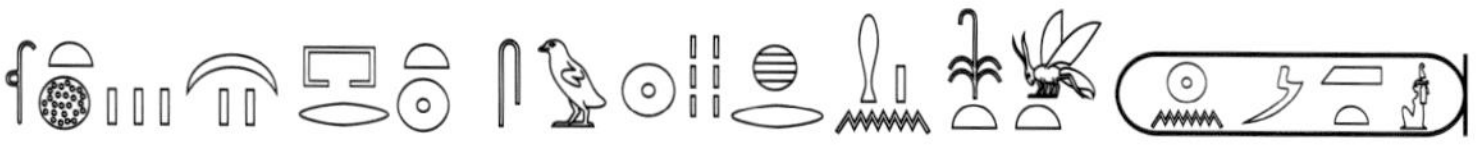

. . . .

. . . .

. . . .

Lesson 29: Royal Monuments from All Periods

The inscriptions on the monuments you have seen so far have been limited to royal names and relatively brief epithets. In this lesson, you will be tackling some slightly more extensive inscriptions. The key to success with these monuments is recognizing patterns, and deciding in what order to read the texts. I will walk you carefully through two typical monuments: a statue base; and a lintel. Then you will try your hand at some others. Grids have been overlaid on some of the illustrations to help you.

Exercise 27: Royal Monuments from All Periods

Example 1: Throne Base of a Statue of Amenemhat I

Vocabulary

	*mswt*	birth
	*ẖnm*	Khnum (a god)

This throne base, in the Egyptian Museum, Cairo is divided into three columns. It is to be read from right to left and top to bottom:

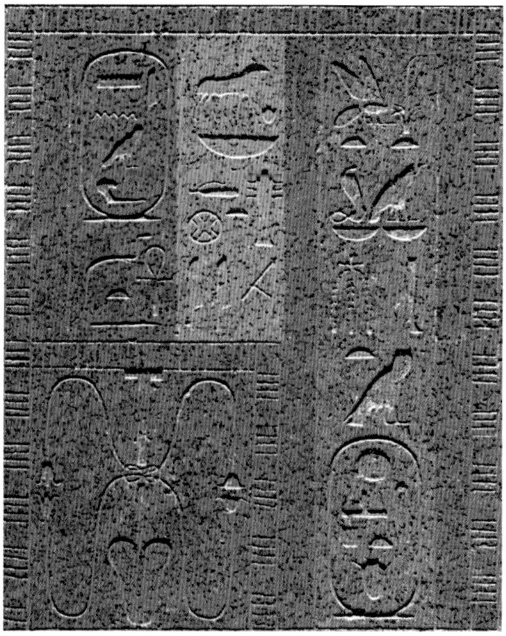

Column 1 (pink): *nswt bỉty nbty wḥm-mswt sḥtp-ỉb-rʿ* = King of Upper and Lower Egypt, the Two Ladies Wekhem-mesut (Repeating/ Repeater of Births); Sehetepibre

Column 2 (yellow): (Watch for the honorific transposition here.) *mry ẖnm nb ḏdt* = Beloved of Khnum, Lord of Djedet (Djedu)

Column 3 (blue): *ỉmn-m-ḥ3t ʿnḫ ḏt* = Amenemhat, living forever.

Example 2: Lintel of Ramesses II

Lintels are a good place to practice reading the names and titles of kings. They are generally symmetrical, so if there is damage on one side you will usually be able to fill in the blanks from the other side. This lintel is in the Theban mortuary temple of Seti I, the father of Ramesses II.

Follow along with the transliteration and translation so you can see how it works; you will try your hand at another lintel in the following exercise.

New signs and vocabulary:

HIEROGLYPH:  **TRANSLITERATION:** *ꜣḫt*

WHAT IS IT? The sun between two hills or mountains.

HIEROGLYPH:  **TRANSLITERATION:** *bḥ*

WHAT IS IT? An elephant's tusk.

HIEROGLYPH:  **TRANSLITERATION:** *ns*

WHAT IS IT? An animal's tongue.

Hieroglyph:  **Transliteration:** *rꜥ-ḥr-(ꜣḫty)*

What is it? A Horus falcon with a sun disk on his head. This is often seen on monuments with the sun disk just behind the falcon. This deity represents a merging of Re with Horus (often "of the two horizons," hence the sometimes unwritten *ꜣḫty*)

Vocabulary

	*ꜣḫt*	horizon
	*bḥdt*	the Behedite
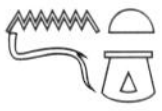	*nst*	seat, throne
	*rꜥ-ḥr-(ꜣḫty)*	Re-Horakhty

Transliteration and translation:

1. Beside winged solar disk on either side (badly damaged on one side, but visible on the other: *bḥdt* = the Behedite.
2. Top line, center to right: *ꜥnḫ rꜥ-ḥr-ꜣḫty kꜣ nḫt mry mꜣꜥt mry ỉmn-rꜥ nswt nṯrw* = Live Re-Horakhty, the strong bull, beloved of Maat, beloved of Amen-Re, king of the gods.
3. Top line, center to left: (Notice that you use the ankh sign, which is conveniently symmetrical, as part of both left and right inscriptions.) *ꜥnḫ rꜥ-ḥr-ꜣḫty kꜣ nḫt mry mꜣꜥt mry ỉmn-rꜥ nb nswt tꜣwy* = Live Re-Horakhty, the strong bull, beloved of Maat, beloved of Amen-Re, lord of the thrones of the Two Lands.
4. Second line, either direction: *ꜥnḫ nswt bỉty nb tꜣwy wsr-mꜣꜥt-rꜥ stp-n-rꜥ mry ỉmn-rꜥ* = Live the King of Upper and Lower Egypt, lord of the Two Lands, Usermaatre, beloved of Amen-Re.
5. Third line, either direction: *ꜥnḫ sꜣ rꜥ nb ḫꜥw rꜥ-mss mry-ỉmn mry mwt* = Live the son of Re, lord of appearances, Ramesses, beloved of Amen, beloved of Mut (as well as the word for mother, this is also the name of an important goddess).

Now it is your turn to try.

Object 1: Stela

This stela was found inside the Valley Temple of the king named here. This temple was part of one of his pyramid complexes at Dahshur, and stood at the end of a large causeway that led from the mortuary temple in front of the pyramid toward the edge of the floodplain to the east. You have only learned the name in the cartouche; transliterate and give English approximations of the other names.

Transliteration: ....

....

Translation: ....

....

Object 2: Statue Base

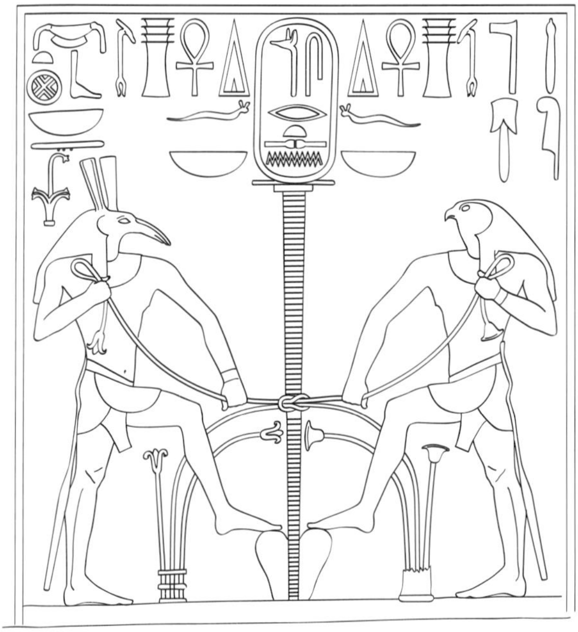

This is the base of a statue in the Egyptian Museum, Cairo, from one of a group of statues of this king from his pyramid complex at Lisht. The two figures here are Seth (left) and Horus (right); the plants under their legs identify them as being from Upper (lotus or lily) and Lower (papyrus) Egypt, respectively. The large hieroglyph in the center of the scene,  *smꜣ*, means "unite." Horus and Seth tie their heraldic plants around this hieroglyph, symbolically uniting the Two Lands. Notice that the neb sign is used here both as "lord" (to the left) and as "all" (toward the center, twice).

One new sign and some vocabulary:

HIEROGLYPH:  **TRANSLITERATION:** *sꜣb*

WHAT IS IT? An animal skin with tail attached.

VOCABULARY

	*nbwty*	He of Ombos (the god Seth)
	*sꜣb*	many-colored of plumage

Transliterate and translate:

Central cartouche:. . . . .

. . . .

Right side:. . . . .

. . . .

Left side:. . . . .

. . . .

Object 3: Statue Base of Ramesses II

Here is one new phrase that you will need for the monument illustrated on the next page:

VOCABULARY

	ḥry-ỉb	who dwells in

Purple) . . . .

. . . .

. . . .

Blue) . . . .

. . . .

. . . .

Red) . . . .

. . . .

. . . .

Brown) . . . .

. . . .

. . . .

Object 4: Lintel of Amenhotep II

This lintel is completely symmetrical. As before, the ankh signs are used in both directions. You will meet a new god here: Horemakhet (Horus in the horizon).

Beside the winged sun disk: . . . .

Line 1:. . . . .

. . . .

Line 2:. . . . .

. . . .

Object 5: Middle Kingdom Royal Stela

On the next page is the top of a royal stela in the Cairo Museum. The organization of the signs here can be confusing; color has again been used to help you. You have not seen the name in the serekh before; transliterate it and give an English approximation. You may also be confused by the sign behind the thin figure holding an ankh to the nose of the falcon on top of the serekh; this is Osiris, being used in a sort of rebus (Osiris holding life to the nose of the king, represented by Horus and his name). The Horus falcon on the standard with the feather () is being used in place of a sign you already know (, *ỉmntt,* "west," "western"); as indicated by the colors, the word here continues on the top of the next column.

Here are some new signs and one new vocabulary word:

Hieroglyph:  **Transliteration:** *msn*

What is it? A bag of wickerwork.

Hieroglyph:  **Transliteration:** *ỉmntt*

What is it? Used in place of .

Vocabulary

 *msn* Mesen

Turn the page; transliterate and translate.

Green: ....

....

Orange: ....

....

....

....

Pink: ....

....

....

....

Blue: ....

....

....

....

End of Chapter III

Chapter IV
Titles

Ancient Egyptian society was extremely hierarchical. It has often been compared to a pyramid, with the king at the top, the royal family just below, then various ranks of officials, all supported by the mass of workers and peasants on whom the economy depended. This chapter explores the realm of the royal family and high officialdom with an introduction to the titles held by the Egyptian elite. These are ubiquitous in monumental inscriptions (found on the walls of tombs and on stelae and statues) and your ability to understand the most common ones will give you a glimpse into the professional lives of elite society. Information on the parentage of the people represented is often included in these inscriptions, providing us with information about the families of these ancient men and women.

There are thousands of titles known from ancient Egypt: at last count, there were almost four thousand attested from the Old Kingdom alone. (This tells you something about the importance of bureaucracy in ancient Egypt!) However, many of these are variations on some standard themes, and you will be able to figure out a majority of them with the aid of a good dictionary. This chapter introduces you to some of the most basic titles, to give you a place to start.

These basic titles are divided into four lessons. First come royal titles, held by close relatives of the king. Next are high court titles, borne for the most part by people of royal or noble birth (although as time went on, this included increasingly large numbers of people). Next come some administrative titles, and then a few priestly titles. These are artificial divisions, created here solely for practical purposes. Unlike a modern bureaucracy, the ancient Egyptian government was not divided into rigid departments. Most officials, both high and low, served in multiple branches of the official and priestly administration; many members of the royal family also held significant official and priestly titles (and just to make things more complicated, people without direct ties to the king could also hold royal titles). Thus a single person could hold royal titles, high court titles (some of which seem to denote rank rather than function), administrative titles, and priestly titles, all at the same time. It is also likely that once a person was awarded a particular title, he or she kept that title throughout life, even if they no longer performed the designated function.

IMPORTANT NOTE: As you have already seen, the Egyptians used no punctuation in their monumental hieroglyphs. This chapter deals with titles, which are generally strung together in lists, with no divisions. One of the difficulties of working with titles is knowing where to end one and start the next. The best way to address this is by knowing the most common individual titles, which is what you will learn in this chapter.

LESSON 30: QUEENS, PRINCES, AND PRINCESSES

Each king had a family, with wives (usually multiple), sons, and daughters. In this lesson, you will learn the most important titles for queens, princes, and princesses. You already know most of the signs and vocabulary you need to interpret these titles; here is one new sign, used in a new vocabulary word.

HIEROGLYPH:  **TRANSLITERATION:** *ḫkr*

WHAT IS IT? Possibly the top of a bundle of reeds. Carved and painted versions were used as decorative ornaments around the tops of walls.

Vocabulary

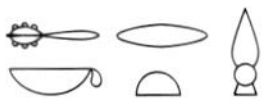	*ẖkrt*	ornament

Here are some of the most common titles for the royal family.

Queens: The most important titles for queens:

	*ḥmt nswt*	wife of the king
	*ḥmt nswt wrt*	great wife of the king
	*mwt nswt*	mother of the king
	*ẖkrt nswt wrt*	great royal ornament

Princes: The basic princely title is:

	*sꜣ nswt*	king's son

This can also refer to a grandson. Especially in later periods, this can be an honorific sort of title given to non-royal officials, so you cannot assume a *sꜣ nswt* is an actual prince. There are two variations on this title; if you see these, it is more likely that you are dealing with a real prince:

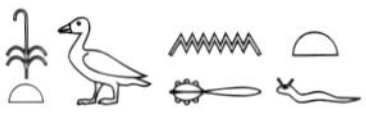	*sꜣ nswt n ẖt.f*	king's son of his body
	*sꜣ nswt smsw*	eldest king's son

Princesses: The titles for princesses are essentially the same as for the princes, with the addition of the feminizing t (not always written).

	*sꜣt nswt*	king's daughter
	*sꜣt nswt nt ẖt.f*	king's daughter of his body
	*sꜣt nswt smsw*	eldest king's daughter.

Exercise 28: Titles of the Royal Family

Transliterate and translate these titles.

1.  ....
2.  ....
3. 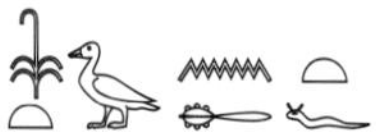 ....
4.  ....
5.  ....
6.  ....
7.  ....

Here is one new phrase to learn:

VOCABULARY

	*ꜥnḫ.tỉ*	may she live

Exercise 29: The Royal Family

Object 1: Old Kingdom Sarcophagus

This inscription is on the side of a large stone sarcophagus, now in the Egyptian Museum, Cairo.

....

....

....

Object 2: Titles from the tomb of Mersyankh

This painted inscription adorns the lintel of the tomb of Mersyankh at Giza, site of the great pyramids of the 4th Dynasty. See if you can figure out which signs spell the name of the tomb's owner.

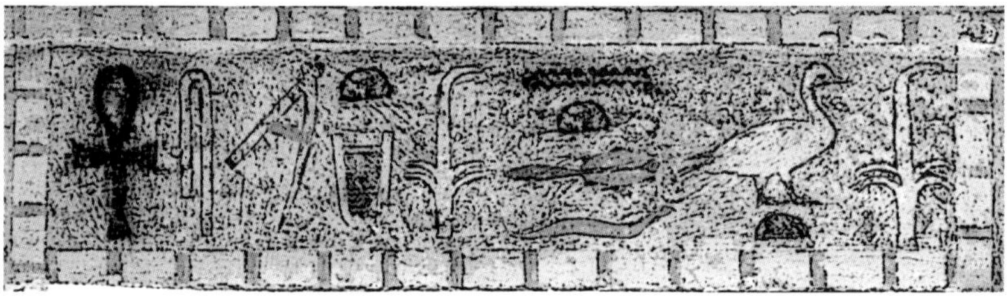

. . . .

. . . .

Object 3: Vase of Queen Tiye

This beautiful calcite vase was found in the tomb of the parents of Queen Tiye, wife of Amenhotep III; it is now in the Cairo Museum. Follow the color-coding; transliterate and translate:

Orange: . . . .

. . . .

Yellow: . . . .

. . . .

Red: . . . .

. . . .

Green: . . . .

. . . .

LESSON 31: COURT TITLES

Here is a new sign that you will need to know. Since many of the new signs you will be seeing from here to the end of the book are used in a limited number of words, information will be included from now on about their most common uses.

HIEROGLYPH:  **TRANSLITERATION:** *ḫtm*
WHAT IS IT? A seal hanging from a necklace.
MOST COMMON USE: In  *ḫtm*, "seal."

Court, or ranking, titles generally come first in lists of titles belonging to a specific person. The translations given here are fairly standard, and reflect what is understood about the function of the office-holder (often very little!). Note that from here on out, I will for the most part give you only the masculine version of words and titles; for female titles, add the feminizing , *t*.

VOCABULARY

	*wʿty*	sole, unique
	*r-pʿ*	hereditary prince
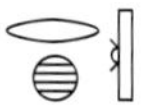	*rḫ*	acquaintance
	*rḫ nswt*	king's acquaintance
	*ḥꜣty-ʿ*	high official
	*ḫtmw-bỉty*	sealer of the King of L.E.*
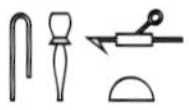	*smr wʿty*	unique companion**

*This can also be transliterated *sḏꜣwty-bỉty*, with the same basic meaning.
**This seems to indicate that the title holder was an intimate of the royal house.

Exercise 30: Practice with a Title String

The court titles are usually put together in a specific order. Remember that there are no markers to indicate where one title stops and the next starts; focus recognizing the individual titles.

Transliteration: . . . .

Translation: . . . .

LESSON 32: ADMINISTRATIVE TITLES

Egyptian administrative titles reflect the multitude of functions that could be carried out by officials. There are literally hundreds of these titles, many of which are variations on a few themes.

This lesson introduces you to some very basic titles, along with a little bit of information about each. Most of these can be combined with modifiers to make them more specific. For example, the first title presented here is , *ỉmy-r*. By itself, this means "overseer." If it is followed by , *pr*, it becomes 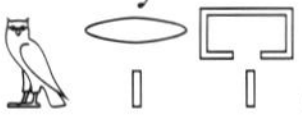, *ỉmy-r pr*, "overseer of the house," or "steward." In this lesson, you will learn only the basic titles; in the exercises, you will meet some of their more elaborate forms.

Here are some new signs that will appear in the following discussion.

HIEROGLYPH:  **TRANSLITERATION:** *ꜣḫ*

WHAT IS IT? A heron. You have met this before.

MOST COMMON USE: Use as a phonogram.

HIEROGLYPH:  **TRANSLITERATION:** *ꜥḏ*

WHAT IS IT? A fish (*Mugil cephalus*).

MOST COMMON USE: In  *ꜥḏ-mr*, "administrator."

HIEROGLYPH:  **TRANSLITERATION:** *mḏḥ*

WHAT IS IT? An adze or axe.

MOST COMMON USE: In  *mḏḥ*, "carpenter," "craftsman," "overseer"

HIEROGLYPH:  **TRANSLITERATION:** *sꜥḥ*

WHAT IS IT? A goat wearing a collar.

MOST COMMON USE: In  *sꜥḥ*, "noble."

HIEROGLYPH:  **TRANSLITERATION:** *ṯꜣyt, ṯꜣitỉ*

WHAT IS IT? The cornice of a building, decorated with a frieze of cobras.

MOST COMMON USE: In  *ṯꜣyt*, "curtain," and *ṯꜣitỉ*, "he of the curtain."

HIEROGLYPH:  **TRANSLITERATION:** *ṯꜣty*

WHAT IS IT? A duckling.

MOST COMMON USE: In  *ṯꜣty*, "vizier."

LIST OF ADMINISTRATIVE TITLES

I. Overseer: The most important title to learn is , *m-r* (usually transliterated more correctly as *ỉmy-r* or *ỉmy-rꜣ),* which means literally "one who is in the mouth," i.e., the one who gives the orders. The ancient Egyptians, in their fondness for wordplay, often used , a tongue, as an abbreviation for . A person could be  of almost anything.

II. Director: , *ḫrp,* is an important title that can be translated "director," "controller," or "administrator."

III. Inspector: , *sḥḏ,* is another important title that you will see often. It is usually translated as "inspector."

IV. Great one: , *wr,* is a word you have met before. It is usually translated "great one," or "greatest," and can be followed by many modifiers.

Great, *wr*, can also be written with this sign: , which, as you have seen, can also be transliterated *smsw*, meaning elder or eldest.

V. Scribe: Another common administrative title is 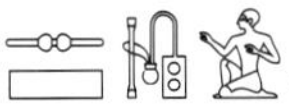. This is traditionally transliterated as *sš*, although modern scholars now transliterate it as *sẖꜣ*. For the sake of simplicity and tradition transliterate this as *sš*. As the determinative (a palette for ink, a water jug, and a reed pen) suggests, this title is translated as scribe. In fact, anyone who was an official was also a scribe, since literacy was a prerequisite for this sort of office, but only certain officials claimed "scribe" as a title.

VI. Judge/Legal: This standing jackal sign, , *sꜣb*, can be translated either as a title, meaning "judge," or as an adjective, meaning "legal." (You will also see this translated as "dignitary," and "senior.") You will usually be able to decide which way to translate this based on context.

VII. Noble: This title , *sꜥḥ*, "noble," is another title that refers to a member of the elite, without specific reference to function.

VIII. Courtier: The title , *špss*, is generally translated as "courtier," also without a specific function attached.

IX. Administrator: The title , *ꜥḏ-mr*, is usually translated as "administrator." There is currently a great deal of debate about exactly what this signifies; for now, all you need to know is the basic translation.

X. Carpenter/Overseer: The title , *mḏḥ*, is seen in a number of contexts, and can mean one of a number of things. Alone, it can be translated "carpenter" or "craftsman." In conjunction with other words, it can mean "overseer."

XI. Land Official/Palace Attendant: The title , *ḫnty-š,* literally means "foremost of the pool"; its exact translation is still under debate, but the most commonly accepted versions are "land official," and "palace attendant." For example, a number of Old Kingdom officials bore the title , *ḫnty-š ꜣḫt-ḫwfw,* "land official of Akhet-Khufu (the pyramid complex of Khufu)."

XII. He of the curtain: The title , *tꜣỉtỉ,* literally means "he of the curtain," and appears to refer to some sort of judicial function. It is most often seen as a title of the vizier.

XIII. Vizier: The highest official in the Egyptian administration was the vizier, , *ṯꜣty*, subordinate only to the king.

Important Note: From now on, there will be a new protocol with regard to vocabulary and exercises. The reality is that you cannot possibly memorize all the vocabulary you will need to translate all the text on the monuments you might see. Within each lesson, I will continue to teach you the most common vocabulary, the words and phrases you will see most often. Armed with only this vocabulary, you will be able to translate a great deal. However, in order to go farther, you will need to know more signs, words and phrases that you will not see as often, things that you might or might not want to commit to memory. Therefore, from now on specific signs and vocabulary will be provided with each exercise that you can use for reference and memorize or not as you see fit. All signs and vocabulary seen in the exercises are also provided in the sign and word lists at the back of the book.

Another Important Note: In general, words within titles follow the usual rules, with adjectives following the nouns they modify. However, this is not always the case, so be prepared to switch the word order if it makes more sense the other way around.

Exercise 31: Practice with Administrative Titles

As promised, here are some new signs, followed by some vocabulary. These will be used in this exercise; some of them may appear in later exercises, but if you do not remember them, you can always look them up in the word list.

Remember that the forms given in the vocabulary lists will not always be the same as those in the titles. In some cases, this is because the titles use a different part of speech, and in others it is because the title is written using an abbreviation. Remember to stay flexible! You do not need to understand the grammar or always see the same spelling to interpret the title.

HIEROGLYPH: or **TRANSLITERATION:** *nḫn*

WHAT IS IT? An artificial mound.

MOST COMMON USE: In *nḫn*, "Nekhen," (ancient city sacred to Horus; known to the Greeks as Hierakonpolis)

HIEROGLYPH: **TRANSLITERATION:** *ḥmwt*

WHAT IS IT? A drill for stoneworking.

MOST COMMON USE: *ḥmwt,* "craft," *ḥmwwt,* "craftsmen."

HIEROGLYPH: **TRANSLITERATION:** *mšʿ*

WHAT IS IT? A Nubian bowman.

MOST COMMON USE: In *mšʿ*, "army," "expeditionary force."

HIEROGLYPH: **TRANSLITERATION:** *kꜣt, ꜣtp*

WHAT IS IT? A man with a basket on his head.

MOST COMMON USE: In *kꜣt*, "work."

HIEROGLYPH: **TRANSLITERATION:** *ʿpr*

WHAT IS IT? This seems to be some sort of bag for clothing.

MOST COMMON USE: In *ʿpr*, "crew," or "equip (verb)."

HIEROGLYPH:  **TRANSLITERATION:** *ꜥḥ*

WHAT IS IT? A palace with a frieze of *ḫkr* signs along the top.

MOST COMMON USE: In  *ꜥḥ*, "palace."

HIEROGLYPH: 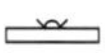 or  **TRANSLITERATION:** *mḏꜣt*

WHAT IS IT? A roll of papyrus (same sign as is used commonly as a determinative).

MOST COMMON USE: In 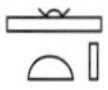 *mḏꜣt*, "document," "book."

VOCABULARY

	*mḏꜣt*	document
	*10 šmꜥw*	10 of Upper Egypt
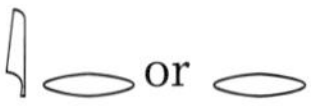	*iry*	guardian
	*ꜥpr*	crew; equip
	*ꜥḥ*	palace
	*mšꜥ*	army, expeditionary force
	*ḥmwt*	craft
	*ḥmwwt*	craftsmen
	*kꜣt*	work

The first six examples here are single titles; the final four are strings of more than one. For each of these, look for the basic titles you know; start a new title when you see one of these.

For each title, translate the basic title and then treat the following word or phrase as a direct genitive.

Example 1:  *imy-r kꜣt* = overseer of work (a simple direct genitive).

Example: 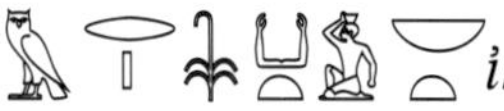 *imy-r kꜣt nbt nswt* = overseer of all the king's work (the phrase that follows "overseer" means "all the work of the king"—a noun, "work," followed by an adjective, "all," and then another noun as a direct genitive, "king," all complicated by the honorific transposition of "king").

1. 

2. 

3. 

4. 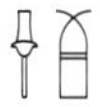

5. 

6. 

7. 

8. 

9. 

10. 

Lesson 33: Priestly Titles

A major percentage of high officials, especially in the earlier periods of Egyptian history, held priestly titles in addition to bureaucratic ones. It was not until the New Kingdom that a professional priesthood developed. First, here are a few new signs.

Hieroglyph:  **Transliteration:** *wꜥb*

What is it? A leg topped by a jar pouring a libation.

Most Common Use: In 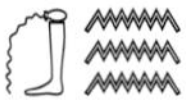 *wꜥb*, "pure," and associated words.

Hieroglyph:  **Transliteration:** *ḥb, šs*

What is it? A basin of alabaster.

Most Common Use: In , *ḥb*, festival, and , *ḥbt*, scroll; also in , *šs*, "alabaster."

Hieroglyph:  **Transliteration:** *tꜣ*

What is it? A potter's kiln.

Most Common Use: This is a relatively common phonogram.

Hieroglyph:  **Transliteration:** *dwꜣ*, *sbꜣ*

What is it? A star.

Most Common Use: In  *sbꜣ*, "star," and  *dwꜣt*, "Duat," the name of the Netherworld,  *dwꜣ* "praise," "worship."

Vocabulary

	*ỉt nṯr*	god's father
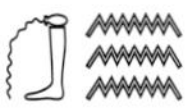	*wꜥb*	pure; purify; cleanse
	*wꜥb*	purifier; wab priest
	*wr mꜣꜣ*	great seer
	*mꜣꜣ*	see (verb)

ḥm nṯr	god's servant
ḥm kꜣ	ka servant (mortuary priest)
ḥry sštꜣ	one who is over the secrets
ḥry-tp	chief
ẖr	under; carrying
ẖry ḥbt	lector priest*
sm	sem priest (funerary priest)
sštꜣ	secret
šmꜥw	musician; singer
šmꜥyt	chantress
dwꜣ	praise; worship
dwꜣ nṯr	divine adorer

* literally "one carrying the scroll"

Each of these basic titles can be modified by specific information, often the name of a king, a pyramid complex, or a god.

Exercise 32: Practice with Priestly Titles

Translate the following priestly titles. Some are single titles, others are strings of two or three. There are two new signs here, and two new words:

Hieroglyph:  **Transliteration:** *nḥt, ỉmꜣ*

What is it? A tree.

Most Common Use: In , *ỉmꜣ*, "tree," , *nḥt*, "sycamore."

Hieroglyph:  **Transliteration:** *ḥwt-ḥr*

What is it? A Horus falcon inside a temple.

Most Common Use: In  *ḥwt-ḥr* "Hathor," goddess of music and love.

VOCABULARY

	*nht*	sycomore
	*ḥwt-ḥr*	Hathor (a goddess)

One of the things that you will really have to watch out for here, as usual, is honorific transposition. Here is an example of how complicated it can get: Example: 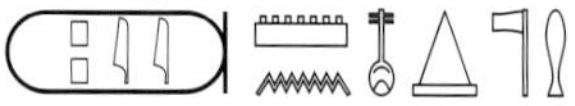. This should be read *ḥm-nṯr mn-nfr-ppy*, "god's servant of Men-nefer Pepy" (the pyramid complex of Pepy, from which, by the way, the city of Memphis took its name). There is honorific transposition within the title , *ḥm-nṯr*, within the name of the pyramid complex, , *mn-nfr-ppy*, and then the order of the two elements is reversed. Here are some titles and title strings to transliterate and translate:

1. . . . . .

. . . .

2. 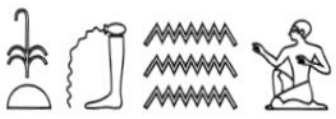 . . . .

. . . .

3. . . . . .

. . . .

4.  . . . .

. . . .

5.  . . . .

. . . .

6.  . . . .

. . . .

7.  . . . .

. . . .

8. 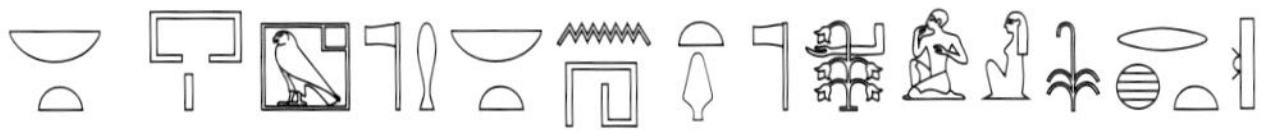 . . . .

. . . .

. . . .

Lesson 34: Titles and Filiation on Monuments

This lesson is dedicated to monuments, for the most part from the Cairo Museum, on which you can practice reading real strings of titles. These strings often include information about the official's parentage; this is known as filiation.

The way that private people expressed filiation was through certain formulaic phrases similar to those you practiced in Chapter 2. The most common pattern is: "X, (who was) made of/by Y [the father], (who was) borne of/by Z [the mother]. Here is an example:

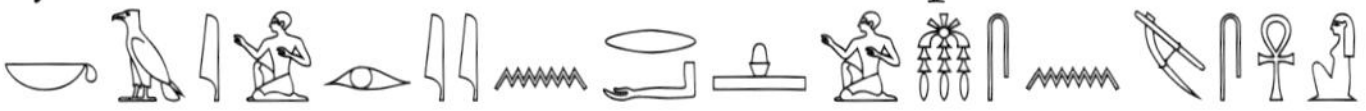

kꜣi ỉry n rʿ-Htp ms n mr.s-ʿnḫ =

Kai, made by Rahotep, borne of Mersyankh.

There are several other ways to express filiation; you will see one of these in the example given for the following exercise.

Exercise 33: Practice with Monuments

Before moving to the monuments on which you will try your hand, here is a example.

Example: Tomb Owner Catching Birds

This scene, from the 12th Dynasty tomb of Khnumhotep at Beni Hasan, shows the tomb owner seated on an elegant stool, single-handed pulling closed a clap-net in which he has caught many birds. He sits behind a screen made of reeds so that he will not scare the birds away, and is accompanied by two officials, one of whom is his eldest son.

Inscription over scene: *r-pꜥ ḥꜣty-ꜥ ỉmy-r ḫꜣswt ỉꜣbtt nḥrỉ sꜣ ẖnm-ḥtp ỉr.n bꜣḳt nb ỉmꜣḫ* = The hereditary prince, high official, overseer of the eastern desert, Nehri's son, Khnumhotep, lord of reverence. [Note: you might want to read this as "Nehri, son of Khnumhotep," but it is actually the other way around—this is another way of expressing filiation, common in the Middle Kingdom.]

Above first small figure: *sꜣ ḥꜣty-ꜥ smsw.f nḫt ỉr.n ẖty* = The son of the high official, his eldest, Nakht, made of (by) Khety.

Above second small figure: *ỉmy-r ḫtmw bꜣḳt* = overseer of sealers, Baqt.

Object 1: Side of Stela

This inscription is on the side of the large stela that you translated in the last chapter. It gives the name of the official responsible for carving the inscription.

. . . .

. . . .

. . . .

. . . .

. . . .

Object 2: Offering Stand of Setjwabu

This is an offering stand; it would have been placed outside the façade of a tomb. There are four titles here, followed by the name of the tomb owner. This is from Saqqara and is now in the Egyptian Museum, Cairo.

. . . .

. . . .

Object 3: Lintel of a False Door

This is taken from an Old Kingdom false door, now in the Egyptian Museum, Cairo. (This is a type of monument discussed further in the next chapter.) The lintel gives you the names and titles of the tomb owner and his wife; the slab stela above (not illustrated here) identifies the tomb owner, his wife, and two of their children.

VOCABULARY

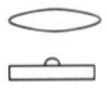 *ỉry-mḏꜣt* keeper of documents.

Line 1: . . . .

. . . .

. . . .

. . . .

Line 2: . . . .

. . . .

. . . .

Object 4: Base of Old Kingdom Statue

This is the base of a statue from the Old Kingdom, also from the Cairo Museum. The overlaid colors will help you sort out the individual titles, of which there are three. The two pairs of feet you see here belong to two statues of the man named on this statue base, Sedenmaat.

HIEROGLYPH: **TRANSLITERATION:** *wḏʿ*

WHAT IS IT? No one seems to know.

MOST COMMON USE: As a phonogram.

HIEROGLYPH: **TRANSLITERATION:** *md*

WHAT IS IT? A staff.

MOST COMMON USE: In , *mdw* "words; speech."

VOCABULARY

	smꜣʿ wḏʿ-mdw	arbitrator
	ḥwt-wrt	law court

Transliterate and translate:

. . . .

. . . .

. . . .

. . . .

. . . .

. . . .

. . . .

Object 5: Old Kingdom Couple

This pair of statues dates from the beginning of the 4th Dynasty. They were found at Meidum, and are now in the Egyptian Museum, Cairo. As is the case for many early Old Kingdom monuments, the spelling of the titles here is variable, and the arrangement of signs can be irregular; the individual titles have been picked out in alternating colors to help you.

HIEROGLYPH:  **TRANSLITERATION:** *ꜣms*

WHAT IS IT? A staff with a flail.

MOST COMMON USE: In , *ꜣms*, "*ames* scepter."

HIEROGLYPH:  **TRANSLITERATION:** *ỉs*

WHAT IS IT? A bundle of reeds tied with a string.

MOST COMMON USE: A common phonogram.

HIEROGLYPH:  **TRANSLITERATION:** *ḥb*

WHAT IS IT? An alabaster basin topped by a tent or booth held up by a pole.

MOST COMMON USE: In 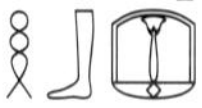 *ḥb*, "festival."

VOCABULARY

	*ꜣms*	*ames* scepter
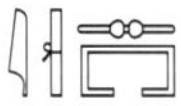	*ỉs*	tomb; council chamber
	*npt*	Nepet (a town)
	*ḥb*	festival
	*smsw ỉs*	elder of the council chamber
	*sṯt*	transport worker(s)
	*špntỉw*	the Shepentiu
	*tmꜣ*	bowmen

Turn the page; transliterate and translate.

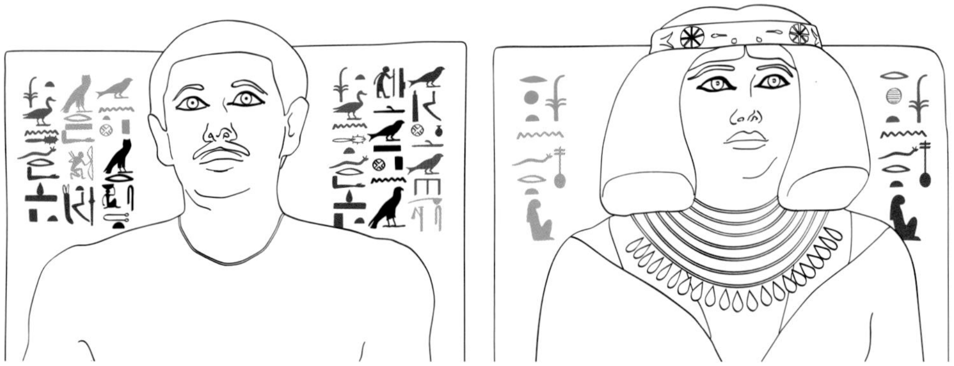

Woman's titles: ....

....

Man's titles, right side: ....

....

....

Man's titles, left side: ....

....

....

Object 6: Wooden Panel of Hesyre

HIEROGLYPH: **TRANSLITERATION:** *unknown*

WHAT IS IT? Also unknown.

MOST COMMON USE: In , *?*, "cult image(?)"

HIEROGLYPH: **TRANSLITERATION:** *mnw*

WHAT IS IT? The emblem of the god Min.

MOST COMMON USE: In *mnw*, "Min," a fertility god.

HIEROGLYPH: **TRANSLITERATION:** *mḥyt*

WHAT IS IT? A lioness.

MOST COMMON USE: In *mḥyt*, "Mehyt," the name of a goddess.

Hieroglyph: **Transliteration:** *ḳd*

What is it? A builder's level.

Most Common Use: As a phonogram, *ḳd*.

Vocabulary

	?	cult image?
	mnw	Min
	mḥyt	Mehyt
	smsw ḳd-ḥtp	elder of the Qed-hetep*

*No one is sure how to translate this.

This wooden panel was one of a number of similar pieces found inside a large and elaborate tomb of the 3rd Dynasty at Saqqara. Work in columns from right to left; as in the statues of Rahotep and Nofret, the individual titles have been highlighted in various colors to help you distinguish them. Transliterate and translate.

Exercise 34: Stela of Tetisheri

This stela belongs to a queen from the very beginning of the New Kingdom; it was found at Abydos. The text is the same on both sides of the center line. There are three new signs to learn for this stela:

HIEROGLYPH:  **TRANSLITERATION:** *ḥꜣ*
WHAT IS IT? A bit of earth with papyrus growing from it.

HIEROGLYPH: 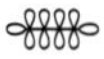 **TRANSLITERATION:** *sꜣ*
WHAT IS IT? A hobble for cattle.

HIEROGLYPH:  **TRANSLITERATION:** *sꜣ*
WHAT IS IT? A rolled up mat or tent.

HIEROGLYPH:  **TRANSLITERATION:** *šri͗, ẖrd*
WHAT IS IT? A child.

VOCABULARY

	*ḥꜣ*	behind
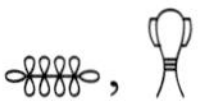	*sꜣ*	protect, protection
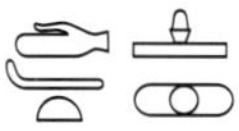	*dbḥt-ḥtp*	funerary meal

There are five distinct texts on this stela, each of which is repeated twice (once on each side of the central axis). These have been colored so that you can follow them. The orientation of each inscription tells you to whom it refers; the figures that go with each inscription have also been colored. (Note that the hieroglyphs will tend to face the same direction as the person or thing to whom they refer.)

Transliteration and translate:

Green: ....

Blue: ....

....

....

....

Red: ....

....

....

....

Yellow: ....

....

End of Chapter IV

45969

Chapter V
Offering Prayers

Every decorated tomb and temple contained an offering prayer and/or offering list, designed to ensure eternal sustenance for the cult recipient (the deceased or the god). Ideally, this sustenance was provided in the form of actual food and drink, but the ancient Egyptians were practical people, and they knew that their cults might not be active forever. Since they believed that words were magic, written prayers and funerary lists could substitute for real provisions. This chapter will introduce the basic offering prayer, seen primarily in private tombs and on votive stelae.

Although the styles of elite Egyptian tombs changed from period to period and region to region, they all had two basic components, an underground area for the burial and an aboveground area for the cult. The body, mummified and placed in a coffin, was deposited in a burial chamber at the bottom of a shaft. Above the shaft was built a mortuary chapel in which the cult was carried out. After the funeral, the burial shaft was sealed and remained inaccessible to the living (except, of course, for tomb robbers, who were very good at getting into them). The chapel was also closed and sealed, but then opened regularly for the performance of the cult.

Each person was thought to be made up of three main aspects:

- the body ();
- the ba (); and
- the ka (). The body was the material form of the person; the ba was their unique personality, character, or essence; and the ka was the life force,

the energy that enabled the person to exist. At the moment of death, the ka became separated from the other two aspects of the self. In order for the deceased to function for eternity as an akh (𓅜𓐍), a blessed and effective spirit, the ka had to be maintained so that it could be reunited with the ba on a daily basis. Thus the essential task of the cult was to maintain the life force of the deceased, the ka, through the real or magical offering of food, drink, incense, eyepaint, and other items.

The joining of the ka and the ba took place in the mummified body, identified with Osiris. Once this merging had taken place, the akh could function again on earth, although on a different plane of existence, for another day. Each night, the spirit of the deceased had to travel again below the earth into the realm of the Duat, or Netherworld (identified with the burial chamber), where it would be reunited with the mummy and made effective again. This cycle is connected with originally royal funerary beliefs that link the sun god, Re, with Osiris, king of the Duat. Each day, Re would travel across the day sky, and at night, he would travel across the night sky of the Duat, braving these dangerous realms in order to join with the mummy of Osiris and be reborn the next morning.

The focal point of the mortuary cult was usually a false door. This was situated in the chapel directly above the burial shaft, and was the magical link between the upper and lower parts of the tomb, between the realm of the dead and the land of the living. It was in the shape of an actual door, with jambs and a lintel, but instead of an opening, the center panel was of solid stone (or occasionally wood), usually left free of inscription or other decoration. A drum above the center panel represented a rolled up curtain of matting or reeds, indicating that the doorway was open.

The soul of the deceased was believed to travel up the shaft and emerge through this dummy door in order to receive offerings. Some tombs of the Old Kingdom have an image of the tomb owner carved into this center panel, shown as if coming out of the realm of the dead. Above the center panel was what is known as a "slab stela," which depicts the deceased person, sometimes with his or her spouse, seated at a table piled high with offerings. Real foodstuffs and other materials would have been placed in front of this door as offerings to the deceased (and then recycled for use by those responsible for the cult – a redistributive economy in action).

The offering cults of private people were carried out regularly by family members serving as priests or by professional cult practitioners. In addition to the daily ritual performed by priests, entire extended families came to the cemetery on the occasion of certain festivals, and to share in feasts and celebrations. In contrast to Western cemeteries, which tend to be primarily for the deposition and commemoration of the dead, ancient Egyptian necropolises were vibrant places, what Egyptologists like to call "liminal" zones, shadowy borderlands where the living and the dead could meet and interact.

The relationship between the living and the dead is illustrated in a number of ways. As part of the decoration of the tomb, the owner might include what are known as "Appeals to the Living," texts that ask anyone who might be passing by to say a prayer or leave an offering. Conversely, the owner might include a curse, a threat that if the passerby damages the tomb in any way, or neglects to say a prayer, he or she will be harmed. My favorite of these threats is that the spirit of the deceased will wring the neck of any trespasser like a bird: 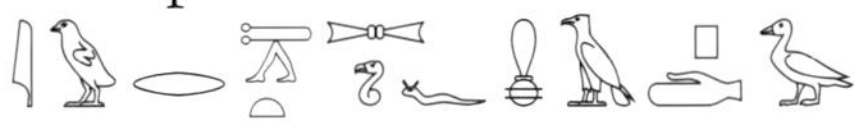. (You will have a chance to translate this curse in Chapter VI.) Some tombs also contain graffiti, inscriptions left within tomb chapels by people who have visited them, often hundreds of years later.

Private cult activity was not limited to the arena of the tomb: votive stelae could be set up in religious zones such as temples. These allowed a private person to share in the cult celebrated for the god. Many such stelae come from Abydos, a site in Upper Egypt associated with the god of the dead, Osiris. An important part of the transition from death into effective functioning in the afterlife was an actual or symbolic pilgrimage to Abydos so that the deceased could be merged with this god. Every year, a great festival of Osiris was held that included a great procession down a long valley to the site of the tombs of the 1st Dynasty. Kings built ka chapels at Abydos, associating their own cults with the cult of Osiris, and private people erected "cenotaphs" (mortuary chapels not associated with a real burial) and stelae so that they too could benefit from the cult of Osiris and remain eternally in the presence of the god. Similar stelae, as well as statues, were set up in other temple votive zones. Like the Abydos stelae, these served to associate the person to whom the object was dedicated with the god.

Thus offering formulas could be found in a number of different contexts. First and foremost, they were found in the tomb, both underground, inscribed on the coffin or sarcophagus; and aboveground in the chapel, on the false door and elsewhere on the walls and architectural elements. Secondly, they could be found on stelae and statues set up in association with the cults of various gods. In each case, they served the same basic purpose: to provision the recipient of the cult for eternity.

According to the Egyptian worldview, elite cult offerings were, at least symbolically, a gift from the king and the gods. The fundamental offering prayer is known by its transliterated name: hetep-di-nesut(). There are four principal parts to the offering formula, which will be addressed one at a time. Do not worry about grammar; this is a formula, with a standard translation that should simply be memorized so that you can recognize it on a multitude of monuments not only in Egypt but also on display in museums throughout the world.

Lesson 35: The Basic Offering Prayer

The basic offering prayer is translated as

“An offering which the king gives…”

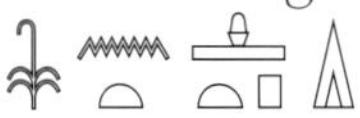

Usually abbreviated as:

 *ḥtp di nswt* = An offering which the king gives. . .

The underlying grammar is as follows: "King" comes first, in honorific transposition, then the subject, "offering," followed by a relative form, "which (the king) gives."

Almost all offering prayers begin this way, demonstrating that offerings ultimately flowed, at least theoretically, from the bounty of the king. This is a particularly clear example of trickle-down economics and redistribution. This was the shortest lesson in the book, and you don't have to practice anything.

LESSON 36: THE GODS OF THE OFFERING PRAYER

The next part of the offering prayer tells us which god also makes the offering. This is usually either Osiris or Anubis. The preposition is usually not written.

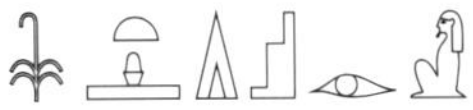

ḥtp di͗ nswt wsi͗r = An offering which the king gives, and Osiris...

ḥtp di͗ nswt i͗npw = An offering which the king gives, and Anubis...

The name of the god is followed by identifying epithets, which are fairly standardized but include a number of variations. Memorize the most common of these epithets, as you will see them often. Here are some new signs, followed by a short list of epithets.

HIEROGLYPH:  **TRANSLITERATION:** *i͗m*

WHAT IS IT? Two perpendicular planks.

MOST COMMON USE: In , *i͗my*, "who, which is in."

HIEROGLYPH:  **TRANSLITERATION:** *ws*

WHAT IS IT? A carrying chair.

MOST COMMON USE: In 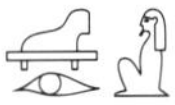 *wsi͗r*, "Osiris."

HIEROGLYPH:  **TRANSLITERATION:** *sḥ*

WHAT IS IT? The façade of a shrine.

MOST COMMON USE: In 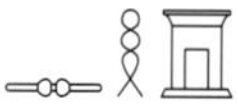 *sḥ*, "booth."

HIEROGLYPH:  **TRANSLITERATION:** *ḏsr*

WHAT IS IT? An arm with a hand holding a brush.

MOST COMMON USE: In 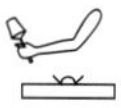 *ḏsr*, "sacred."

EPITHETS OF THE GODS

For Osiris

	*ḫnty imntiw*	foremost of the Westerners
	*nb ḏdw*	Lord of Djedu (many spellings possible)
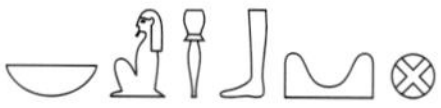	*nb ꜣbḏw*	Lord of Abydos
	*nṯr ꜥꜣ*	great god
	*wnn-nfr*	Wenennefer
	*wsir/ꜣsir*	Osiris (alternate spelling)
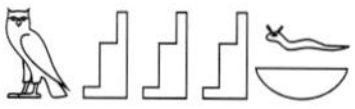	*m swt.f nb*	in all his seats

For Anubis

	*imy wt*	who is in the place of embalming
	*tpy ḏw.f*	who is on his mountain
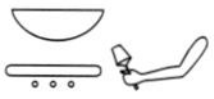	*nb tꜣ ḏsr*	Lord of the sacred land (the necropolis)
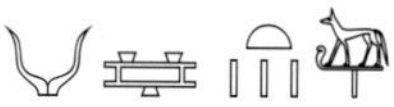	*wp-wꜣwt*	Opener of the Ways (Wepwawet)
	*ḫnty sḥ nṯr*	foremost of the divine booth
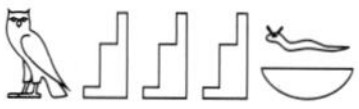	*m swt.f nb*	in all his seats

Exercise 35: Epithets of Osiris and Anubis

Practice transliterating and translating these two partial offering prayers.

1. 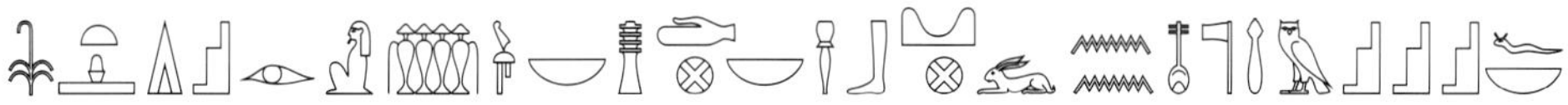

2. 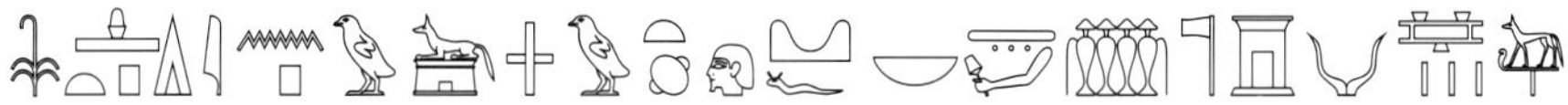

Lesson 37: The Four Sons of Horus

Other important gods connected with an ancient Egyptian burial were the four sons of Horus. When the ancient Egyptians mummified their dead, they dried the body with a kind of salt called natron. In order to keep the inside of the body from decaying, they removed most of the internal organs and dried them separately, then stored them in containers we now call canopic jars. There were four specific organs extracted: the lungs, the liver, the stomach, and the intestines. (The heart was left in place, and the brain was removed and discarded.) Each of the four organs was put into its own container, and was protected by a special mortuary deity. By the New Kingdom, the stoppers on these containers were often given the distinctive heads of these four gods:

- human-headed Imsety (liver);
- jackal-headed Duamutef (stomach);
- hawk-headed Qebehsenuef (intestines); and
- baboon-headed Hapy (lungs).

These gods were known as the four sons of Horus. Each was partnered with a goddess: Imsety with Isis; Duamutef with Neith; Qebehsenuef with Selkhet; and Hapy with Nepthys.

Hieroglyph: **Transliteration:** *ḥp*

What is it? Part of a boat?

Most Common Use: In *ḥpy*, "Hapy."

Hieroglyph: **Transliteration:** *ḳbḥ*

What is it? A jar pouring water.

Most Common Use: In *ḳbḥ*, "purify."

Hieroglyph: **Transliteration:** *nỉwt*

What is it? Crossroads.

Most Common Use: In *nỉwt*, "town," "city."

Exercise 36: The Four Sons of Horus

Object 1: Gold Plaque

Vocabulary

 *pw* this; that

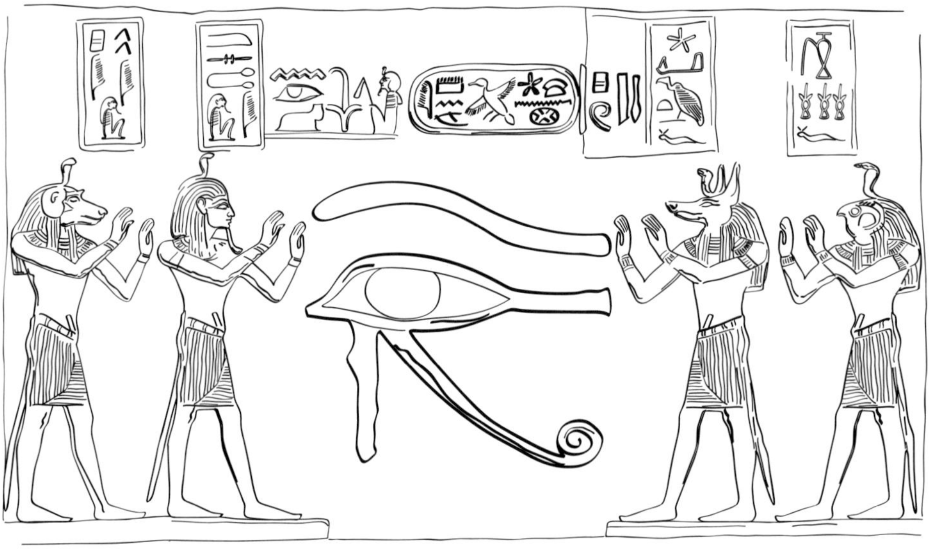

The gold plaque illustrated here was found in one of the royal tombs of the 21st and 22nd Dynasties at Tanis (a site in the Delta), in the precinct of the Amen temple there. This was one of the most spectacular discoveries in the history of Egyptology, but received relatively little attention because it occurred in 1939, during World War II. This was placed covering the canopic incision made in the abdomen of a king of the 21st dynasty. The name of this king in Greek is Psusennes; this bears very little resemblance to his name in hieroglyphs. Just transliterate and give an English approximation. Work from left to right. See if you can come up with the names of the four sons based on the information given on the previous page.

. . . .

. . . .

Object 2: Canopic Container

VOCABULARY

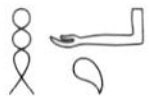 *ḥꜥ* body; flesh

This silver canopic container, now in the Egyptian Museum, Cairo, was also found at Tanis, Transliterate, translate, and identify the original contents (lungs, liver, stomach, or intestines). [Note that  should be transliterated *šꜣ* here.]

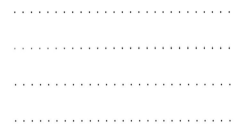

. . . .

. . . .

. . . .

. . . .

. . . .

Lesson 38: Voice Offerings

First, some new signs:

Hieroglyph:  **Transliteration:** *ỉ3w, msw*

What is it? An elderly man.

Hieroglyph:  **Transliteration:** *nḏm*

What is it? A seed pod of some sort.

Most Common Use: In  *nḏm*, "sweet."

Hieroglyph:  **Transliteration:** *ẖrt-nṯr*

What is it? A combination of signs.

Most Common Use: In  *ẖrt-nṯr*, "necropolis."

Hieroglyph:  **Transliteration:** *šs/šsr*

What is it? A twisted bit of rope.

Most Common Use: As a phonogram in a number of words.

Hieroglyph:  **Transliteration:** *ṯ3w*

What is it? A mast with an unfurled sail.

Most Common Use: In  *ṯ3w*, "breath."

The next step in the offering prayer is for the god to give voice offerings (, *prt-ḫrw*), prayers spoken aloud that list offerings to be given to the ka of the cult recipient. The hieroglyph for voice offerings is made of four parts: the house plan, 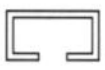, an abbreviation for the verb , *prỉ*, "to go forth"; the oar, , for *ḫrw*, voice; bread; and beer. Thus the meaning is literally: "that the voice go forth," for the fundamental staples of the Egyptian diet.

Following the  will often come a list of the other major offerings that the deceased wishes to have recited. Here is a list of the most common of these additional offerings. These are very often abbreviated; although the fuller spelling is listed here, you will often see the determinative alone.

Vocabulary

	*ỉm*	therein/on which
	*wrt*	very
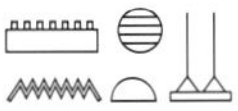	*mnḫt*	linen; clothing
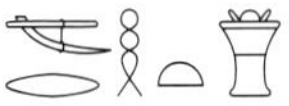	*mrḥt*	oil for (anointing)
	*nḏm*	sweet
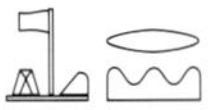	*ẖrt-nṯr*	necropolis
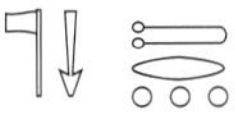	*snṯr*	incense
	*st (smyt)*	desert, necropolis
	*šs*	alabaster (actually calcite)
	*kꜣ*	meat
	*ḳrs*	bury
	*ḳrst*	burial
	*ṯꜣw*	breath; air
	*ṯꜣw nḏm*	sweet breath (of life)
	*ḏf(ꜣw)*	provisions

These offerings can be preceded by the word , *ḫꜣ*, "one thousand," or , *ḫꜣ m*, "one thousand from (of)."

Many offering formulas include a request for:

ḫt nb(t) nfr(t) wꜥb(t) = everything which is good and pure, or for

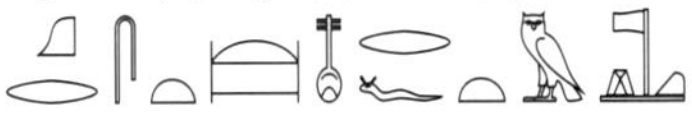

ḳrst nfrt m ẖrt-nṯr = a good burial in the necropolis.

Or they ask:

ḳrst.f m ẖrt-nṯr = may he be buried in the necropolis. (Do not worry about the grammar here—just memorize the pattern.)

They can also ask for:

ỉꜣw nfr wrt = a very good old age.

And some extra phrases that can be added at the end:

ꜥnḫt nṯr ỉm = on which the god lives.

nṯr dwꜣ = which the god praises.

The  is often (but not always) preceded by the phrase: , *dỉ.f*, meaning "that he may give." If this phrase is not present, it is implied, and should be understood as part of the prayer.

Exercise 37: Offering Prayers with Voice Offerings

Here are two offering prayers to try. Transliterate and translate.

1. 

. . . .

. . . .

. . . .

. . . .

2. 

. . . .

. . . .

. . . .

. . . .

Lesson 39: The Cult Recipient

The final portion of the offering prayer names the recipient of the cult. The offerings are directed to his or her ka, so the next bit says:

, *n kꜣ n* = "to the ka of"

(Note that the  *n* is used in two different ways here:  meaning "to" or "for"; and the possessive , meaning "of.")

Next comes the identification of the person to whom the offerings are to be given. He or she can be given an entire titulary, such as the ones studied in the last chapter, and/or can be called , *ỉmꜣḫw*, "the revered one." (For a woman, , *ỉmꜣḫt*) The name and titles of the deceased then follow.

As an alternative, a specific god can be invoked here, just before the name of the deceased. The pattern is: , *ỉmꜣḫw ḥr nṯr ꜥꜣ*, "revered before the great god." The names of other gods can be substituted here for "the great god."

After the name of the deceased comes the epithet , *mꜣꜥ ḫrw*,"true of voice," "justified," to which you were introduced in Chapter 2.

The following exercise will put together all the pieces of the offering prayer and some elite titles, using monuments from various periods, all now in the Egyptian Museum, Cairo.

Exercise 38: Offering Prayers on Monuments

The following objects bear versions of full or partial offering prayers. They come from different periods, and you will see that spelling can vary both according to time period and space available.

Object 1: Offering Stela of Nitptah and his Family

This Middle Kingdom stela from the west bank at Thebes does not have a full offering prayer on it, but will help you practice reading some names. It is a nice example of the sort of family group often seen on such stelae.

VOCABULARY

	*nỉt-ptḥ*	Nitptah
	*ỉy*	Iy
	*snỉ*	Seni
	*skr*	Sokar
	*dd*	Ded
	*tỉ*	Ti

Top line: . . . .

. . . .

. . . .

. . . .

. . . .

. . . .

Above first man: . . . .

. . . .

Above first woman: . . . .

. . . .

Above second man: . . . .

. . . .

Above second woman: . . . .

. . . .

Object 2: Naos (Shrine) of Ptahmes

This small shrine holds an image of the man to whom is it dedicated. It dates to the New Kingdom. You can see how much sketchier the hieroglyphs are here than they have been in the other examples. By this point in time, the influence both of the spoken language and of the cursive form of hieroglyphs, hieratic, was creeping into monumental texts.

VOCABULARY

 *sḫm* scepter

Center to right: . . . .

. . . .

. . . .

. . . .

. . . .

. . . .

Center to left: . . . .

. . . .

. . . .

. . . .

. . . .

. . . .

Cartouches on Body: . . . .

Titles on kilt: . . . .

Object 3: Stela of Amenemhat and Iy

This beautifully preserved 11th Dynasty stela from the west bank at Thebes still bears much of its paint. Again, this is only a partial offering prayer. Note the way the inscriptions are arranged to correspond with the figures.

Top line, center to left: . . . .

. . . .

Top line, center to right: . . . .

. . . .

Before seated man: . . . .

. . . .

Before standing woman: . . . .

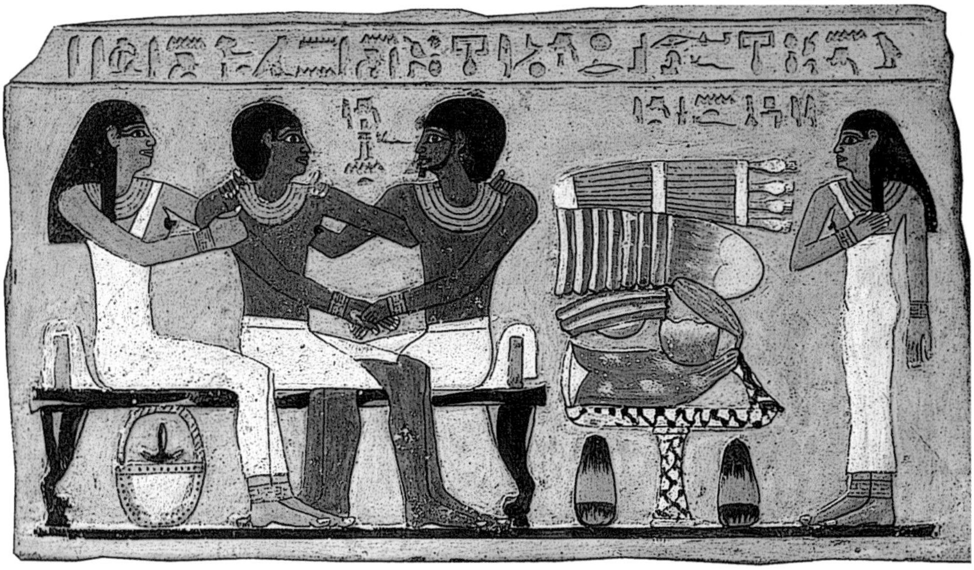

Object 4: Wooden Coffin of Huy

The coffin on the next page dates from the Middle Kingdom, and was found at Assiut; it is now in the Egyptian Museum, Cairo. Translate the horizontal band of text first, then the vertical bands, working from right to left. Note that there is a spelling mistake in the top line; see if you can catch it.

HIEROGLYPH:  **TRANSLITERATION:** *mḏd*

WHAT IS IT? This seems to be connected with weaving.

MOST COMMON USE: This is a fairly rare sign. One place you will see it (in addition to the word you are about to learn) is in one of the names of Khufu:  *mḏdw*, Medjedw

HIEROGLYPH:  **TRANSLITERATION:** *ẖw*

WHAT IS IT? An arm with a flail.

MOST COMMON USE: This is seen mainly in words connected with  *ẖwỉ*, protect.

VOCABULARY

	*hrw*	day
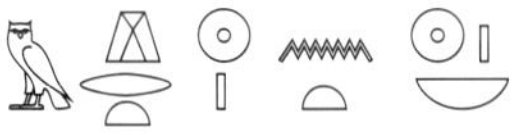	*m ẖrt hrw nt rʿ nb*	daily
	*mḏdnỉ*	Medjedny (a place name)
	*ḥwt-ḥr/ꜣst*	Hathor or Isis

Horizontal band: . . . .

. . . .

. . . .

. . . .

Vertical bands . . . .

. . . .

Object 5: A False Door

This beautiful Dynasty 6 false door was found relatively recently at Saqqara, deep in a tomb shaft near the underground galleries of the 2nd Dynasty king Ninetjer. This man was an official connected with the pyramid complex of Wenis; see if you can figure out the name of the complex (remember to watch out for honorific transposition).

One new sign:

HIEROGLYPH:  **TRANSLITERATION:** *tp* (or *tpỉ*)

WHAT IS IT? A dagger.

Top horizontal line: ....

....

On lintel: ....

....

Right outer jamb: ....

....

....

Left outer jamb: ....

....

....

Both inner jambs: ....

....

....

....

Object 6: Stela of a General

This stela from Naga el-Deir dates to the 12th Dynasty. Unfortunately, it is damaged at the bottom so the name of its owner is missing. You will note that the offerings are not written out here; the pile of offerings depicted in front of the standing couple would have sufficed in this case. See if you can follow the inscription from beginning to end.

Lesson 40: Offering Lists

The ancient Egyptians often included expanded lists of offerings in their tombs and temples. These enumerated the foods and other supplies (such as eyepaint, linen, and precious oils) the cult recipient needed for eternal life.

The most elaborate type of offering list was the funerary menu. You can recognize these menus easily: they are most often on the walls of tombs or temples, and are divided into grids, with one item in each box. They can also be found on portable objects like offering tables. These can be very long, as they list specific types of bread, beer, wine, and the like. Other lists of offerings are not set off by grids, but still can contain many items of food, drink, and other cult materials. These menus and lists give scholars a great deal of information about what the Egyptians ate, drank, and wore, and also about the funerary cult itself; for practical purposes, recognizing a few of the most common items will be enough.

This is the last lesson for this chapter, and is devoted primarily to working with monuments. I will work through an example of an Old Kingdom slab stela (originally set up in a tomb at Giza, and now in the Louvre) for you, and then you will try your hand at several relatively extensive monuments. Relevant signs and vocabulary will be provided with each monument.

Example: Slab Stela of Nefertiabet

This elegant carved and painted stela was designed to secure eternal offerings for Princess Nefertiabet. I will guide you through this section by section, and then you will try a similar example. (I am grateful to have as a reference for these two stelae Boston Egyptologist Peter der Manuelian's beautiful new publication of a group of these stelae, including the two included here.) Here are some new signs and some vocabulary for this stela.

Hieroglyph:  **Transliteration:** *wꜣḏ*

What is it? A papyrus stalk.

Most Common Use: In , *wꜣḏ*, "green, fresh."

Hieroglyph:  **Transliteration:** *swn, sšr*

What is it? An arrow.

Most Common Use: As a phonogram.

Hieroglyph:  **Transliteration:** *r; ṯrp; ꜣpd*

What is it? A goose's head.

Most Common Use: There are several types of poultry represented here; you do not need to worry about the details, just translate them all as "goose" or "bird."

Vocabulary

	*ỉꜥw*	tools for ritual washing
	*ỉrp*	wine
	*ỉdmy*	idemy cloth
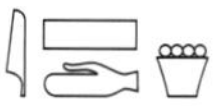	*ỉšd*	persea fruit
	ꜥꜣ	Aa linen
	*wꜣḏ*	green eye paint
	*wꜥḥ*	carob bean
	*msdmt*	black eye paint
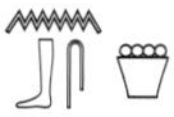	*nbs*	zizyphus fruit
	*r*	goose; bird
	*t-nbs*	bread of zizyphus fruit
	*ḥꜣtt*	the best
	*spr*	rib
	*sḫpt*	beer
	*sšr*	sesher cloth
	*ḳbḥ*	container of cool water
	*dꜣbw*	figs

Step I: Transliterate and translate the inscription in green above the head of the deceased: *sꜣt nswt nfrt-iꜣbt* = King's daughter, Nefertiabet

Step II: Now transliterate and translate the hieroglyphs in blue, which represent an early form of the offering list: *snṯr hꜣtt mrḥt wꜣḏ msdmt dꜣbw išdw sḫpt irp nbsw t-nbsw wꜥḥw* = Incense, the best of oil, green eye paint, black eye paint, figs, persea fruit, beer, wine, zizyphus fruit, bread of zizyphus, carob beans.

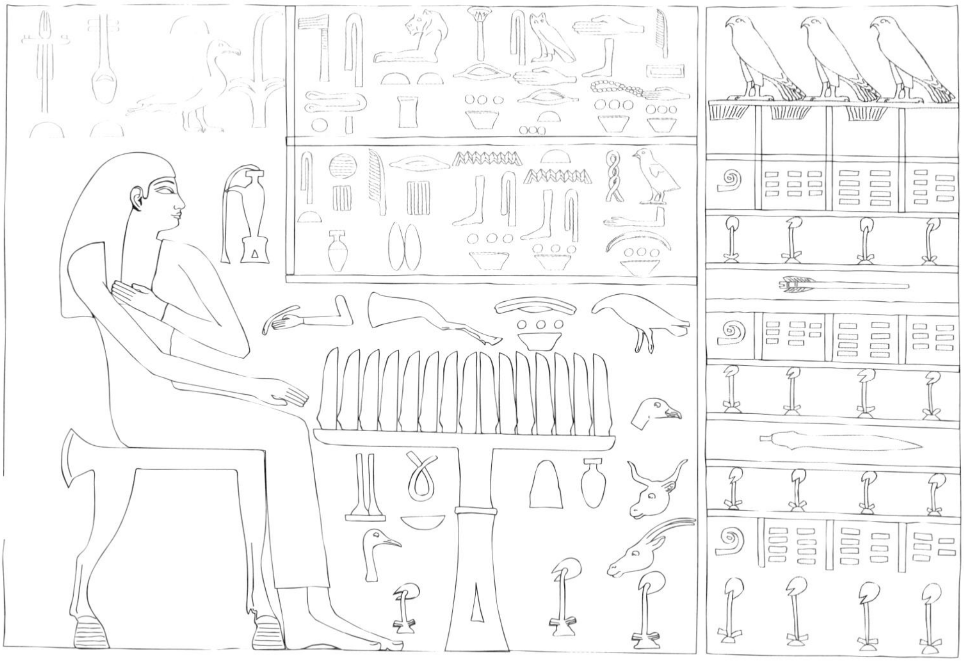

Step III: Transliterate and translate the hieroglyphs in red, an accounting of different types of cloth which were probably used for mummification. There are three basic categories, then numbers that seem to represent the widths of the cloth. All the numbers are multiplied by ten.

idmy, 100 (1,000), 90 (1,000), 80 (1,000), 70 (1,000); *sšr*: 100 (1,000), 90 (1,000), 80 (1,000), 60 (1,000); ꜥꜣ 4,000, 100 (1,000), 80 (1,000), 70 (1,000), 50 (1,000) = Idemy cloth, 1,000 each of widths 100, 90, 80, and 70; sesher cloth, 1,000 each of widths 100, 90, 80, and 60; Aa cloth, 4,000, 1,000 each of widths 100, 80, 70, and 50.

Step IV: Finally, transliterate and translate the signs scattered around the offering table. Try to work from right to left and top to bottom, but don't worry if your order is different than mine; it does not matter. Interpret the abbreviated signs (heads or headless bodies) as you would full determinatives: *ḳbḥ, ỉʿwy, ḫpš, spr, r, ꜣpd, mnḫt, šsr, r, t ḥnḳt 1000, kꜣ, mꜣ-ḥḏ 1000* = container for cool water, tools for ritual washing, foreleg of ox, rib meat, goose, fowl, 1,000 each of: cloth, alabaster, geese, 1,000 bread and beer, 1,000 cattle and antelope.

Exercise 39: Monuments

The following two monuments will help you practice the concepts, patterns, and vocabulary you have just learned. New signs and vocabulary will be provided with the individual monuments.

Object 1: Slab Stela of a Prince

This stela dates from Dynasty 4; like the stela of Nefertiabet, it was found at Giza, and is now at the Phoebe A. Hearst Museum in Berkeley, California. Work in sections according to the instructions below.

HIEROGLYPH:  **TRANSLITERATION:** *bnr*

WHAT IS IT? The root of a plant.

MOST COMMON USE: In 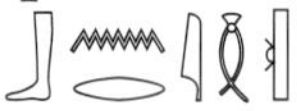 *bnr*, "sweet," and words having to do with dates.

HIEROGLYPH:  **TRANSLITERATION:** *ḥꜣ*

WHAT IS IT? A standard bearing the hieroglyph for foreign land.

MOST COMMON USE: In  *ḥꜣ*, "Ha" (the name of a god of the desert).

HIEROGLYPH:  **TRANSLITERATION:** *ḥḳt*

WHAT IS IT? A frog on a basket

MOST COMMON USE: In  *ḥḳt*, "Heqat" (the name of a goddess).

HIEROGLYPH:  **TRANSLITERATION:** *sš3t*

WHAT IS IT? The emblem of Seshat.

MOST COMMON USE: In the name of Seshat, , *sš3t*, goddess of writing.

HIEROGLYPH:  **TRANSLITERATION:** *i͗3tt*

WHAT IS IT? A modified was-scepter.

MOST COMMON USE: In , *i͗3tt*, "milk."

VOCABULARY

	*ʿg(w)t*	grain
	*i͗3tt*	milk
	*i͗ẖt*	things; property
	*b3*	soul
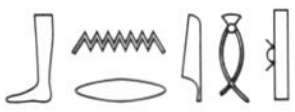	*bnr*	sweet
	*bnrt*	date wine
	*p*	Pe (a town)
	*hk3*	Heka priest
	*ḥ3*	Ha (a god of the desert)
	*ḥḳt*	Heqat
	*ẖt*	attendant
	*sš3t*	goddess of writing.
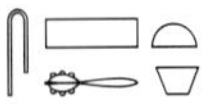	*sšẖt (sẖt)*	cake
	*šmʿt-nfrt*	fine linen
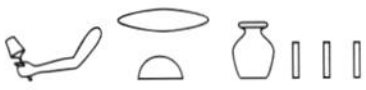	*ḏsrt*	ale

Text in green: . . . .

. . . .

. . . .

. . . .

. . . .

Text in blue: . . . .

. . . .

. . . .

. . . .

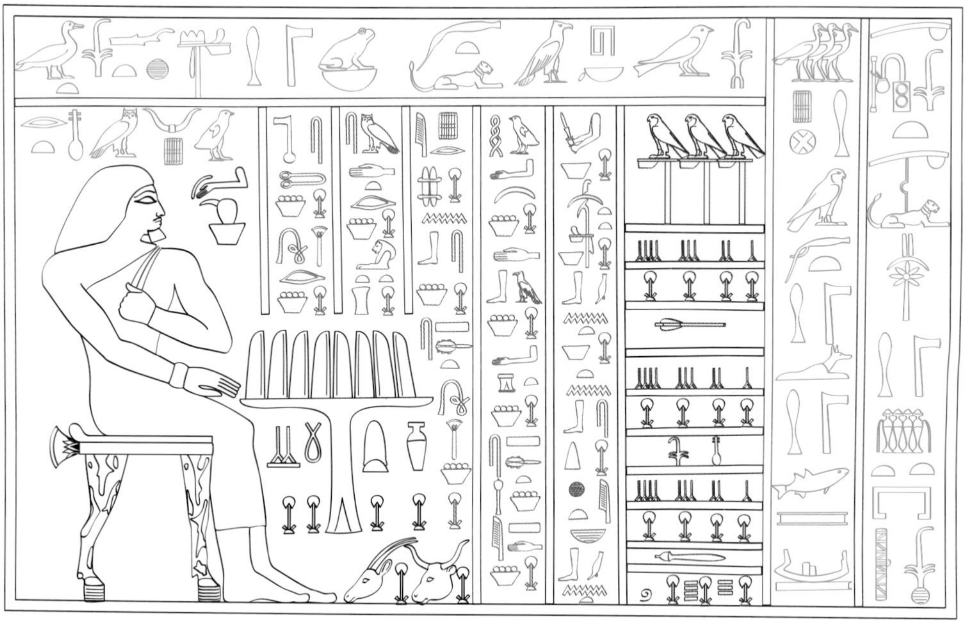

Text in black:. . . . .

. . . .

. . . .

Text in red: In this case, the quality of the cloth is indicated by the number of fringes. . . . .

Object 2: Entrance to the Tomb Chapel of the "Two Brothers"

On the following spread is the entrance to a tomb chapel at Saqqara. This entire tomb is a gem of Old Kingdom architecture and decoration. It was built for two brothers, or perhaps close friends; everything in the tomb is repeated, once for each of the tomb owners. The entrance here functions like an expanded false door, with a real rather than symbolic entrance.

HIEROGLYPH: **TRANSLITERATION:** *ꜥnt*

WHAT IS IT? a stylized hand with fingers and nails.

MOST COMMON USE: In *iry ꜥnt,* "manicurist."

HIEROGLYPH: **TRANSLITERATION:** *mḥnk, mi, imi, ḥnk*

WHAT IS IT? An arm and hand holding a jar.

MOST COMMON USE: For many different uses.

HIEROGLYPH: **TRANSLITERATION:** *šsp*

WHAT IS IT? A fence.

MOST COMMON USE: As a phonogram.

VOCABULARY

	imꜣḫ	reverence
	iry ꜥnt	manicurist
	mḥnk	intimate
	šspw-ib-rꜥ	Shesepuibre*

*(the sun temple of the 5th Dynasty king Niuserre)

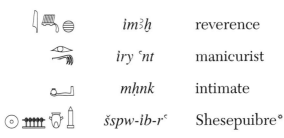

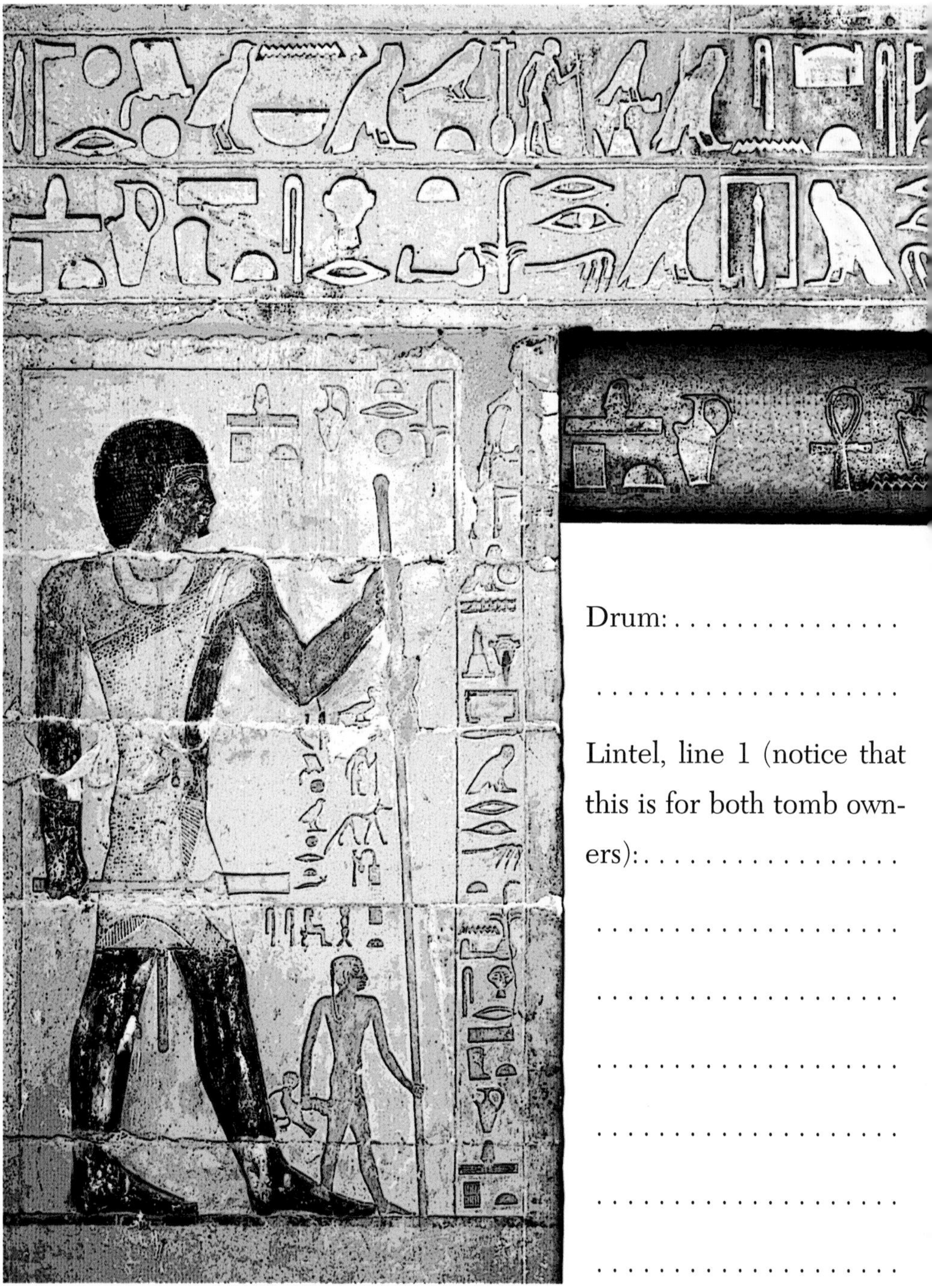

Drum: . . . .

. . . .

Lintel, line 1 (notice that this is for both tomb owners): . . . .

. . . .

. . . .

. . . .

. . . .

. . . .

. . . .

Lintel, line 2, center to right (use the central *pr-ꜥꜣ* in both directions): . . . .

. . . .

Lintel, line 2, center to left: . . . .

. . . .

. . . .

. . . .

Horizontal text on right (before face of large figure): . . . .

. . . .

Vertical text on right: . . . .

. . . .

. . . .

. . . .

. . . .

Horizontal text on left: . . . .

. . . .

. . . .

Vertical text on left: . . . .

. . . .

. . . .

Above small figure on right: . . . . . .

. . . .

Above small figure on left: . . . .

. . . .

. . . .

End of Chapter V

Chapter VI
More Inscriptions

Armed with the material you have encountered so far, you should be able to decipher a wide range of monumental inscriptions. In this chapter, you will look at some slightly more complex texts. Many of the illustrations in this chapter have been taken from private tombs, which are rich sources of monumental inscriptions. These tombs were adorned with lively reliefs and paintings depicting activities of various sorts, all designed in some way to ensure the successful afterlife and commemoration on earth of the deceased. Scenes found in such monuments include depictions of activities related to food production—for example, sowing and harvesting grain, baking bread and brewing beer, catching fish, and feeding and slaughtering cattle; workshop scenes where artisans carve statues, make jewelry, or the like; and processions of offering bearers. Many of these scenes bear inscriptions. These can be labels identifying the people, animals, objects, or activities depicted; or can be captions, words spoken by the participants.

Lesson 41: Labels and Captions using the Infinitive

One of the most useful verb forms is the infinitive, which you have already met in Chapter I. In this form, a verb can function as a noun. Egyptian infinitives can be translated like an English infinitive, e.g. "to be," or an English gerund (-ing word), for example, "being."

Most infinitives look just like the root of the verb (the simplest form), e.g. , *wḥm*. One category of verbs doubles their last radical, e.g.  *mꜣꜣ*. In other verbs, a *t* is added, as you have seen with 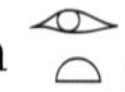, *ỉrt*. Here are examples of the infinitives of some different verbs (and you can memorize these verbs while you are at it).

Forms of the Infinitive

Root	Infinitive	Transliteration	Translation
		*sḏm*	to hear; hearing
		*mꜣꜣ*	to see; seeing
	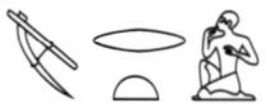	*mrt*	to love; loving
	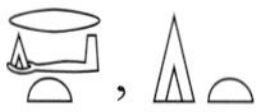	*rdỉt, dỉt*	to give; giving

Infinitives are commonly seen as labels in tomb and temple scenes, where they are used to identify the action taking place. For example, a scene which shows grain being harvested might be labeled helpfully as "harvesting grain." Infinitives can also be used in places where English would use, for example, "to harvest" or "harvesting."

The next exercise lets you practice with infinitives as labels. Remember, the spelling provided in the vocabulary list will not necessarily be the same as that which occurs in the exercises.

Exercise 40: Scene Labels

All of these scenes depict activities that have to do with the producing, manufacturing, gathering, or bringing of food and other items to be used in the funeral and offering cult. The majority of them take place on the estate of the tomb owner, in his or her fields or workshops; others are set in the marshes that fringed the Nile valley. Most of them are from tombs, although one is from an object discovered inside a tomb, and another is from a royal chapel.

Scene 1: Domesticating animals

This scene is from the tomb of a high official of the Old Kingdom at Saqqara. This scene is connected with the preparation of meat for the funerary meal—notice the meat piled on a shelf above the heads of the men shown here.

VOCABULARY

	*wšꜣ*	fatten
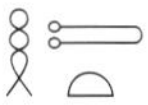	*ḥṯt*	hyena

Transliterate and translate.

. . . .

. . . .

Scene 2: Domesticating birds

This is another scene from Saqqara, from the tomb of Ti. Work from right to left. Don't let the horned viper in the central inscription throw you; it is reversed.

HIEROGLYPH:  **TRANSLITERATION:** *fs; srf*

WHAT IS IT? A brazier.

MOST COMMON USE: This is used as a phonogram in a number of words.

HIEROGLYPH:  **TRANSLITERATION:** *nm*

WHAT IS IT? A butcher's knife.

MOST COMMON USE: Used mainly as a phonogram.

HIEROGLYPH:  **TRANSLITERATION:** *ḏꜣ, wḏꜣ*

WHAT IS IT? A fire-drill.

MOST COMMON USE: Used as a phonogram.

VOCABULARY

	fsỉ	cook, heat
	swt	wheat
	snmỉ	feed
	ḏꜣt	crane

Above man on left: . . . .

. . . .

. . . .

Above man on right . . .

. . . .

. . . .

Between men in center:

. . . .

. . . .

. . . .

Scene 3: Gilded Chair of Sitamen

This chair is one of the treasures of the Egyptian Museum, Cairo. The princess who originally owned this chair (a daughter of Amenhotep III and Queen Tiye) gave it to her grandparents as a funerary gift; it was found in their tomb.

Vocabulary

 *ms* bring, carry

Above offering bearers:. . . . .

. . . .

Before princess: . . . .

. . . .

Scene 4: Funeral Procession

This is from the tomb of Niankhnum and Khnumhotep, the entrance to whose tomb you deciphered at the end of the last chapter; it is their statues which are in the shrine at the left of the illustration. The tomb was divided into two halves, one for each of the men; but they appear together in many scenes (such as this one), and clearly wanted to spend eternity together.

HIEROGLYPH: **TRANSLITERATION:** *šms*

WHAT IS IT? A bundle of tools and weapons.

MOST COMMON USE: In , *šms*, "follow," and related words.

VOCABULARY

	r	to
	šms	follow (verb)
	twt	image; statue

. . . .

. . . .

In front of first priest: . . . .

. . . .

Scene 5: Catching a bull

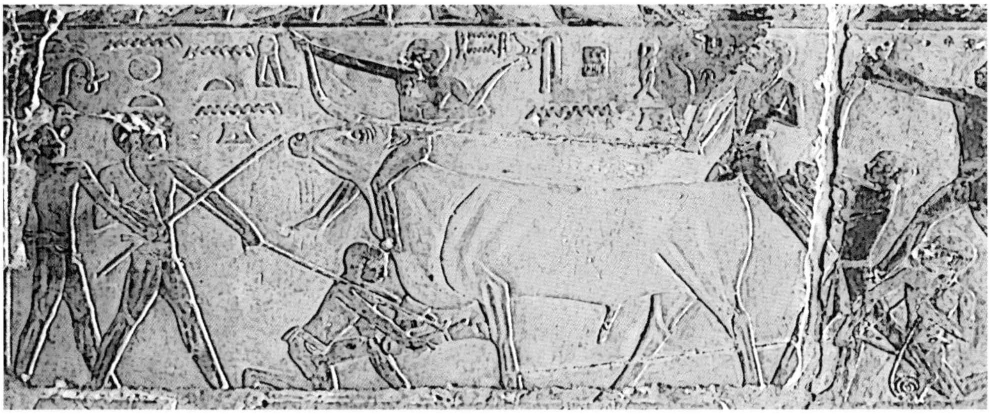

This is also from the tomb of Niankhnum and Khnumhotep. The bull was a very important part of the offering feast. Cattle were a form of wealth, and the bull was also an important symbol of power and virility.

Vocabulary

	*i͗ni͗*	bring
	*ng(ꜣw)*	long-horned bull
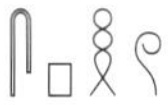	*spḥ*	lasso
	*dwꜣt*	Duat (Netherworld/tomb)

There are several labels here:

Above bull: . . . .

. . . .

Name of man grasping horns: . . . .

. . . .

In front of bull: . . . .

. . . .

. . . .

Scene 6: Offering bearers

This next scene, from the Old Kingdom tomb of Nenkhetefka, is now in the Egyptian Museum, Cairo. It depicts a procession of offering bearers bringing gifts. There would have been a large image of the tomb owner somewhere in the tomb facing these men, receiving their offerings. There is a caption above the row of men, and then each is labeled with his name and titles.

One new sign and some vocabulary:

Hieroglyph:  **Transliteration:** *n, ỉw, ỉwt*

What is it? Two arms outstretched.

Most Common Use: As a phonogram; often used in negative constructions.

Vocabulary

	*ỉmy-wrt*	starboard
	*wꜣḏ*	green
	*sꜣ*	phyle (team)
	*sẖp*	bring

Main inscription:

. . . .

. . . .

. . . .

. . . .

. . . .

. . . .

. . . .

Between first two offering bearers: . . . .

. . . .

Between second and third men: . . . .

Between third and fourth men: . . . .

Scene 7: The Tomb Owner and his Workers

This scene is from tomb of Khnumhotep at Beni Hasan; Khnumhotep is inside the carrying chair in the center of the scene.

Vocabulary

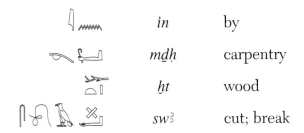

	ỉn	by
	mḏḥ	carpentry
	ḫt	wood
	swꜣ	cut; break

Work from right to left.

. . . .

. . . .

. . . .

Scene 8: The King Offering to the God

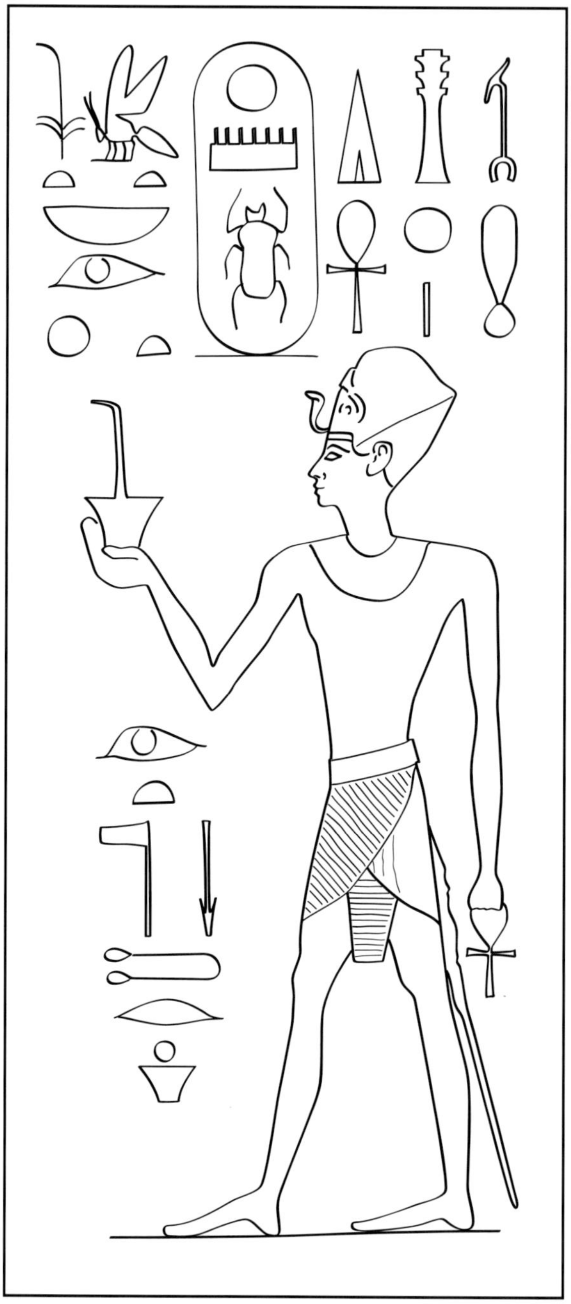

This is a relief scene from the Red Chapel of Hatshepsut at Karnak. This has recently been reconstructed; it stands in the Open Air Museum, on the grounds of Karnak. Transliterate and translate, beginning with the names and titles and ending with the scene label.

Above head of king: . . . .

. . . .

. . . .

. . . .

. . . .

. . . .

. . . .

. . . .

Before king: . . . .

. . . .

. . . .

. . . .

. . . .

. . . .

Lesson 42: The Imperative

Some scene captions use the imperative. This is seen, for example, when one actor in a scene calls out a command to another. The imperative in ancient Egyptian works the same way as the imperative in English: It comes first in the sentence and is translated as a command. The basic forms are for the most part identical to the verb roots; here they are:

The Imperative

Strong	𓄔𓅓	*sḏm*	listen!
Doubling	𓌳𓁹𓄿(𓄿)	*m*ꜣ(ꜣ)	see!
Weak	𓁹	*ỉr*	do!
Anomalous	𓏙, 𓂞	*dỉ*	Put!

Exercise 41: The Imperative

These are examples from actual tomb scenes. In each case, you will need to choose between the imperative and the infinitive. (Quick hint: in at least one case, either one works.)

Example: Fighting Bulls

This scene is from the tomb of Khnumhotep at Beni Hasan. Cattle were extremely important to the ancient Egyptian economy, and regular cattle censuses were held to keep an accurate accounting. Beef was a key part of the funerary meal; various cuts of meat are shown on offering tables, and cattle bones and even bits of mummified meat have been found connection with burials.

A new type of pronoun appears here for the first time. This is the dependent pronoun, 𓇓𓅱, *sw*, ("him," "it") which acts as the object of a verb (this is in general the main function of the dependent pronoun). A full listing of the dependent pronouns can be found in the Appendix, on page 229.

One new sign and some new vocabulary:

Hieroglyph: **Transliteration:** *mniw; s3w*

What is it? A seated shepherd.

Most Common Use: In , *mniw*, "herdsman."

Vocabulary

mniw	herdsman
mry	fighting bull
h3i	tackle
sw	him; it
sfḫ	separate; part

Cattle tenders allowed bulls to fight with one another as an important practice of animal husbandry, as only the strongest bulls were permitted to breed. There are three separate labels here, each spoken by or identifying a different figure or group of figures.

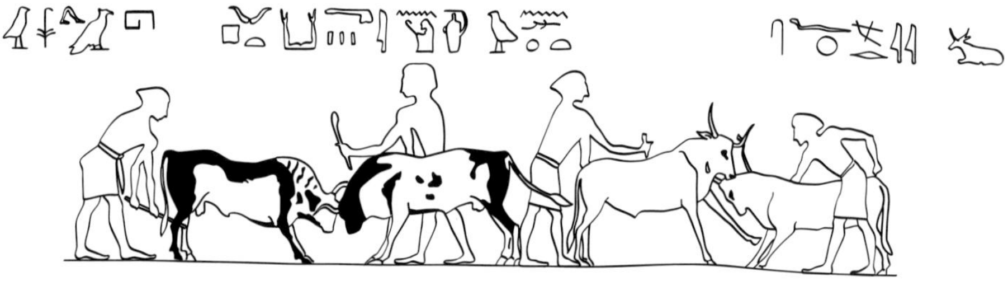

On right: *sfḫ mry* = Separate the fighting bull(s)!/Separating the fighting bull(s).

Central label: *wpt k3w in mniw ẖnmw-nḫt* = Opening (separating) the bulls by the herdsman, Khnumunakht.

On left: *h3 sw* = Tackle him/it!

Scene 1: Butchering Cattle

This is also from the tomb of Khnumhotep at Beni Hasan. Here is some new vocabulary:

VOCABULARY

	*m-ʿ*	in the possession/charge of
	*nfr*	well, beautifully
	*rʿ*	sun; daylight
	*ḫws*	slaughter; cut
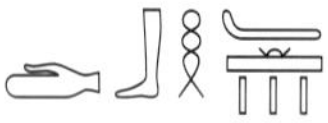	*dbḥ*	funerary requirements

There are two separate labels here. The first is very idiomatic; translate it literally, and see if you can figure out what the butcher is trying to say.

. . . .

. . . .

Scene 2: Fighting Boatmen

Scenes depicting men on papyrus skiffs, holding mock battles, are common in tombs of the Old and Middle Kingdom. The exact meaning of these scenes is still being debated: some scholars believe they are simply lively vignettes included to add context to marsh scenes; others think they may have more significant symbolic overtones. Either way, they are great fun. This scene, which has been doctored to make it more legible, includes two phrases, separated from one another by vertical lines (ignore the hieroglyphs to the right of the crack in the relief).

New vocabulary:

Vocabulary

	*psḏ*	back; spine
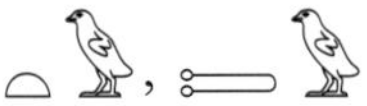	*tw, ṯw*	you (2P dep. pro.)/one
	*hn*	head

Work from left to right.

Inscription 1:...

....

....

Inscription 2:...

....

....

Lesson 43: Quotations–the Djed-medu

In monumental contexts, inscriptions are often introduced by a pattern known as the djed-medu, or "saying of words," which basically functions as an ancient Egyptian quotation mark. The djed-medu is usually abbreviated: . The basic formulation is very simple:

X = *ḏd mdw ỉn* X

This is translated: "Words spoken by X," where X is most often a king or god. The *ỉn* can also be left out, so that only *ḏd mdw* X is written.

What follows the *ḏd mdw* often contains a verb.

Here are some translation guidelines:

1. Translate the basic sense of each word;
2. Look for patterns;
3. If you have a verbal form, look at its spelling and think about how it could be used in a sentence;
4. Look at the context for additional clues;
5. Come up with a sensible translation.

Exercise 42: Monuments with Djed-medu

Example: Statue Base of Senwosret I

This is an example of an inscription in which the suffix pronouns have been omitted. It is the two gods who are speaking, and their images serve as the subjects of their respective sentences. There is one new construction here—a new use of the suffix pronoun, as the object of a preposition. The verbal phrase on each side begins the same way: , *dỉ.n.(ỉ) n.k,* "I gave/have given to you." (Again, notice that the suffix pronoun "I" is not written, because the figures on either side of the *smꜣ* sign serve this function.

Vocabulary

	ḥtpwt	offerings

Central cartouche. . . . .

. . . .

Either side:. . . . .

. . . .

. . . .

. . . .

. . . .

. . . .

. . . .

Object 2: Canopic Chest of Tutankhamen: Front and Side

These two drawings illustrate the front and one side of the canopic chest of Tutankhamen. The boy-king's viscera were individually embalmed, and then placed in small golden coffinettes, which were in turn put into this box and covered with four stoppers. The chest is surrounded by figures of the four protective goddesses, who reach out their arms to embrace the contents.

Vocabulary

	*wn(n)*	be, exist
	*m*	in; as
	*ḫpr*	form, shape
	*srḳt*	Serqet (Selqet)

The hieroglyphs on this canopic chest are in a simplified form and thus somewhat difficult to read; focus on recognizing vocabulary.

Front View

Left column: . . . .

. . . .

. . . .

. . . .

Right column: . . . .

. . . .

. . . .

. . . .

. . . .

. . . .

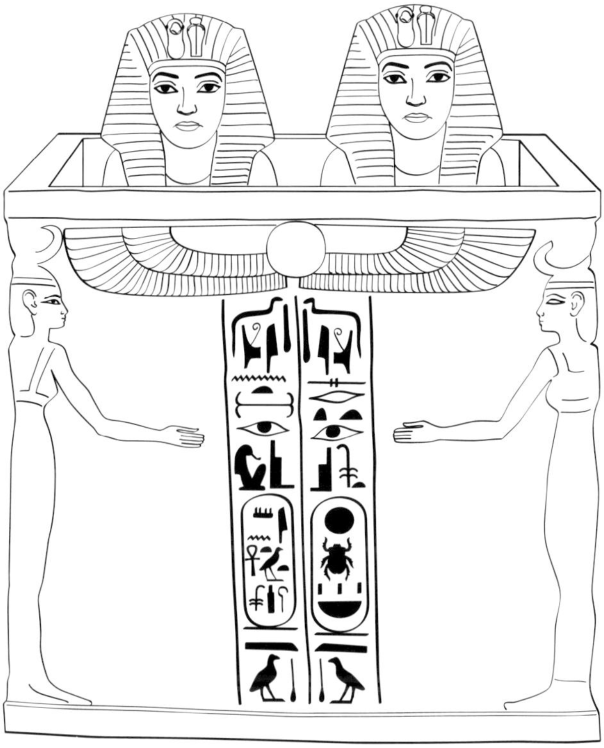

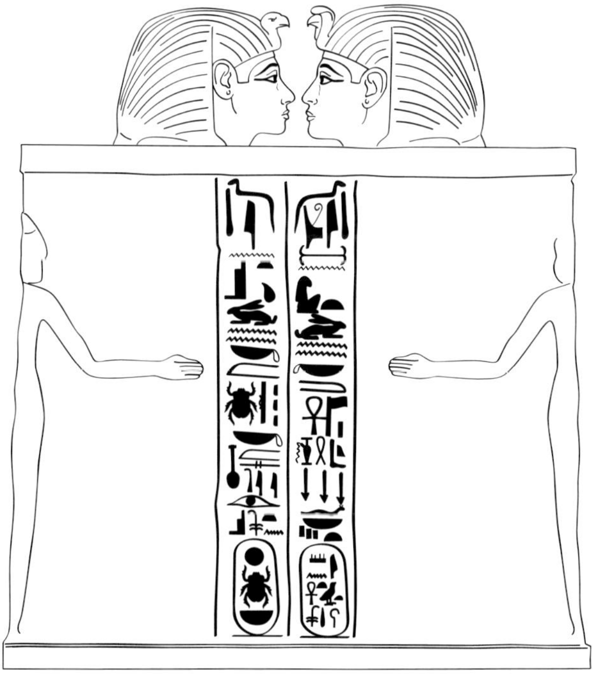

Side View

Left column: . . . .

. . . .

. . . .

. . . .

Right column: . . . .

. . . .

. . . .

. . . .

. . . .

Object 3: Statue Base of Amenemhat III

This piece is in the Egyptian Museum, Cairo. You do not need to transliterate and translate the *ḏd mdw* at the top of every column; after the first on each side, these are for visual effect.

VOCABULARY

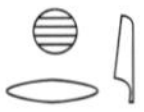 *ẖrỉ* therewith; therefrom

Center cartouche: . . . .

Right of center: . . . .

. . . .

Left of center: . . . .

. . . .

Object 4: Pillar from a Chapel of Senwosret I, Karnak

This scene graces one side of a pillar that once formed part of a small chapel erected at Karnak. It is now in the Egyptian Museum, Cairo.

A new sign:

HIEROGLYPH: 

TRANSLITERATION: *ỉn*

WHAT IS IT? A bulti fish.

COMMON USE: As a phonogram.

VOCABULARY

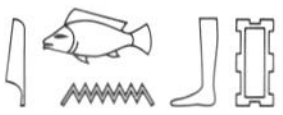	*ỉnb*	wall
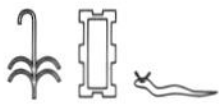	*rsy ỉnb.f*	south of his wall

Yellow: . . . .

. . . .

. . . .

Red then blue: . . . .

. . . .

. . . .

Green then orange:. . . . .

. . . .

Scene 5: Painting from the Tomb of Ramesses I, Valley of the Kings

The tombs of the New Kingdom pharaohs were decorated with scenes of kings and gods. This scene is from the tomb of the first king of the 19th dynasty.

VOCABULARY

	*ỉm*	among
	*hn; hnỉ*	praise; give praise (verb)

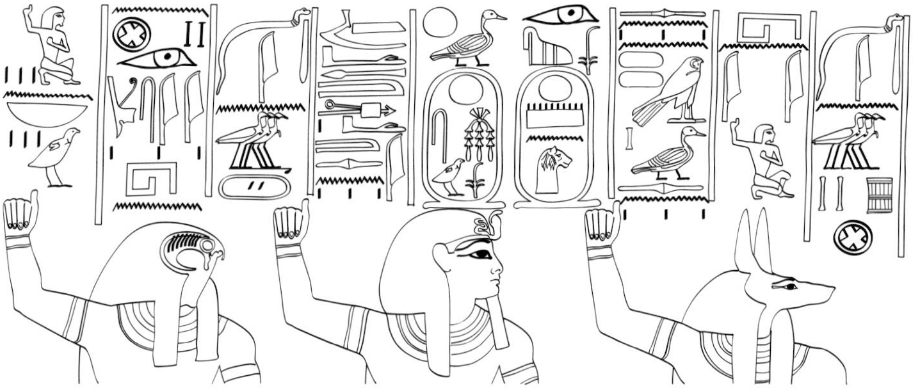

END OF CHAPTER VI

Chapter VII
Putting it All Together

Ambitious readers will enjoy this final chapter enormously. It consists of a series of exercises designed to help you practice reading hieroglyphs. All of the texts included here are from real monuments and are more extensive and more complex than those found in the previous chapters. The first section includes some temple and tomb scenes, as well as a text from a coffin. The next lesson introduces excerpts from a tomb autobiography—a long text telling the story of the tomb owner's life, and the last lesson contains the opening passages of a monumental narrative text.

Translation Guidelines: This chapter contains many monuments with which to work . You have already learned most of the basic grammar you will need; additional points of grammar and specific vocabulary will be provided with the individual monuments. Remember the translation guidelines as you read this chapter and try your hand at the exercises:

1. Translate the basic sense of each word;
2. Look for patterns;
3. If you have a verbal form, look at its spelling and think about how it could be used in a sentence;
4. Look at the context for additional clues;
5. Come up with a sensible translation.

Finally: Stay flexible!

The grammar presented in Chapters I through VI should allow you to extract the fundamental sense of each of these texts. One caveat: do not expect to achieve linguistically accurate, highly nuanced translations at this level; settle for the getting the gist of things.

Lesson 44: Temples, Tombs, and a Coffin

Temple and tomb walls and coffins are some of the places in which relatively extensive texts can be found. There are five exercises here: two temple scenes, two tomb inscriptions, and two spells from a painted coffin. Signs and vocabulary will, as usual, be given with their respective monuments.

Exercise 43: Scene from a New Kingdom Temple

This scene comes from the wall of the a New Kingdom mortuary temple at Thebes. It encapsulates the reciprocal relationship between the king and the god: the monarch makes offerings to and cares for the god; in return, the god gives him the tools of kingship.

Vocabulary

 *ḥtpw* offerings; peace

Translate the individual texts here in the order given by the colors:

Green: ....

....

....

Blue: ....

....

....

Red: ....

....

Yellow then orange:. . . . .

. . . .

. . . .

Purple: . . . .

. . . .

. . . .

Exercise 44: Scene from the Mortuary Temple of Ramesses III

This scene again illustrates the relationship between king and god. Each figure is labeled with name and description; captions in front record their eternal conversation with one another.

Hieroglyph:  **Transliteration:** *ꜥḥꜥ*

What is it? The mast of a boat

Most Common Use: Used as a phonogram, *ꜥḥꜥ*, in a number of words.

Hieroglyph:  **Transliteration:** *ꜥšꜣ*

What is it? A gecko lizard

Most Common Use: In , *ꜥšꜣ*, "many," "numerous"; also used as a determinative.

Hieroglyph:  **Transliteration:** *ḥb-sd*

What is it? Double canopied platform with two thrones side-by-side.

Most Common Use: In , ***ḥb-sd*****,** "Sed festival," the royal ceremony of renewal.

Hieroglyph:  **Transliteration:** *tm*

What is it? A sled.

Most Common Use: This is a phonogram.

Vocabulary

	*ꜥḥꜥw*	lifetime
	*ꜥšꜣ*	many; much
	*ꜥšꜣt*	often
	*rnpt*	year
	*(ỉ)tm*	Atum (a god)
	*ḥnk-m*	offer (verb)

Above and before king: . . . .

. . . .

Behind king: . . . .

. . . .

Before king: . . . .

. . . .

Above god: . . . .

. . . .

In front of god: . . . .

Exercise 45: Spells from a Coffin

Here are two spells from the side of a coffin in the Egyptian Museum, Cairo.

There is a new type of pronoun in this exercise, the independent pronoun, in this case , *ink* (I). (A full chart of these pronouns is on page 229.) The most common use of this type of pronoun is as the subject of a non-verbal sentence, which is how it is used here. For example, you see it at the beginning of each of the two spells: , *ink ḥpy,* "I am Hapy..."

Hieroglyph:  **Transliteration:** *ẖꜣ*

What is it? A fish.

Most Common Use: As a phonogram.

Vocabulary

	*ii*	come (verb)
	*bnw*	benu-bird; phoenix
	*mꜣꜥty*	Maaty (a place-name)
	*mky*	protect (verb)
	*r*	in order (followed by verb)
	*ḥwrw*	weakness; corruption
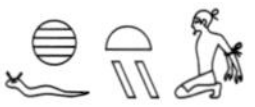	*ḫfty*	enemy
	*ẖꜣt*	corpse
	*sꜣ*	son
	*sḫpr*	create; come into being
	*šsp*	receive, accept
	*dr*	expel, drive out
	*di*	cause
	*ḏs.f*	himself

Spell 1 (from right): ....

....

....

....

....

Above first figure: ....

Spell 2: ....

....

....

....

Above second figure: ....

Exercise 46: Census Scene

Like a number of the exercises in this book, this comes from the tomb of Khnumhotep at Beni Hasan.

Here are two new signs, and some vocabulary.

HIEROGLYPH:  **TRANSLITERATION:** *ẖn*
WHAT IS IT? A goatskin.
MOST COMMON USE: As a phonogram.

HIEROGLYPH: 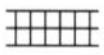 **TRANSLITERATION:** *spꜣt; ḏꜣtt*
WHAT IS IT? Land gridded with irrigation canals.
MOST COMMON USE: In 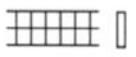, *spꜣt*, "nome" (large administrative district); *ḏꜣtt*, "estate."

VOCABULARY

	*ỉnỉ*	bring*
	*ỉnw*	produce
	*ỉrw*	census
	*mꜣ-ḥḏ*	oryx**
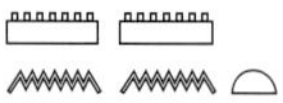	*mnmnt*	animals
	*nỉwt*	town, city
	*ẖnw*	interior
	*sẖpr*	create; bring into being
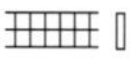	*ḏꜣtt*	estate

*translate this here as "which was brought"
**on a standard, the name of a nome.

This figure of Khnumhotep stands on the north wall of his tomb. He is approached here by several registers of smaller figures (not visible in this illustration), who are presenting offerings to him.

Above small figure at top: . . . .

. . . .

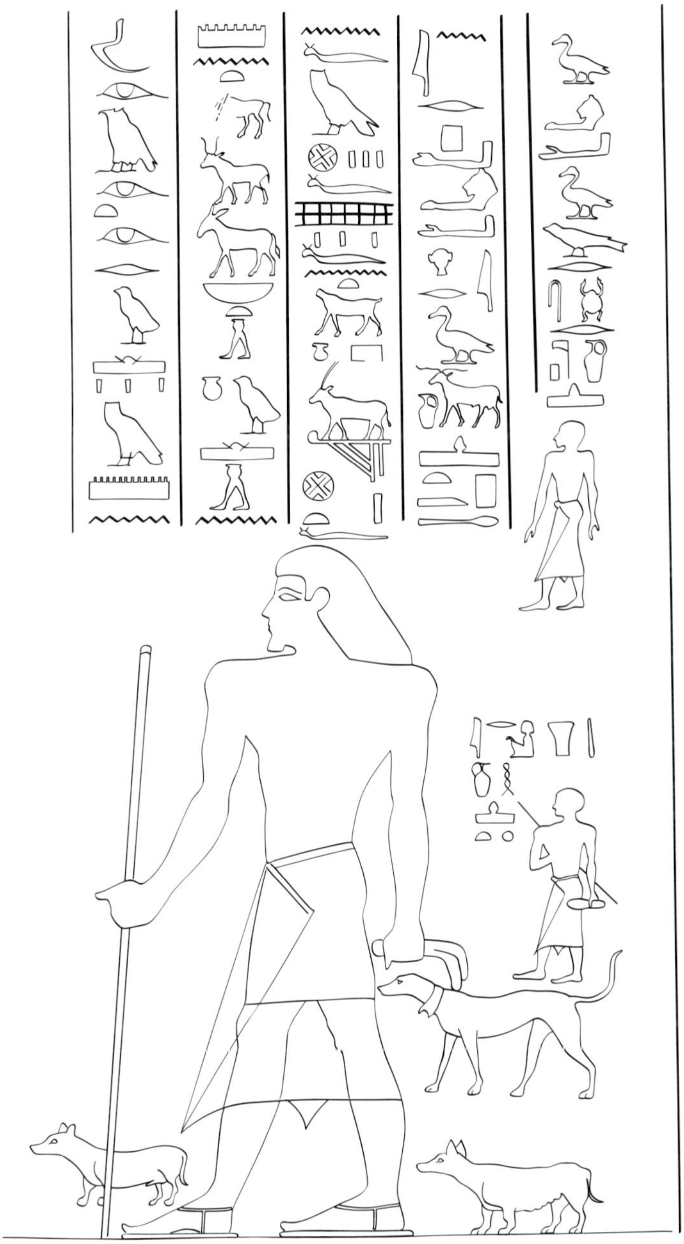

Above lower small figure: . . . .

. . . .

. . . .

. . . .

Main inscription: . . .

. . . .

. . . .

. . . .

. . . .

. . . .

. . . .

. . . .

. . . .

. . . .

. . . .

. . . .

. . . .

. . . .

. . . .

. . . .

Exercise 47: Scene from the Tomb of Shure (Shuroy)

This beautiful scene is from the New Kingdom tomb of Shuroy at Thebes. The chapel is cut into the living rock of the cliffs, and is quite small. Some of the decoration was left unfinished, so the visitor can still see sketches made by the draughtsmen. The scenes that were completed still retain their vibrant color.

Grammar Note: You will see here a verb form that ends with a t. There are a number of ways that this could function; in this case, translate it as a future tense.

Hieroglyph:  **Transliteration:** *psḏ*
What is it? The moon.
Most Common Use: In , *psḏt,* "Ennead," a group of nine gods.

Vocabulary

	*i͗3i*	praise; honor
	*psḏt*	Ennead (group of nine gods)
	*mni͗*	moor (a metaphor for death)

Before god: ....

. . . .

. . . .

. . . .

. . . .

. . . .

. . . .

Before tomb owner and wife: . . . .

. . . .

. . . .

. . . .

. . . .

. . . .

. . . .

. . . .

. . . .

Lesson 45: The Autobiography of Harkhuf

The tomb of Harkhuf lies in the western cliffs high above the river on the west bank at Aswan, the southernmost town in Egypt proper. Harkhuf lived during the 6th Dynasty. His autobiography, which is carved around the entrance to his rock-cut tomb, provides a fascinating glimpse into this period of Egyptian history. As a high official of the Aswan area, he was responsible for leading trading and military expeditions to the south, beyond the borders of Egypt; his autobiography tells the stories of several of his successful exploits.

The exercises in this lesson are taken from three different sections of his extensive autobiographical inscription. The first part consists of offering formulas, and will serve primarily as a review (although the first formulation is slightly different than the ones you have seen previously). The second section is also largely formulaic, and will introduce some new types of common funerary formulas (including a curse). Harkhuf lived through the reigns of several kings; the third exercise quotes part of a letter from one of these monarchs.

Exercise 48: Autobiography of Harkhuf I

You already know most of the vocabulary for this exercise, but here is one new sign and two additional words.

Hieroglyph:  **Transliteration:** *iꜥꜣw*

What is it? A kilt.

Most Common Use: In  *iꜥꜣw*, "foreign worker," "interpreter."

Vocabulary

	*iꜥ*	ascend (w/ *n*, ascend to) (v.)
	*iꜥꜣw*	foreign worker, interpreter
	*ḫpi*	travel; encounter (verb)

Transliterate and translate the texts on the facing page:

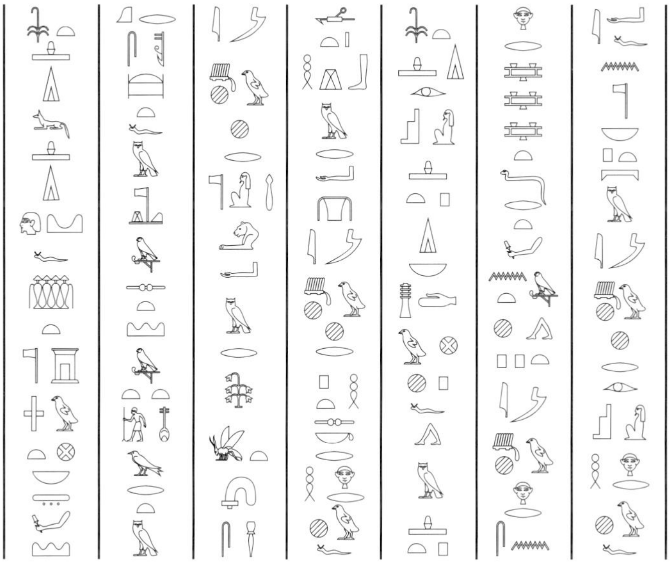

Exercise 49: Autobiography of Harkhuf II

In this section Harkhuf describes the successful execution of his basic duties as a nobleman. This exercise contains several common formulas, including an appeal to the living, in which Harkhuf calls on those who might pass his tomb to say prayers for him; and a curse. Remember that the first person suffix pronoun is often omitted (there are large-scale figures of Harkhuf himself that serve this function), and remember that the missing pronoun can be the subject, part of a direct object, or the object of a preposition.

One new sign and some vocabulary:

Hieroglyph:  **Transliteration:** *iṯ*

What is it? A hobble on a pair of legs.

Most Common Use: As a phonogram.

Vocabulary

	*ꜣḫ*	spirit
	*i*	Oh!
	*iwty*	those without
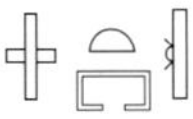	*imyt*	will (last testament)
	*iw*	[marker] (see below)
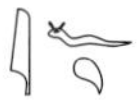	*iwf*	flesh (here for )
	*ir*	as for; if
	*iṯi*	take; conquer; wring (verb)
	*ꜥꜣ*	door
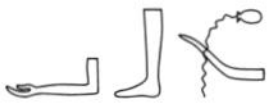	*ꜥb*	impurity; impure
	*wi*	me (dependent pronoun)
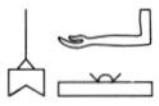	*wḏꜥ*	judge; be judged (verb)
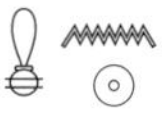	*min*	today

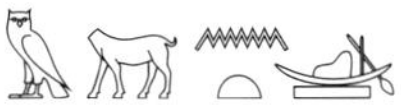	*mḫnt*	ferry-boat
	*nb*	everyone
	*ḫsfw*	travel upstream/south (verb)
	*ḫdỉ*	travel downstream/north (v.)
	*ḳd*	build (verb)
	*sʿḥʿ*	raise up; erect; install (verb)
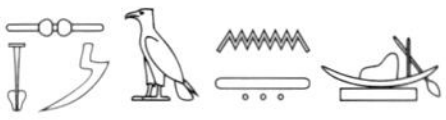	*smꜣ n tꜣ*	passage
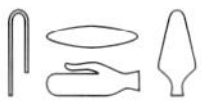	*srd*	plant (verb)
	*swꜣ*	pass by (verb)
	*sbỉ*	watch over (with *ḥr*) (verb)
	*šꜣd*	dig (verb)
	*ṯs*	neck

There are two new verbal constructions in this exercise, both of which use a marker word, , *ỉw*. This word is not translated; it serves as a sort of placeholder. This is interpreted in various ways by Egyptologists; the translation patterns provided here are, as usual, meant to be practical. Here are the two patterns with  that you will see in this exercise:

1. As a marker that a new sentence is beginning:

Example: 

ỉw rdỉ.n.ỉ t n ḥḳr = I gave bread to the hungry.

2. In a construction to indicate future:  plus the suffix pronoun plus the preposition , *r*, and the infinitive. Translate the  + infinitive as "will X," and you should get close to a useable meaning:

Example: 

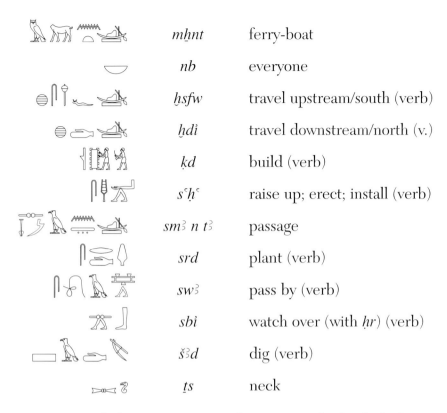

ỉw.ỉ r ỉṯt ṯsf = I will wring his neck.

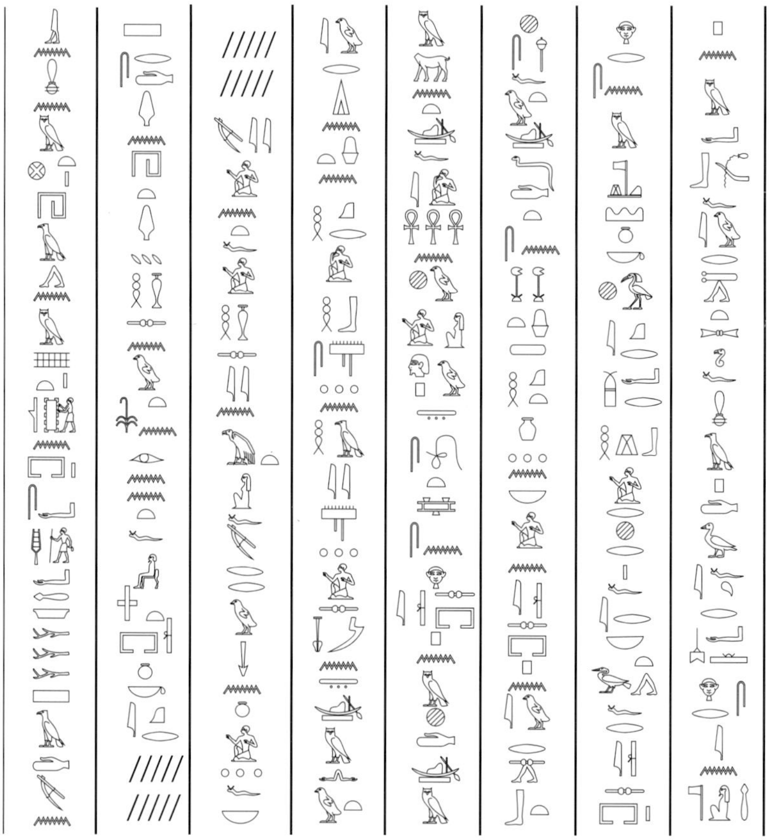

Exercise 50: Autobiography of Harkhuf III

Harkhuf goes on to talk about his travels into Nubia, south of Egypt, where he led expeditions against various local rulers. These seem to have been designed primarily to safeguard important trade routes and protect Egypt's borders. On one of his journeys, he brought back some particularly exotic flora and fauna. He also brought back a human captive, a pygmy. Dwarves and pygmies were important in ancient Egypt as sacred dancers, who performed rituals for the sun god. (Also note that a number of dwarves are known to have held high positions in the Egyptian court on their merits.) The king of Egypt at the time was Pepi II, who had recently come to the throne as a child of six. This expedition took place not many years after his coronation. The young king was very excited about the pygmy, and wrote a letter to Harkhuf, which the latter reproduced on his tomb entrance as part of his autobiography.

HIEROGLYPH:  **TRANSLITERATION:** *bỉꜣ*

WHAT IS IT? A well with water.

MOST COMMON USE: In 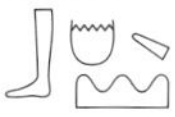, *bỉꜣ*, "mine"

HIEROGLYPH:  **TRANSLITERATION:** *ḫꜣ*

WHAT IS IT? A mussel shell.

MOST COMMON USE: As a phonogram.

HIEROGLYPH:  **TRANSLITERATION:** *gs*

WHAT IS IT? Unknown.

MOST COMMON USE: In , *gs*, "side"

HIEROGLYPH:  **TRANSLITERATION:** *ḏr*

WHAT IS IT? A bundle of flax.

MOST COMMON USE: As a phonogram.

Vocabulary

	*ỉbꜣw*	do a dance; be a dancer (v.)
	*ỉr*	as for
	*wḏꜣ*	prosperity
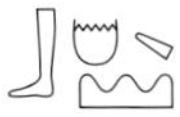	*bỉꜣ*	mine
	*pw*	this
	*m ỉw(t) r.k*	in coming yourself
	*rmṯ*	people*
	*r*	more than
	*ḥr-ꜥw*	at once
	*ḫꜣꜥ*	descend (verb)
	*ḫr*	fall (verb)
	*ẖn*	tent
	*sꜣw*	guard; protect
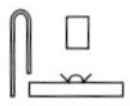	*sp*	inspect
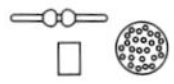	*sp*	time; occasion
	*snḫꜣḫꜣ-ỉb*	soothe the heart (verb)
	*sḫmḫ-ỉb*	gladden the heart (verb)
	*sḏr*	sleep; spend the night (verb)
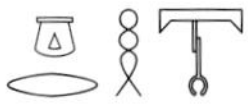	*grḥ*	night
	*gs*	side
	*dng*	pygmy

*Notice that the *m* is not written.

. . . .

. . . .

. . . .

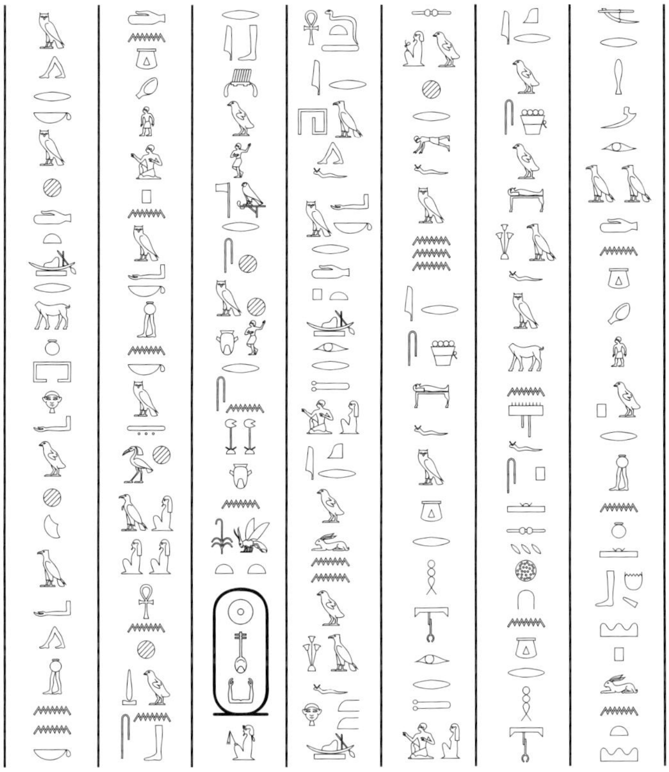

Lesson 46: The Battle of Qadesh

Early in his reign, Ramesses II, third king of the 19th Dynasty, fought an important battle near the city of Qadesh in what scholars call Syria-Palestine, on the Orontes River. This city lay in an important strategic location, in an area of contention between the Egyptians and their most powerful opponents, the Hittites. The Hittite capital lay far to the north, in what is now Turkey; their empire had been on the rise since the days of Akhenaten and his successors, several decades earlier. Although Ramesses II presents the outcome as a great personal victory, it was in actual fact a stalemate. Relations remained difficult between the two superpowers for another decade and a half, until both sides decided it was in their mutual best interest to become allies, and signed a peace treaty. This is the first such treaty known in history. It was originally engraved on a silver tablet, and copies have survived, most remarkably, from both Egypt and from Hattusas, the Hittite capital. To cement the diplomatic ties between the two superpowers, the Hittite king sent first one princess, and then another, to the Egyptian court to marry Ramesses II and join the royal harem.

Ramesses II had the story of the Battle of Qadesh inscribed on the walls of a number of his temples. This version, of which the illustration here presents only the opening paragraphs (in reality, the entire inscription fills the wall above the king's head), is from the Ramesseum, his mortuary temple on the western bank of Thebes.

The grammar for this inscription is considerably more complex than that in the previous examples. However, you should be able to manage, for the most part, with a few pointers:

1. As much as possible, idioms have been provided. Rather than struggling with an unfamiliar construction, even if it contains words you have seen before and think you know, check the vocabulary list and see if there is a new idiom you need to know.

2. In several cases, the subject precedes the verb. Some of these constructions are ones you have met before, with the subject preceding a prepo-

sition and then an infinitive. Others are new constructions, which I will not teach you here. Just be flexible and don't try to stick rigidly to the grammar you have learned so far.

Here are several new signs:

Hieroglyph:  **Transliteration:** *ꜥḥꜣ*
What is it? Two arms, one holding a shield and the other a mace.

Hieroglyph:  **Transliteration:** *wḏ*
What is it? Rope wound around a staff or stick.
Most Common Use: As a phonogram.

Hieroglyph:  **Transliteration:** *rs*
What is it? The stylized version of the upright post of a scale.
Most Common Use: Primarily as a determinative.

Hieroglyph:  **Transliteration:** *snḏ*
What is it? A plucked goose.
Most Common Use: As a phonogram.

Hieroglyph:  **Transliteration:** *pꜣ*
What is it? A flying duck.
Most Common Use: As a phonogram.

Hieroglyph: 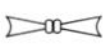 **Transliteration:** *ṯs*
What is it? A belt with a knot.
Most Common Use: As a phonogram.

On the next page is a great deal of vocabulary, which you will probably want to use as reference.

Vocabulary

ỉw	come (verb)
ỉmꜣw	tent
ỉst	lo!
2nwt (snwt)	second
ꜥnḫ wḏꜣ snb	life, prosperity, health
ꜥḥꜣ	fight (verb)
ꜥḏꜣ	falseness (*m-ꜥḏꜣ* = falsely)
wỉ	separate
wḏꜣ	proceed; go; set out
wḏyt	campaign; expedition
bꜣk	servant
pꜣ	the; those (masc. sing.)
pꜣ-nty	the place where
ptr	see; spy
prwy-ꜥꜣ	Pharaoh
m-ꜥ	among; from
m-nꜣy.n	in this way; thus
m, m-tw	behold; and
m-ḫntỉ	southward
m-ḫd	northward
m-dỉ	with
nꜣ	the; these (plural)
n-ỉb-n	in order to
nty	who are, which are
rs	awakening

	*hꜣw*	kindred
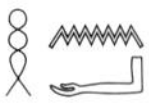	*ḥnꜥ*	with; together with
	*ḥr*	get ready to fight (verb)
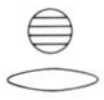	*ḫr*	indeed
	*ḫr*	fallen one
	*ḫyrbꜣi͗*	Herbai (Aleppo)
	*ḫtꜣ*	Kheta (the Hittites)
	*sw*	and that
	*snḏ*	fear (verb)
	*spr*	arrive (verb)
	*šꜣbtwn*	Shabetun (a place name)
	*šꜣsw*	Shasu (Bedouin)
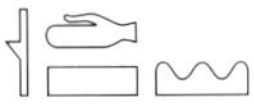	*ḳdš*	Qadesh (a city)
	*twnp*	Tunip
	*tm di͗.t(w)*	prevent that one cause
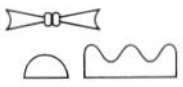	*ṯst*	mountain
	*dmi͗*	town
	*ḏꜣhy*	Djahy (ancient Palestine)

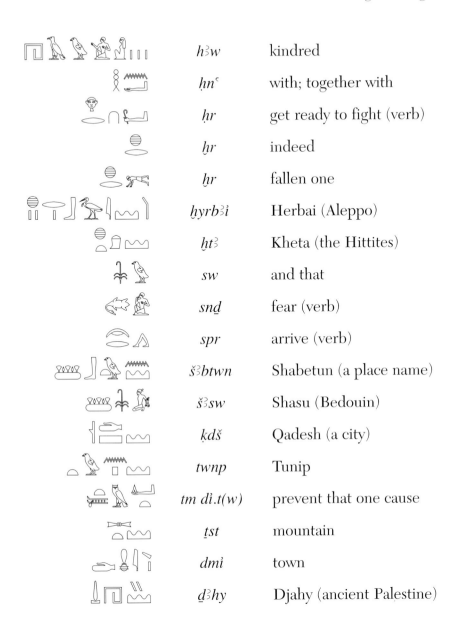

Exercise 51: The Battle of Qadesh

. . . .

. . . .

. . . .

. . . .

. . . .

. . . .

. . . .

. . . .

. . . .

. . . .

. . . .

. . . .

. . . .

. . . .

. . . .

The rest of this story is quite remarkable. As this opening text relates, the Shasu (Bedouins), were spies, sent by the Hittites to trick the Egyptians into believing that their main army was far away. In fact, they were right behind Qadesh, lying in wait. Ramesses went ahead with a small force to Qadesh, and set up camp, expecting to have plenty of time to wait for the rest of his troops and prepare for battle. While the king was sitting upon his throne (presumably reviewing his battle plans), one of his scouts came in with two Hittite spies. These men told the king that the Hittites were, in fact, close by, with an enormous army. Ramesses called in his councilors and while they were all busy discussing the situation, the Hittites and their allies attacked, defeating the first Egyptian division and attacking the royal encampment itself. It was, according to these texts, Ramesses II's own personal valor that saved the day, and held off the Hittite attack until reinforcements could arrive. The battle eventually ended in a stalemate.

END OF CHAPTER VI

Conclusion

Now that you are equipped with a basic understanding of hieroglyphs, your visits to museums around the world and to sites in Egypt itself will be infinitely more enjoyable. There are many wonderful collections of Egyptian artifacts around the world that you can visit. Here are a few:

In the United States, one of the largest collections is at the Metropolitan Museum of Art in New York. Its holdings span all eras of Egyptian history, and the galleries there have just been beautifully reinstalled. The Brooklyn Museum is also well known for its Egyptian material. The University Museum of the University of Pennsylvania is unique in that it has predominantly excavated artifacts in its collections. Another excellent East Coast collection is at the Museum of Fine Arts, Boston, which has many spectacular pieces. The Michael C. Carlos Museum in Atlanta is also worth a visit. Other significant East Coast collections include the Walters Art Museum in Baltimore and the Smithsonian in Washington. In the Midwest, the Oriental Institute Museum is excellent. There are also a number of important West Coast museums, such as the Stanford University Museum and the Rosicrucian Museum; Canada has good collections in both Montreal and Toronto.

Europe of course boasts a number of worthwhile collections. The two biggest are probably at the British Museum in London and the Louvre Museum in Paris. Each of these museums contains many spectacular pieces, objects fundamental to our understanding of Egyptian history. Other important collections are in Berlin and Leiden. For a full list of museums with

Egyptian collections, look in the *Atlas of Ancient Egypt* (John Baines and Jaromír Málek, 2002). Also visit the very useful website maintained by Egyptologist Nigel Strudwick: http://www.newton.cam.ac.uk/egypt/.

The best way to appreciate fully the civilization of ancient Egypt is to visit the Land of the Pharaohs, beginning with the Egyptian Museum, Cairo. Armed with your new knowledge of the ancient language, you will be able to enjoy this collection, without a doubt the most spectacular group of Egyptian artifacts in the world, and identify many of the pieces you are seeing. As you have seen, most of the illustrations in this book are of objects housed in this institution. The museum in Luxor is also excellent. It is beautifully laid out, and has a manageable number of objects to enjoy. A new exhibit on the army in ancient Egypt is opening here in May 2004.

The Nubian Museum in Aswan is wonderful. The exhibits are nicely arranged and the collection is rich. There is also a lovely museum on Elephantine Island, a place well worth visiting when you go to Aswan. The Supreme Council of Antiquities is currently building and opening a number of new museums around the country, including an Akhenaten Museum in Minya, and the new Grand Museum, where the Tutankhamen collection will be displayed.

Of course, site visits are also an important part of any trip to Egypt. Go to Giza, and do not spend all of your time at the Great Pyramid and Sphinx. Wander around in the ancient cemeteries that cover the plateau, visit some of the tombs of the nobles there, and enjoy the lively scenes that decorate their walls. But remember, DO NOT touch the reliefs, and be aware that your breath contains moisture, which attracts the salt from beneath the surface of the limestone and damages the ancient paint. Saqqara, where many of the most beautiful tombs of the Old and New Kingdoms are located, is a must. Visit the exquisite tomb of Niankhnum and Khnumhotep first: the repertoire of scenes there is excellent, and much of the paint is preserved. Also see Mereruka, an enormous maze of chapels and chambers, including a number dedicated to his beautiful wife, and stop off at the tomb of Ti.

While in Luxor, visit the Luxor Temple, which has many beautiful reliefs, and the vast, sprawling temple complex of Karnak. While you are at Karnak, make sure to visit the Open Air Museum, which contains, among other things, a jewel-like shrine of alabaster from the reign of Senwosret I and the reconstructed Red Chapel of Hatshepsut. On the West Bank, be sure to visit the mortuary temple of Hatshepsut at Deir el-Bahri. In the Valleys of the Kings, Queens, and Nobles, you will be limited to whichever tombs are open when you go, but they are all wonderful. Aswan is also on the standard tourist itinerary; make sure to go across the river to the Tombs of the Nobles, where you can find Harkhuf's tomb and read his autobiography from the original text, and also enjoy a spectacular view. The tombs here have been cut into the striated rock, with pillars left standing in their echoing chambers.

Further Reading

If you wish to continue your studies of the language of ancient Egypt, I recommend *How to Read Egyptian Hieroglyphs*, by Mark Collier and Bill Manley. Their approach is different from the one you have worked with here, but armed with the material from *Ancient Egyptian Hieroglyphs: A Practical Guide*, you will enjoy their book a great deal. It will reinforce what you have learned here, and give you more opportunities to build your vocabulary and knowledge of grammar.

A current, extremely thorough grammar of Middle Egyptian is James P. Allen's *Middle Egyptian*. If you work through it slowly and carefully, you will learn a great deal. It has exercises at the end of each chapter (and a key in the back) that are very useful.

The best way to build your hieroglyphic skills is to practice. There are many beautiful art books out there that contain photos of objects in museums. Look at the pictures, and instead of just reading the English captions, you can read the objects themselves. Visit the Egyptological collection closest to you, and come to visit Egypt!

Appendix 1: Key to the Exercises

The answers given here are based on the information and concepts provided in this book. Do not worry if your answers are not exactly the same; the important thing is to get the right basic meaning.

Chapter I: The Egyptian Alphabet

Exercise 1: The Alphabet

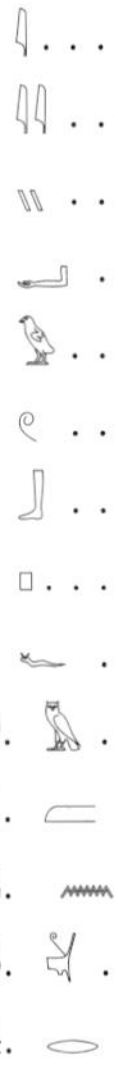

1.	*ỉ*	i
2.	*y*	y
3.	*y*	y
4.	*ꜥ*	e
5.	*w*	w,u,o
6.	*w*	w,u,o
7.	*b*	b
8.	*p*	p
9.	*f*	f
10.	*m*	m
11.	*m*	m
12.	*n*	n
13.	*n*	n
14.	*r*	r

15.	*h*	.h
16.	*ḥ*	.h
17.	*ḫ*	.kh
18.	*ẖ*	.kh
19.	*s*	.s
20.	*s*	.s
21.	*š*	.sh
22.	*ḳ*	.q
23.	*k*	.k
24.	*g*	.g
25.	*t*	.t
26.	*ṯ*	.tj
27.	*d*	.d
28.	*ḏ*	.dj

Exercise 2: Names in English

1.	*frꜣnk*	Frank
2.	*ꜣdꜣm*	Adam
3.	*ꜣnn*	Ann
4.	*frꜣnsỉs*	Francis
5.	*sꜣndy*	Sandy
6.	*mꜣrgꜣrꜥt*	Margaret
7.	*šꜥrry*	Sherry/Shelly
8.	*hꜥnry*	Henry
9.	*kꜣrꜥn*	Karen
10.	*sꜣrỉmꜣ*	Salima
11.	*ḳwỉnsy*	Quincy
12.	*ḏꜥnnỉfꜥr*	Jennifer
13.	*swsꜣn*	Susan
14.	*mꜥrỉssꜣ*	Melissa
15.	*gwstꜣfw*	Gustavo
16.	*ꜣwdrꜥy*	Audrey
17.	*pꜣtrỉṯỉꜣ*	Patricia

Exercise 3: Egyptian Names

1. . . . . *ỉnpw* . . . . Inpw (Anubis, god of embalming)
2. . . . . *ỉtn* . . . . Iten (Aten)
3. . . . . *ꜣny* . . . . Any
4. . . . . *skr* . . . . Seker (Sokar)
5. . . . . *ptḥ* . . . . Peteh (Ptah)
6. . . . . *bꜣḳt* . . . . Baqt
7. . . . . *rꜥ* . . . . Re (Ra)
8. . . . . *tꜣwrt* . . . . Taweret
9. . . . . *sbk* . . . . Sebek (Sobek)

Exercise 4: Practice with Vocabulary

1. . . . . . *s bỉn* . . . . an evil man
2. . . . *ꜣpd ḥḳr* . . . . a hungry bird
3. . . . . . *ḫfty bỉn* . . . . an evil enemy
4. . . . . *hy ỉḳr* . . . . an excellent husband
5. . . . . . *st bỉnt* . . . . an evil woman
6. . . . *ḫfty hꜣ* . . . . a naked enemy
7. . . . . *hy ḥḳr* . . . . a hungry husband
8. . . . . *st tn* . . . . this seat/throne
9. . . . *s smsw* . . . . an elder man

Exercise 5: Suffix Pronouns

1. . . . . *š.n* . . . . our pool
2. . . . . *snb.k* . . . . your health
3. . . . . *t ḥnḳt* . . . . bread and beer
4. . . . . *wỉꜣ.f* . . . . his divine bark
5. . . . . *ỉt.ỉ* . . . . my father
6. . . . . *ẖt.s ꜥ.f* . . . . her body and his arm
7. . . . . *ḫpš ꜣpd* . . . . foreleg of ox and fowl
8. . . . *hy.k ỉḳr* . . . . your excellent husband
9. . . . . *r.ỉ* . . . . my mouth

Exercise 6: Dual and Plural

1. . . . . *šwy* . . . . two pools
2. . . . . . . *ꜣpdw* . . . . birds
3. . . . . . *wỉꜣw* . . . . divine barks
4. . . . *sy ḥḳry* . . . . two hungry men
5. . . *hyw ỉḳrw* . . . . excellent husbands
6. *ḫftyw bỉnw* . . . . evil enemies

Exercise 7: Non-Verbal Sentences and Short Phrases

1. . . . *skr m wỉꜣ.f* . . . . . . Sokar is in his divine bark.

2. *ỉnpw rn.f* . . . Anubis is his name.
3. *ptḥ m pt* . . . Ptah is in the sky.
4. *rꜥ ỉt.ỉ* . . . Re is my father.
5. *ỉnpw m wt.f* . . . Anubis is in his place of embalming.

Exercise 8: Verbal Sentences and Phrases

1. *ḏd.n rꜥ* . . . Re spoke.
2. *rḫ.ỉ rn.k* . . . I know/will know your name.
3. *wbn rꜥ m pt* . . . Re (the sun) rises/wil rise in the sky.
4. *ỉp.n.f ꜣpdw.n* . . . He counted our birds.
5. *ḏd.sn* . . . They spoke.
6. *ỉp.k ḫftyw* . . . You (m.) count/will count the enemies.
7. *rḫ.ṯ ỉt.ỉ* . . . You (f.) know/will know my father.

Chapter II: Beyond the Alphabet

Exercise 9: Names with Biliterals

1. *ỉmn* . . . Imen (Amen)
3. *wnỉs* . . . Wenis
2. *ꜣbḏw* . . . Abdju (Abydos)
3. *mry-rꜥ* . . . Meryre
4. *pr-ỉb-sn* . . . Peribsen
5. *mꜣꜥt* . . . Maat
6. *nwt* . . . Nut
7. *ḏdw* . . . Djedu (Busiris)
8. *ỉrṯṯ* . . . Irtjetj
9. *mỉṯrỉ* . . . Mitjri

Exercise 10: Possession

1. *nb tꜣwy* . . . lord of the Two Lands
2. *sꜣ n ỉt.k* . . . the son of your father
3. *nb ḫꜥw* . . . lord of appearances
4. *nb ḏdw* . . . lord of Djedu (Busiris)
5. *ỉb n s* . . . the heart of a man
6. *sꜣ smsw n ẖt.f* . . . the eldest son of his body.
7. *ꜥꜣw nw st tn* . . . the donkeys of this woman
8. *nbt pr* . . . mistress/lady of the house
9. *nb ꜥꜣ n ꜣbḏw* . . . great lord of Abydos

Exercise 11: Names with Honorific Transposition

1. *ḥsy-rꜥ* . . . Hesyre
2. *ḫꜥ.f-rꜥ* . . . Khefre (Khafre)
3. *mn-kꜣw-rꜥ* . . . Menkaure

4. . . . *mry-rꜥ* . . . Meryre
5. . . . *n-mꜣꜥt-rꜥ* . . . Nemaatre
6. . . . *rꜥ-ms.s* . . . Ramesses

Exercise 12: More Sentences and Phrases

1. . . . *mry n ptḥ* . . . (one) beloved of Ptah
2. *ỉmꜣḫy ḫr rꜥ* . . . (one) revered before Re
3. . . . *ỉry n ỉt.f* . . . (one) made of (by) his father
4. . . . *ḥsy n nb.f* . . . (one) praised of (by) his lord
5. . . . *sꜣ.f mry.f* . . . his son, whom he loves
6. . . . *mrt nt hy.s* . . . (one) beloved of her husband
7. . . . *ỉmꜣḫt ḫr snt.s* . . . (one) revered before her sister
8. . . . *nbt.f ḥst.f* . . . his mistress whom he praises
9. . . . *ḥmt.f mrt.f* . . . his wife whom he loves
10. . . . *sꜣ.s msy.s* . . . her son whom she bore

Exercise 13: More Names with Biliterals

1. . . . *ỉnt.f* . . . Intef
2. . . . *mꜣ-ḥḏ* . . . Mahedj (Oryx)
3. . . . *ḥm-kꜣ* . . . Hemka
4. . . . *snwy* . . . Senwy
5. . . . *nḫt* . . . Nakht
6. . . . *bꜣḳt* . . . Baqt
7. . . . *ḥr-wr* . . . Herwer

Exercise 14: Sentences and Common Phrases

1. . . . *sꜣ rꜥ* . . . son of Re
2. . . . *kꜣ nḫt* . . . mighty bull
3. . . . *mỉ rꜥ ḏt* . . . like Re, forever
4. . . . *sꜣt.ỉ nt ḫt.ỉ* . . . my daughter of my body
5. . . . *kꜣ-tp m pr* . . . Katep is in the house.
6. . . . *dpt ḥr mw* . . . The boat is on the water.
7. . . . *sn.s ḥsy.s* . . . her brother whom she praises
8. . . . *ḥm n nb.f* . . . a servant of his lord
9. . . . *tp(y) ḏw.f* . . . (who is) upon his mountain
10. . . . *pr ḥḏ* . . . white/silver house (treasury)

Exercise 15: Names with Multi-sound Signs

1. . . . *ḫpr-kꜣ-rꜥ* . . . Kheperkare
2. . . . *wsrt-sn=sn-wsrt* . . Senwosret (honorific transposition)
3. . . . *twt-ꜥnḫ-ỉmn* . . . Tutankhamen

4. .... *ḏḥwty-ms* .... Djehutymes (Tuthmosis)
5. .... *nṯr-ẖt* .... Netjerkhet
6. .... *ḥtp-ḥr.s* .... Hetepheres
7. .... *mꜣꜥt-kꜣ-rꜥ* .... Maatkare
8. .... *sꜣḥw-rꜥ* .... Sahure
9. .... *špss-kꜣ.f* .... Shepseskaf
10. .. *ỉmn-m-ḥꜣt* .... Amenemhat
11. .. *sḥtp-ỉb-rꜥ* .... Sehetibre
12. ...... *ẖnm-ḥtp* .... Khnumhotep
13. .... *nfrt* .... Nefret
14. .... *wp-wꜣwt* .... Wepwawet

Exercise 16: Transliteration Practice

1. .... *wsỉr* .... Wesir (Osiris)
2, ... *nṯr* .... netjer
4. .... *ḥwt* .... hut
5. .... *ḥkꜣ* .... heqa
7. .... *ꜥnḫ* .... ankh
9. .... *wꜣs* .... was
10. .... *swtn=nswt* ...... nesut (honorific transposition)
11. .... *ẖrw* .... kheru
12. .... *ḥtp* .... hetep
13. .... *stp* .... setep
14. .... *mwt* .... mut
15. .... *nfr* .... nefer

Exercise 17: Common Phrases

1. .... *ḥwt-nṯr* .... divine mansion (temple)
2. *stp n rꜥ* chosen of (by) Re [You might also have come up with *stp.n rꜥ*, Re has chosen]
3. .... *sꜣ nswt* .... son of the king
4. ... *mwt nswt mryt.f* .. mother of the king, whom he loves
5. .... *dỉ ꜥnḫ ḏd wꜣs nb* .. given all life, stability, wealth
6. *ỉry n ỉt.f ms n mwt.f* made of his father; borne of his mother
7. ...... *wp wꜣwt* .... one who opens/opener of the ways (Wepwawet)
8. ... *ỉmn-m-ḥꜣt mꜣꜥ ẖrw* Amenemhat, true of voice
9. .... *nswt bỉty*........ King of Upper and Lower Egypt
10. ...... *dỉ ꜥnḫ mỉ rꜥ ḏt* .... given life like Re forever
11. .... *nṯr nfr*.......... the good god
12. .... *nbty ḥr nbw* ..... the Two Ladies, Horus of gold
13. ...... *ḥkꜣ ẖꜣswt* .... ruler of the foreign lands
14. ... *sꜣ nswt n ẖt.f*..... son of the king of his body

15. .... *nb mꜣꜥt* .... lord of Maat (truth/justice)
16. ..... *ḥḳꜣ wꜣst* .... ruler of Thebes

Exercise 18: More Common Phrases

1. .... *ỉwnw šmꜥw* ...... Iunu of Upper Egypt (southern Iunu)
2. .... *ḫꜣswt ỉꜣbty* ...... eastern foreign lands
3. .... *nbt pt* .... mistress/lady of the sky
3. .... *wsỉr ḫnty ỉmntyw* . Osiris, foremost of the Westerners
4. .... *tꜣ mḥty* .... the northern land
5. .... *wr šmꜥw* .... great one of Upper Egypt
6. .... *nṯr ꜥꜣ*........... great god
7. .... *r nḥḥ* .... to eternity

Exercise 19: Labels

Object 1: Animal Offerings from the Old Kingdom

Animal 1: ....*rn mꜣ-ḥḏ* ....the young (of) oryx
Animal 2: ....*rn nwḏw* ....the young (of) long-horned cattle
Animal 3: ....*gsḥt (gḥst)* ......female gazelle

Object 2: List of Enemies

Enemy 1: ....*sngr* ....Senger = Babylon
Enemy 2: ....*kš* ....Kesh (Kush) = Nubia
Enemy 3: ....*nhryn* ....Naharin = Syria
Enemy 4: ....*ỉrm* ....Irem = place in Nubia
Enemy 5: ....*kftỉw* ....Keftiu = Crete
Enemy 6: ....*ỉwnw-st(ỉ)* ....Iunuseti = place in Nubia
Enemy 9: ....*šꜣsw* ....Shasu = Bedouin

Chapter III: Royal Names and Titles

Exercise 20: Early Dynastic Monuments

Object 1: Statue of Hetepdief

Serekh 1: *ḥtp-sḫmwy* Hetepsekhemwy

Serekh 2: *nb-rꜥ* Nebre/*rꜥ-nb* Reneb

Serekh 3: *n-nṯr* Ninetjer

Object 2: Abydos Stela

ḏ(t) Djet

Object 3: Slate Palette

nꜥr-mr Narmer

Exercise 21: Old Kingdom Monuments

Object 1: Statue Base of Djoser

nswt bỉty nbty nṯr-ḫt nbw = King of Upper and Lower Egypt, Two Ladies, Netjerkhet of gold

Object 2: Lintel
nswt bỉty ḫꜥ.f-rꜥ sꜣ rꜥ = King of Upper and Lower Egypt, Khafre, son of Re
Object 3: Relief Fragment
ppy nfr-kꜣ-rꜥ = Pepi (II) Neferkare

Exercise 22: Middle Kingdom Monuments
Object 1: Pectoral *ḫꜥ-kꜣw-rꜥ* = Khakaure (Senwosret III)
Object 2: Pectoral *ḥtp nṯrw ḫꜥ-ḫpr-rꜥ* = an offering of the gods, Khakheperre (Senwosret II). [The hetep and netjer signs can also be understood as a participial phrase, "he who makes content the gods."]
Object 3: Pectoral *nb pt n-mꜣꜥt-rꜥ nṯr nfr nb tꜣwy ḫꜣswt nb(w)t* = Lord (Lady) of the sky (refering to the vulture) Nimaatre (Amenemhat III), the good god, lord of the Two Lands and of all foreign lands
Object 1: Pyramidion
Center to right: *nswt bỉty n-mꜣꜥt-rꜥ dỉ ꜥnḫ ḏt* = King of Upper and Lower Egypt Nimaatre, given life forever.
Center to left: *sꜣ rꜥ ỉmn-m-ḥꜣt dỉ ꜥnḫ ḏt* = Son of Re, Amenemhat (III), given life forever.

Exercise 23: New Kingdom Monuments
Part 1: Tiles *sṯy mry-n-ptḥ mn-mꜣꜥt-rꜥ* = Sety (I), beloved of Ptah, Menmaatre
Part 2: Box and Jewel
Box: *twt-ꜥnḫ-ỉmn ḥḳꜣ-ỉwnw-šmꜥw* = Tutankhamen, ruler of Southern Iunu
Jewel: *nb-ḫprw-rꜥ* = Nebkheperure
Part 3: Architrave
nswt bỉty nb tꜣwy nb ỉr(t) ḫt nb ḫꜥw mn-ḫprw-rꜥ = King of Upper and Lower Egypt, lord of the two lands, lord of ritual, lord of appearances, Menkheperure (Tuthmosis IV).
Part 4: Back pillar of statue of Amenhotep II *nṯr nfr nb tꜣwy nb ỉr(t) ḫt nswt bỉty ꜥꜣ-ḫprw-rꜥ mry ỉmn dỉ ꜥnḫ ḏt* = The good god, lord of the Two Lands, lord of ritual, king of Upper and Lower Egypt, Aakheperure, beloved of Amen, given life forever.

Exercise 24: Post-New Kingdom Monuments
Object 1: Column of Psammetik
ḥr wꜣḥ-ỉb wꜣḥ-ỉb-rꜥ mry nt nbt sꜣw dỉ ꜥnḫ ḏd wꜣs ḏt = The Horus Wahib, Wahibre, beloved of Neith, lady of Sais, given life, stability, wealth, forever.
Object 2: Relief from Dendera
ptwlmys = Ptolemy
kysrws ꜥnḫ ḏt mry ptḥ ꜣst = Caesar, living forever, beloved of Ptah and Isis.
ḳlwpꜣdrꜣt = Cleopatra

Exercise 25: Numbers
1. 𓎆𓎆𓎆𓏺𓏺𓏺 33
2. 𓍢𓍢𓍢𓍢𓍢𓍢𓍢𓎆𓎆𓎆𓎆𓎆𓏺𓏺𓏺 753
3. 𓍢𓍢𓏺𓏺𓏺𓏺𓏺𓏺𓏺𓏺𓏺 209

4. 𓆼𓆼𓆼𓆼𓆼𓍢𓍢𓍢𓍢𓍢𓍢𓎆𓎆𓎆𓎆𓎆𓎆𓎆𓎆𓏺𓏺 5682
5. 𓆼𓆼𓎆𓎆𓎆𓎆𓎆𓏺𓏺𓏺𓏺 2,054

Exercise 26: Regnal Dates

1. *ḥsbt 31 ꜣbd 3 ꜣḫt sw 10 ḫr ḥm n nswt bỉty nb-mꜣꜥt-rꜥ*

Year 31, month 3 of Akhet, day 10 under the majesty of the king of Upper and Lwer Egypt, Nebmaatre (Amenhotep III).

2. *ḥsbt 14 ꜣbd 1 šmw sw 11 ḫr ḥm n nswt bỉty mꜣꜥt-kꜣꜥ-rꜥ*

Year 14, month 1 of Shemu, day 11 under the majesty of the king of Upper and Lower Egypt, Maatkare (Hatshepsut).

3. *ḥsbt 3 ꜣbd 2 prt sw 6 ḫr ḥm n nswt bỉty n-mꜣꜥt-rꜥ*

Year 3, month 2 of Peret, day 6 under the majesty of the king of Upper and Lower Egypt, Nimaatre (Amenemhat III).

Exercise 27: Royal Monuments from All Periods

Object 1: Stela *nb mꜣꜥt nswt bỉty nbty nb mꜣꜥt ḥr nbw snfrw* = Nebmaat (or Lord of Maat), King of Upper and Lower Egypt, Nebmaat, Horus of gold, Sneferu.

Object 2: Statue Base

Center cartouche: *snwsrt* = Senwosret

Right side: *ḏỉ.f ꜥnḫ ḏd wꜣs nb nbwty nb tꜣ šmꜥw* = May he give all life, stability, and dominion, (one of) Nebuty (a town in Egypt) lord of Upper Egypt.

Left side: *dỉ.f ꜥnḫ ḏd wꜣs nb nṯr ꜥꜣ sꜣb* = May he give all life, stability, dominion, the great god, many-colored of plumage (a reference to Horus as a falcon).

Object 3: Statue Base of Ramesses II

Purple: *nswt bỉty nb tꜣwy wsr-mꜣꜥt-rꜥ stp-n-rꜥ nbw* = King of Upper and Lower Egypt, lord of the Two Lands, Usermaatre, chosen of Re, the golden one.

Blue: *sꜣ rꜥ nb ḫꜥw rꜥ-ms-sw mry-ỉmn* = Son of Re, lord of appearances, Ramesses, beloved of Amen

Red: *mrwt mỉ ỉmn dỉ ꜥnḫ [ḏt]* = beloved like Amen, given life [forever]

Brown: *mry mnṯw ḥry-ỉb wꜣst* = beloved of Montu, who dwells in Waset (Thebes)

Object 4: Lintel of Amenhotep II

Beside winged disk: *bḥdt* The Behedite

Line 1: *ꜥnḫ nswt bỉty ꜥꜣ-ḫprw-rꜥ mry ḥr-m-ꜣḫt* = Live the King of Upper and Lower Egypt, Aakheperure, beloved of Horemakhet (Horus in the horizon)

Line 2: *ꜥnḫ sꜣ rꜥ ỉmn-ḥtp nṯr ḥkꜣ-mꜣꜥt dỉ ꜥnḫ ḏt* = Live the son of Re, Amenhotep (II), divine ruler of Truth, given life forever.

Object 5: Middle Kingdom Royal Stele

Green: *bḥdt nb msn* = the Behedite, ruler of Mesen

Orange: *ḥr ꜥnḫ-mswt* = the Horus, Ankhmesut

Orange, continued: *sꜣ rꜥ snwsrt nṯr nfr nb tꜣwy dỉ ꜥnḫ ḏd wꜣs snb mỉ rꜥ ḏt* = son of Re, Senwosret, the Good God, Lord of the Two Lands, given life, stability, dominion, health, like Re forever.

Purple: *wsỉr ḫnty ỉmntỉw nb ꜣbḏw dỉ.f ꜥnḫ wꜣs ḏt* = the Osiris, foremost of the westerners, lord of Abydos, may he give life, dominion forever.
Blue:*ꜥnḫ ḥr ꜥnḫ-mswt nbty ꜥnḫ-mswt nswt bỉty ḫpr-kꜣ-rꜥ nṯr nfr nb tꜣwy sꜣ rꜥ snwsrt dỉ ꜥnḫ ḏd wꜣs snb ꜣw ỉb.f mỉ rꜥ ḏt* Live the Horus, Ankhmesut, the Two Ladies, Ankhmesut, King of Upper and Lower Egypt, Kheperkare, the good god, lord of the Two Lands, son of Re, Senwosret (I), given life, stability, dominion, health, may he be happy, like Re forever.

Chapter IV: Titles

Exercise 28: Titles of the Royal Family

1. *mwt nswt* mother of the king
2. *sꜣt nswt* daughter of the king
3. *sꜣ nswt n ḫt.f* son of the king of his body
4. *ḫkrt nswt wrt* great royal ornament
5. *sꜣ nswt smsw* eldest son of the king
6. *ḥmt nswt wrt* great wife of the king
7. *sꜣt nswt smsw(t)* eldest daughter of the king

Exercise 29: The Royal Family

Object 1: Old Kingdom Sarcophagus

sꜣ nswt ḏd.f-ḫwfw Son of the king, Djedefkhufu

Object 2: Titles from the tomb of Mersyankh

sꜣt nswt nt ḥ(t).f ḥmt nswt mr.s-ꜥnḫ daughter of the king of his body, wife of the king, Mersyankh

Object 3: Vase of Queen Tiye

Orange: *nswt bỉty nb-mꜣꜥt-rꜥ* King of Upper and Lower Egypt, Nebmaatre
Yellow *sꜣ rꜥ ỉmn-ḥtp ḥkꜣ wꜣst* Son of Re, Amenhotep (III), ruler of Waset (Thebes)
Red: *dỉ ꜥnḫ ḏt* given life forever.
Green: *ḥmt nswt tỉy ꜥnḫ.tỉ* Wife of the king, Tiye, may she live.

Exercise 30: Practice with a Title String

r-pꜥ ḥꜣty-ꜥ ḫtmw bỉty smr wꜥty rḫ nswt Hereditary prince, sealer of the king of Lower Egypt, high official, unique companion, king's acquaintance.

Exercise 31: Practice with Administrative Titles

1. ....*ỉmy-r mšꜥ* Overseer of the army (general)
2. ....*ỉmy-r ḥmwwt* Overseer of the craftsmen
3. ....*sḥḏ ḫtmw* Inspector of the sealers
4. ....*ḫrp ꜥpr* Director of a crew
5. ....*wr 10 šmꜥw* Great one of the 10 of Upper Egypt
6. ......*sš mḏꜣt nswt* Royal document scribe
7. *ꜥḏ mr ḫnty-š ꜣḫt-ḫwfw rḫ nswt* = Administrator, land official of Akhet Khufu (the pyramid complex of Khufu), royal acquaintance
8. *mdḥ sš nswt ỉmy-r kꜣt nbt nswt ṯꜣity sꜣb ṯꜣty* = Overseer of

the royal scribes, overseer of all the king's work, he of the curtain, judge, vizier

9.  *r-pꜥ ḥꜣty-ꜥ ḫtmw bỉty smr wꜥty wr 10 šmꜥw rḫ nswt* = Hereditary prince, high official, sealer of the king of Lower Egypt, unique companion, great one of the 10 of Upper Egypt, royal acquaintance.

10.  *špss sꜥḥ sꜣb sḥḏ ꜥḥ sš ỉry nḫn* = Courtier, noble, judge, inspector of the palace, scribe, guardian of Nekhen.

Exercise 32: Practice with Priestly Titles

1. 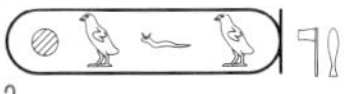 *ḥm-nṯr* = god's servant of Khufu
2.  *wꜥb nswt* = royal wab priest
3.  *sḥḏ ḥm-kꜣw sm ḫry-ḥbt* = Inspector of the ka priests, sem priest, lector priest
4.  *ḥry-sštꜣ ḏḥwty* = Keeper of the secrets of Thoth
5.  *ḥry-tp ḥmw-nṯr wr mꜣꜥ ỉwnw* = Chief of the priests, great seer of Iunu.
6.  *dwꜣ nṯr šmꜥyt nṯr* = Divine adoratrice, divine chantress
7.  *ḥry-tp ḥm-nṯr ỉmn ỉt nṯr* = Chief god's servant of Amen, god's father
8. 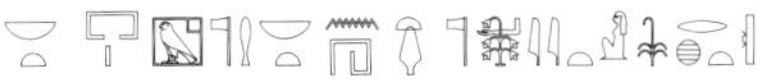 *nbt pr ḥm(t)-nṯr ḥwt-ḥr nbt nht šmꜥyt nṯr rḫt nswt* = Mistress/lady of the house, god's servant of Hathor, lady of the sycamore [epithet of Hathor], divine chantress, king's acquaintance

Exercise 33: Practice with Monuments

Object 1: Side of Stela

r-pꜥ ḥꜣty-(ꜥ) ḫtmw-bỉty smr wꜥty ỉmy-r ḫtmw mṯw-ḥtp = Hereditary prince, sealer of Lower Egypt, sole companion, overseer of sealers, Mentuhotep.

Object 2: Offering Stand of Setjwabu

ṯꜣity sꜣb ỉmy-r sš ḥry sštꜣ sṯ-wꜥbw = He of the curtain, judge, overseer of scribes, one who is over the secrets, Setjwabu.

Object 3: Lintel from False Door

Line 1: *sꜣb sḥḏ ỉry-mḏꜥt wꜥb nswt rḫ nswt rꜥ-n-kꜣw* = Judge, inspector, keeper of the documents, royal wab priest, king's acquaintance, Renkau.

Line 2: *ḥmt.f mrt.f nbt mꜣꜥt ỉmꜣḫ(t) ḫr hy.s rḫ(t) nswt ỉḫꜣt* = His wife, whom he loves, Mistress of Maat, one revered before her husband, king's acquaintance, Ikhat.

Object 4: Base of Old Kingdom Statue

sꜣb ỉry-nḫn ḥry sštꜣ smꜣꜥ wḏꜥ-mdw n ḥwt wrt sdn-mꜣꜥt = Legal guardian of Nekhen (or judge, guardian of Nekhen), one who is privy to the secrets, arbitrator of the law court, Sedenmaat.

Object 5: Old Kingdom Couple

Woman's titles: *rḫt nswt nfrt* = royal acquaintance, Nefret

Man's titles, right side: *wr mꜣꜣ ỉwnw wꜥ wr ḥb mḏḥ ꜣms šmsw ỉs wꜥ wr špntyw sꜣ nswt n ḫt.f rꜥ-ḥtp* = Great seer of Heliopolis, unique great one of the festival, craftsman/maker of the ames scepter, elder of the council chamber, unique great one of the Shepentiu, king's son of his body, Rehetep (Rahotep).

Man's titles, left side: *wr npt ỉmy-r sṯt ỉmy-r [m]šꜥ ḫrp tmꜣ sꜣ nswt n ḫt.f rꜥ-ḥtp* = Chief of Nepet, overseer of the transport workers, overseer of the army (general), director of the bowmen, king's son of his body, Rahotep.

Object 6: Wooden Panel of Hesyre
smsw ḳd-ḥtp ỉt mnw mḏḥ ? mḥyt rḫ nswt mḏḥ sš nswt wr 10 šmꜥw ḥsy-rꜥ = Elder of the qed-hetep; father of Min [tricky one—this is like "god's father"], fashioner of the cult image of Mehyt, king's acquaintance, overseer of the royal scribes, great one of the 10 of Upper Egypt, Hesyre.

Exercise 34: Stela of Tetisheri
Green: *bḥdt nṯr ꜥꜣ* = The Behedite, great god
Blue: *ḥmt nswt mwt nswt tti-šri ꜥnḫ.ti ḏt* = Wife of the king, mother of the king, Tetisheri, may she live forever.
Red: *ḥr kꜣ-m-wꜣst nṯr nfr nb tꜣwy nb-pḥty-rꜥ sꜣ rꜥ n ẖt.f ỉꜥḥ-ms dỉ ꜥnḫ ḏt* = Horus Kaemwaset, the good god, lord of the Two Lands, Son of Re of his body, Ahmose, given life forever.
Behind king: *sꜣ ꜥnḫ ḥꜣ.f nb* = all protection and life behind him
Yellow: *dbḥ-ḥtp* = funerary meal

Chapter V: Offering Prayers

Exercise 35: Epithets of Osiris and Anubis
1.  *ḥtp dỉ nswt wsỉr ḫnty ỉmntyw nb ḏdw nb ꜣbḏw wnn-nfr nṯr ꜥꜣ m swt.f nb* = An offering which the king gives (and) Osiris, lord of Djedu (Busiris), lord of Abdju (Abydos), Wenennefer, the great god, in all his seats.
2.  *ḥtp dỉ nswt ỉnpw ỉmy wt tpy ḏw.f nb tꜣ ḏsr ḫnty sḥ nṯr wp-wꜣwt* = An offering which the king gives (and) Anubis, who is in the place of embalming, lord of Ta-djeser (the sacred land), who is before the divine booth, opener of the ways.

Exercise 36: The Four Sons of Horus
Object 1: Gold Plaque
ḥpy m-sṯỉ n wsỉr nswt pꜣ-sbꜣ/dwꜣ-ḫꜥ-n-nỉwt mry-ỉmn pw mꜣꜥ ḫrw dwꜣ-mwt.f ḳbḥ-snw.f = Hapy; Imsety; to this Osiris, king, Pasebakhaenniut, beloved of Amen, true of voice; Duamutef; Qebehsenuef. (Note that the star in this king's name is usually transliterated *sbꜣ* rather than *dwꜣ*, since it probably means "star" here.)
Object 2: Canopic Container
ỉmsṯ ḥꜥ.f šꜣ-šꜣnḳ-mry ỉmn = Imsety, his flesh: Shashanq (Shoshenq), beloved of Amen. (Liver)

Exercise 37: Offering Prayers with Voice Offerings
1.  *ḥtp dỉ nswt ỉnpw tpy ḏw.f ỉmy wt ḫnty sḥ-nṯr*
 *dỉ.f prt-ḫrw t ḥnḳt kꜣ ꜣpd*
 *sš mnḫt ḫt nfr(t) wꜥb(t) ꜥnḫt nṯr ỉm*
An offering which the king gives (to) Anubis, who is on his mountain, who is in the place of embalming, foremost of the divine booth, that he may give invocation offerings: bread, beer, meat, fowl, alabaster, clothing, all good and pure things on which a god lives.

2.  *ḥtp dỉ nswt wsỉr ḫnty ỉmntyw nb ꜣbḏw wnn-nfr nṯr ꜥꜣ*
prt-ḫrw ḏfꜣw mrḥt snṯr ṯꜣw nḏm
ḳrst.f m ẖrt-nṯr st ỉmntt ḫt nb(t) nfr(t) wꜥb(t) nṯr dwꜣ
An offering which the king gives (and) Osiris, foremost of the westerners, lord of Abydos, Wenennefer, the great god, (that he might give) invocation offerings, provisions: oil, incense, the sweet breath, that one might bury him in the necropolis of the western desert, all good and pure things which the god praises.

Exercise 38: Offering Prayers on Monuments
Object 1: Stela of Nitptah
Top line: *ỉmꜣḫw ḫr ptḥ-skr; ỉmꜣḫw ḫr ptḥ-skr dỉ.f ḥnḳt kꜣ ꜣpd n kꜣ n* = One revered before Ptah-Sokar; one revered before Ptah-Sokar, may he give beer, meat, and fowl to the ka of:
Above first man: . . . .*nỉt-ptḥ ms.n ỉy* . . .Nitptah born of Iy
Above first woman: . .*snỉ ms(t).n tỉ* . . . . .Seni born of Ti
Above second man: . .*ỉnt.f ms.n snỉ* . . . . .Intef born of Seni
Above second woman: *dd mst.n snỉ* . . . .Ded born of Seni.
Object 2: Naos (Shrine) of Ptahmes
Center to right: *ḥtp dỉ nswt ỉnpw wp-wꜣwt sḫm tꜣwy ḫnty tꜣ šmꜥw prt-ḫrw t ḥnḳt kꜣ ꜣpd ḏfꜣw n r-pꜥ ḥꜣty-ꜥ ḫtmw-bỉty sm wr ḫrp ḥmwwt ptḥ-ms mꜣꜥ ḫrw* = An offering which the king gives (and) Anubis, opener of the ways (Wepwawet), scepter of the two lands, foremost of the southern land, (that he might give) invocation offerings, bread, beer, meat, fowl, provisions, to the hereditary prince, high official, sealer of the king of Lower Egypt, sem priest, great one, (OR greatest) director of craftsmen, Ptahmes, true of voice.
Center to left: *ḥtp dỉ nswt wsỉr ḫntyw ỉmntyw nṯr ꜥꜣ nb ꜣbḏw prt-ḫrw t ḥnḳt kꜣ ꜣpd ḏfꜣw n r-pꜥ ḥꜣty-ꜥ ḫtmw-bỉty sm wr ḫrp ḥmwwt ptḥ-ms mꜣꜥ ḫrw* = An offering which the king gives (and) Osiris, foremost of the westerners, great god, lord of Abydos, (that he might give) invocation offerings: bread, beer, meat, fowl, provisions, to the hereditary prince, high official, sealer of the king of Lower Egypt, sem priest, great one, (OR greatest) director of craftsmen, Ptahmes, true of voice.
Cartouches on Body: *mn-ḫpr-rꜥ ḏḥwty-ms* Menkheperre Tuthmosis (III) [hard to see]
Titles on kilt: *ḫtmw-bỉty wr ḫrp ḥmwwt ptḥ-ms* = Sealer of the king of Lower Egypt, greatest director of the craftsmen, Ptahmes.
Object 3: Stela of Amenemhat and Iy
Top line, center-left: *prt-ḫrw t ḥnḳt kꜣ ꜣpd n ỉmꜣḫ ỉmn-m-ḥꜣt n ỉmꜣḫt ỉy*= Invocation offerings: bread, beer, meat, and fowl, to the revered one, Amenemhat, to the revered one Iy.
Top line, center-right: *ỉmꜣḫ ḫr wsỉr dỉ.f prt-ḫrw t ḥnḳt kꜣ ꜣpd n ỉmꜣḫw* = One revered before Osiris, that he might give invocation offerings, bread, beer, meat, fowl, to the revered ones.
Before seated man: *ỉmꜣḫ ỉnt.f* = the revered one, Intef
Before standing woman: *ỉmꜣḫt snt.f ḥpy* = the revered one, his sister, Hapy.
Object 4: Wooden coffin
Horizontal band: *ḥtp dỉ nswt n wsỉr nb ḏdw nṯr ꜥꜣ nb ꜣbḏw (ḥbḏw* for *ꜣbḏw) m swt.f nb prt-ḫrw t ḥnḳt kꜣ ꜣpd ḏfꜣw nṯr dwꜣ n kꜣ n ỉmꜣḫy ḫr nṯr ꜥꜣ nb pt (n)ḥḥ tp tꜣ ḫw* = An offering

which the king gives to Osiris, lord of Djedu, great god, lord of Abydos in all his seats, (that he might give) invocation offerings, bread, beer, meat, fowl, provisions, which god praises, to the ka of the one revered before the great god, lord of the sky and of eternity (or eternally), upon earth, Khu.

Vertical lines: *im3ḫy ḫr wsir; im3ḫy ḫr 3st/ḥwt-ḥr nb(t) mḏdni m ḫrt ḫrw nt rˁ nb im3ḫ[. . .]* = One revered before Osiris; one revered before Isis/Hathor; lady of Medjedny daily, the revered one [. . .]

Object 5: A False Door

Top horizontal line: *ḥtp di nswt inpw tpy ḏw.f n špss nswt k3-tpi* An offering which the king gives (to) Anubis, who is on his mountain, to the royal courtier, Katepi.

On lintel: *špss nswt k3-tpi* the royal courtier, Katepi.

Right outer jamb: *ḫnty-š wnis-nfr-swt špss nswt sš n st k3-tpi* = Land official/palace attendant of Wenis-nefersut (the pyramid of Wenis), royal courtier, scribe of the throne, Katepi.

Left outer jamb: *ḫnty-š wnis-nfr-swt smr wˁty k3-tpi* = Land official/palace attendant of Wenis-nefersut, unique companion, Katepi.

Inner jambs: *ḥtp di nswt wsir prt-ḫrw t ḥnkt ḏf3w n k3-tpi* = An offering which the king gives (to) Osiris, (that he may give) invocation offerings, bread, beer, provisions, to Katepi.

Object 6: Stela of a General

ḥtp di nswt inpw tpy ḏw.f imy wt nb t3 ḏsr m swt.f nbt nfrt prt-ḫrw n r-pˁ ḥ3ty-ˁ ḫtmw bity smr wˁty ḫry-ḥbt im3ḫ ḫr nṯr ˁ3 nb pt imy-r mšˁ [. . .]ḥmt.f mryt.f ḫkrt nswt wˁtt ḥm-nṯr ḥwt-ḥr im3ḫ[t. . .] = An offering which the king gives (and) Anubis, who is on his mountain, who is in the place of embalming, lord of Ta-djeser, in all his good places, (that he may give) invocation offerings to the hereditary prince, high official, seal-bearer of Lower Egypt, unique companion, lector priest, revered before the great god, lord of the sky, overseer of the army (general) [. . .] and his wife, whom he loves, royal ornament, companion, god's servant of Hathor, the revered one [. . .]

Exercise 39: Monuments

Object 1: Slab Stele of a Prince

Green: *mḏḥ sš nswt mḏḥ ? mḥyt ḥm nṯr sš3t ḫntt pr rḫ nswt mḏ3t ḥm b3w p ḥm nṯr ḥr mḥt ḥm nṯr inpw ˁḏ mr wi3 wr 10 šmˁw hk3 mḥyt ḥm nṯr ḥkt ḫt ḥ3 s3 nswt wp-m-nfrt* = Overseer of the royal scribes, overseer of the cult image of Mehyt, god's servant of Seshat, foremost of the house of the documents of the royal acquaintances, servant of the souls of Pe, god's servant of Horus of the north, god's servant of Anubis, administrator of the divine bark, great one of the 10 of Upper Egypt, god's servant of Hekat, attendant of Ha, king's son, Wepemnefert

Blue: *snṯr 1000 w3ḏ 1000 msdmt 1000 ḥ3tt mrḥt 1000 irp 1000 nbs 1000 sšḫt w3ḏ(t) 1000 wˁḥ 1000 db3 1000 ˁgwt 1000 sšḫt ḥḏ(t) 1000 išd 1000 ḏsrt 1000 i3tt 1000 bnrt 1000 t-nbs 1000 ḫti nb bnrnt* = 1000 incense; 1000 green eye-paint; 1000 black eye-paint; 1000 best oil; 1000 wine; 1000 zizyphus; 1000 green cakes; 1000 carob bean; 1000 figs; 1000 grain; 1000 white cakes; 1000 persea fruit; 1000 ale; 1000 milk; 1000 date wine; 1000 zizyphus bread; and all sweet things.

Red: In this case, the quality is indicated by the number of fringes: *idmy, 4 (1,000), 3*

(1,000), 2 (1,000), 1 (1,000); sšr: 4 (1,000), 3 (1,000), 2 (1,000), 1 (1,000); šmꜥt-nfrt 4 (1,000), 3 (1,000), 2 (1,000), 1 (1,000); ꜥꜣ 100 (1,000), 40 (1,000), 30 (1,000) = Idemy cloth, 1,000 each of grades 4, 3, 2, and 1; sesher linen, 1,000 each of grades 4, 3, 2, 1; fine linen, 1000 each of grades 4, 3, 2, 1; aa linen, 4,000, 1,000 each of grades 100, 40, 30.
Black: *iꜥw, ḳbḥ, mnḫt 1000 šs 1000 t 1000 ḥnḳt 1000 mꜣḥḏ 1000 kꜣ 1000* = tools for lustration; container of cool water; 1000 each of cloth, alabaster, bread, beer, oryx, and beef.

Object 2: Entrance to the Tomb Chapel of the "Two Brothers"

Drum: *ẖnm-ḥtp n-ꜥnḫ-ẖnm* = Khnumhotep, Niankhnum
Lintel line 1: *ḥtp di nswt ḥtp (di) inpw ḫnty sḥ nṯr ḳrst.sn m ẖrt-nṯr imntt iꜣw nfr wrt m nbw imꜣḫ ḫr nṯr ꜥꜣ* = An offering which the king gives, which Anubis gives, foremost of the divine booth, that they may be buried in the western necropolis: a very good old age, as lords of reverence before the great god.
Lintel line 2, center to right: *imy-r iry ꜥnt pr-ꜥꜣ mḥnk nswt ḥry sštꜣ n-ꜥnḫ-ẖnm* = Overseer of the manicurists of the palace, intimate of the king, one privy to the secrets, Niankhkhnum.
Lintel line 2, center to left: *imy-r iry ꜥnt pr-ꜥꜣ mḥnk nswt ḥry sštꜣ ẖnm-ḥtp* = Overseer of the manicurists of the palace, intimate of the king, one privy to the secrets, Khnumhotep.
Horizontal text on right: *rḫ nswt n-ꜥnḫ-ẖnm* = King's acquaintance, Niankhkhnum
Vertical text on right: *ḥm-nṯr rꜥ m špw-ib-rꜥ imy-r iry ꜥnt pr-ꜥꜣ mḥnk nswt ḥry-sštꜣ n-ꜥnḫ-ẖnm* = God's servant of Re in Shepuibre, overseer of the manicurists of the palace, intimate of the king, one privy to the secrets, Niankhnum.
Horizontal text on left: *rḫ nswt ẖnm-ḥtp* = King's acquaintance, Khnumhotep.
Vertical text on left: *ḥm-nṯr rꜥ m špw-ib-rꜥ imy-r iry ꜥnt pr-ꜥꜣ mḥnk nswt ḥry-sštꜣ ẖnm-ḥtp* = God's servant of Re in Shepuibre, overseer of the manicurists of the palace, intimate of the king, one privy to the secrets, Khnumhotep.
Above small figure on right: *sꜣ.f smsw sꜣb sš imꜣḫw ḫr it.f ḥm-rꜥ* = His eldest son, judge, scribe, revered before his father, Hemre.
Above small figure on left: *sꜣ.f smsw sꜣb sš imꜣḫw ḫr it.f ptḥ-špss* = His eldest son, judge, scribe, revered before his father, Ptahshepses.

Chapter VI: More Inscriptions

Exercise 40: Scene Labels

Scene 1: Domesticating animals

wšꜣ ḥṯt = fattening a hyena

Scene 2: Domesticating birds

Above man on left; above man on right: *snmt ḏꜣt* = feeding the crane
Between two men: *fst swṯ (swt)* = cooking wheat

Scene 3: Gilded Chair of Sitamen

ms nbw n ḫꜣswt rsw(t) = Bringing gold of the foreign land of the south.
Before princess: *sꜣt nswt wrt mrt.f sꜣt-imn* = Great daughter of the king, whom he loves, Sitamen.

Scene 4: Funeral procession

šms twwt n is = following the statues to the tomb.

In front of first priest: *sš pr-ḥḏ sḫm* = Scribe of the treasury, Sekhem

Scene 5: Catching a bull

Above bull: *spḥ ng(ꜣw)* = lassoing the long-horned bull

Name of man grasping horns: *ḥnns* = Henenes

In front of bull: *ỉnt ng(ꜣw) n ḫt dwꜣt* = bringing the long-horned bull of the things (property) of the Duat (the tomb chamber).

Scene 6: Offering bearers:

Main inscription: *sḫp ỉḫt n smr ḫrp ꜥḥ nn-ḫt.f-kꜣ* = Bringing things to the companion, director of the palace, Nenkhetefka.

Between first two offering bearers: *ỉmy-r pr-ꜥꜣ ḥs-pr sḥḏ ḥm-kꜣ ỉmy-wrt sꜣ wꜣš.k* = Overseer of the palace Hesper, inspectorof the ka priests of the "Starboard" phyle, Washek.

Between second and third men: *sḥḏ ḥm-kꜣ sꜣ wꜣḏ ptḥw-ꜥnḫ* = Overseer of the ka priests of the "Green" phyle, Ptahuankh (OR Ptahankhu).

Between third and fourth men: *sš ḥm-kꜣ ḫnw* = Scribe of the ka priests, Khenu.

Scene 7: The Tomb Owner and his Workers

mꜣ(ꜣ) mḏḥ ỉn r-pꜥ ḥꜣty-ꜥ ẖnm-ḥtp = Watching the carpentry by the hereditary prince, high official, Khnumhotep

swꜣ ḫt = cutting wood

ꜥnḫ = life (part of a name)

Scene 8: The King Offering to the God

Above head of king: *nswt bỉty nb ỉr(t) ḫt mn-ḫpr-rꜥ dỉ ꜥnḫ ḏd wꜣs mỉ rꜥ* = King of Upper and Lower Egypt, lord of ritual, Menkheperre (Thuthmosis III), given stability, dominion, life, like Re

Before king: *ỉrt sntr* = making incense

Exercise 41: The Imperative

Scene 1: Butchering Cattle

ḫws nfr hrw m-ꜥ.k = Cut perfectly (well), the daylight is in your possession! [In other words, do a good job, and do it now before the light goes.]

ỉp dbḥ = Count/Inspect the funerary requirements! or Counting the funerary requirements.

Scene 2: Fighting Boatmen

wp sw m hn.f = Open him in his head! (i.e. Break open his head!)

swꜣ t(w) psḏ.f = Break you his back! or *swꜣ.t(w) psḏ.f* = One is breaking/will break his back!

Exercise 42: Monuments with Djed-medu

Object 1: Statue Base of Senwosret I

Central cartouche: *snwsrt* = Senwosret (I)

Either side: *ḏd mdw dỉ.n.(ỉ) n.k ḥtpwt nb(t)* = Words spoken: I gave to you all offerings.

Object 2: Canopic Chest

Front view. Left column: *ḏd mdw ỉn nt wsỉr twt-ꜥnḫ-ỉmn ḥkꜣ-ỉwnw-šmꜥw mꜣꜥ ḫrw* = Words spoken by Neith: the Osiris Tutankhamen, ruler of southern Iunu, true of voice.

Right column: *ḏd mdw ỉn srḳt wsỉr nswt nb-ḫprw-rꜥ mꜣꜥ ḫrw* = Words spoken by Selket: the Osiris, king, Nebkheperure, true of voice.

Side view Left column: *ḏd mdw in ꜣst wnn.k m ḫprw.k nfr (i)m-sty wsir nswt nb-ḫpr(w)-rꜥ* = Words spoken by Isis, may you exist in your perfect forms, Imsety, the Osiris, king Nebkheper(u)re.

Right column: *ḏd mdw in nt wnn.k m nṯr ꜥnḫ ḳbḥ-snw.f nbwt* [perhaps *nb ḫꜥw] twt-ꜥnḫ-imn ḥkꜣ-iwnw-šmꜥw* = Words spoken by Neith: may you exist as the living god, Qebekhsenuef, [lord of appearances], Tutanhkamun, ruler of southern Iunu.

Object 3: Statue Base of Amenemhat III

Center text: *nṯr nfr nb tꜣwy n-mꜣꜥt-rꜥ* = The good god, lord of the Two Lands, Nimaatre

Right of center: *ḏd mdw in mḥy di.(i) ꜥnḫ nb (ḏd mdw) di.n.(i) n.k ḫt nb(t) nfrt imyt (ḏd mdw) di.n.(i) n.k ꜥnḫ ḏd wꜣs nb ḫri* = Words spoken by the northland: I give all life; (words spoken) I have given to you all good things therein; (words spoken) I have give to you all life, stability, dominion therewith.

Left of center: *ḏd mdw in šmꜥw di.(i) ꜥnḫ nb (ḏd mdw) di.n.(i) n.k ḫt nb(t) nfrt imyt (ḏd) mdw di.n.(i) n.k ꜥnḫ ḏd wꜣs nb ḫri* = Words spoken by the southland: I give all life; (words spoken), I have given to you all good things therein; words spoken, I have give to you all life, stability, dominion therewith.

Object 4: Pillar of Senwosret I

Yellow: *nṯr nfr snwsrt di ꜥnḫ wꜣs* = The good god Senwosret, given life and dominion

Red then blue: *ptḥ rsy inb.f di.f ꜥnḫ wꜣs* = Ptah, south of his wall, may he give life, dominion

Green then orange: *ḏd mdw di.n.(i) ꜥnḫ ḏd wꜣs nb snb nb ꜣwt ib nb n nswt bity ḫpr-kꜣ-ꜥrꜥ di ꜥnḫ ḏd wꜣs mi rꜥ* = Words spoken: I have given all life, stability, dominion, all health, all happiness, to the King of Upper and Lower Egypt, Kheperkare, given life, stability, and dominion like Re.

Scene 5: Painting from the Tomb of Ramesses I, Valley of the Kings

ḏd mdw in bꜣw p hny.sn n rꜥ-ḥr-ꜣḫty sꜣ.sn wsir nwst mn-pḥ(ty)-rꜥ sꜣ rꜥ rꜥ-ms-sw mꜣꜥ ḫrw m wꜥ im.sn = Words spoken by the souls of Pe: may they give praise to Rehorakhti, their son, the Osiris, king, Menpehtyre, son of Re, Ramesses, true of voice, as one unique among them.

ḏd mdw in bꜣw nḫn iry.sn hnw n nbw = Words spoken by the souls of Nekhen, may they make praises to the lords.

Chapter VII: Putting it All Together

Exercise 43: Scene from a New Kingdom Temple

Green: *nb tꜣwy wsr-mꜣꜥt-rꜥ stp-n-rꜥ nb ḫꜥw rꜥ-ms-sw mry-imn* = Lord of the Two Lands, Usermaatre, chosen of Re, lord of appearances, Ramesses (II), beloved of Amen.

Blue: *nb pt* = lord of the sky

Red: *sꜣ ꜥnḫ ḏd wꜣs nb snb nb mi rꜥ*= all protection, life, stability, dominion, all health like Re.

Yellow, then orange: *ḏd mdw in nswt nṯrw nb pt ḥkꜣ wꜣst di.n.(i) n.k ḫꜣswt nb(wt) m ḥtpw* = Words spoken by the king of the gods, lord of the sky, ruler of Thebes: I have given to you all foreign lands as offerings/in peace.

Purple: *di.n.(i) n.k ꜣwt-ib nb* = I have given to you all happiness.

Exercise 44: Scene from the Mortuary Temple of Ramesses III

Above and before king: *nb tꜣwy wsr-mꜣꜥt-rꜥ mry-ỉmn nb ḫꜥw rꜥ-ms.s ḥḳꜣ-ỉnw* = Lord of the Two Lands, Usermaare, beloved of Amen, lord of appearances, Ramesses (III), ruler of Iunu.

Behind king: *sꜣ ꜥnḫ ḫꜣ.f nb mỉ rꜥ* = All protection, life, behind him, like Re.

Before king: *ḥnk-m ỉrp n ỉt.f ỉmn-rꜥ ỉr.f dỉ ꜥnḫ* = Offering wine to his father, Amen-Re, who made him, given life.

Above god: *ḏd mdw ỉn ỉmn nswt nṯrw nb pt dỉ.n.(ỉ) n.k ḥb-sdw ꜥšꜣt rnpwt n tm* = Words spoken by Amen, king of the gods, lord of the sky: I have given to you Sed festivals often, the years of Atum.

In front of god: *dỉ.n.(ỉ) n.k ꜥḥꜥw n rꜥ rnpwt n tm* = I have given to you the lifetime of Re, the years of Atum.

Exercise 45: Spells from a Coffin

Spell 1: *ỉnk bnw ḫpr ḏs.f sꜣ.k mr.k mky ỉỉ.n.(ỉ) m sꜣw ḥꜥt.k r dr ḥwrw ḥr ḫꜣt.k rdỉt [r dỉt] ꜥnḫ r nḥḥ n bꜣ.k ḏt ḥr ḫꜣt.k* = I am the benu-bird who creates himself, your son, whom you love, one who protects. I have come as protection of your body in order to drive out weakness/corruption from your body, [in order] to give life forever to your soul, eternity upon your body.

Above head of first figure: *bnw ḥḳꜣ ỉmntt* = Benu-bird, ruler of the west.

Spell 2: *ỉnk ḥpy sꜣ.k mr.k mky ỉỉ.n.(ỉ) wnn m sꜣw.k r dr ḫfwt.k nb m dwꜣt ḏt rdỉt [r dỉt] šsp.k ḥtpw ḏt mỉ nṯrw nbw mꜣꜥty* = I am Hapy, your son, whom you love, one who protects. I have come to exist as your protection, in order to drive out all your enemies from the Duat forever, [in order] to cause that you receive offerings eternally like all the gods of Maaty.

Above head of second figure: *(ỉ)msṯ nb ỉmntt* = Imsety, lord of the west

Exercise 46: Census Scene

mꜣꜣ ỉrt ỉrw m mnmnt nbt ỉnw ỉn n.f m nỉwt.f ḏꜣtt.f nt ḫnw mꜣ-ḥḏ nỉwt.f ỉn r-pꜥ ḥꜣty-ꜥ [n]ḥrỉ sꜣ ḫnm-ḥtp = Watching the making of the census as (being) all animals, the produce which was brought to him from his towns and his estates of the interior of the Oryx nome and his town, by the hereditary prince, high official, Heri's (a mistake for Nehri's) son, Khnumhotep.

Above top small figure: *sꜣ ḥꜣty-ꜥ sꜣ wr sḫpr nṯr ḫnm-ḥtp* = Son of the high official, eldest son who was created of god (whom god created), Khnumhotep.

Above lower small figure: *ỉry-mrḥt ḫnm-ḥtp*

Keeper of the Oil, Khnumhotep.

Exercise 47: Scene from the Tomb of Shuroy

Before god: *ḏd mdw ỉn rꜥ-ḥrꜣḫty (ỉ)tmw nb tꜣwy ỉwnw nṯr ꜥꜣ nb pt* = Words spoken by Rehorakhti, Atum, lord of the Two Lands and Iunu, the great god, lord of the sky.

Before tomb owner and wife: *ỉꜣw n.ṯn nbw nḥḥ psḏt ꜥꜣ nbw tꜣ ḏsr šspt.n hrw mnỉ ỉnk mꜣꜥt n kꜣ n wsỉr šs nswt ỉmy-r pr* = Praises to you, lords of eternity, great Ennead, lords of the sacred land, (that) we may achieve the day of mooring (the day of death). I am one who did truth for the ka of the Osiris, royal scribe, overseer of the house. [The name of the tomb owner can be partially seen in the illustration, it is Shure.]

Exercise 48: The Autobiography of Harkhuf I

ḥtp di nswt ḥtp di inpw tpy-ḏw.f ḫnty sḥ nṯr imy wt nb tꜣ ḏsr ḳrst.f m ḫrt-nṯr imntt st imntt iꜣw nfr wrt m imꜣḫw ḫr nṯr ꜥꜣ ḥꜣty-ꜥ imy-r šmꜥw ḫtmw-bity smr wꜥty ḫry-ḥbt imy-r iꜥꜣw imꜣḫw ḫr ptḥ-skr ḥr-ḫwf = An offering which the king gives, an offering which Anubis gives, who is on his mountain, foremost of the divine booth, who is in the place of embalming, lord of the sacred land, may he be buried in the western necropolis of the western desert; a very good old age to the one revered before the great god, the hereditary prince, overseer of the south, sealer of Lower Egypt, unique companion, lector priest, overseer of the foreign workers, one revered before Ptah-Sokar, Harkhuf.

ḥtp di nswt ḥtp di wsir nb ḏdw ḫp.f m ḥtp ḥr wꜣwt ḏsr(w)t nt imntt ḫppt imꜣḫw ḥr.sn iꜥ.f n nṯr nb pt m imꜣḫw ḫr wsir ḥr-ḫwf = An offering which the king gives, an offering which Osiris gives, lord of Djedu: may he travel in peace upon the sacred roads of the west, upon which travel the revered ones [this is a relative form]; may he ascend to the god, lord of the sky, as one revered before Osiris, Harkhuf.

Exercise 49: The Autobiography of Harkhuf II

ii.n.(i) min m niwt.(i) hꜣ.n.(i) m ḏꜣtt.(i) ḳd.n.(i) pr sꜥḥꜥ [or sꜥḥꜥ.(i)] ꜥꜣw šꜣd.n.(i) š srd [or srd.(i)] nhwt ḥs.n wi nswt ir.n n.(i) it imyt ink iḳr [. . .]mry n it.(f) ḥsy n mwt.f mrrw snw.f nb = I came today from my town. I descended from my estate. I built a house, setting up [or (I) set up] doors, I dug a pool, planting [or I planted] trees. The king praised me. My father made for me a will. I was an excellent one [text lost here] one beloved of (his) father, one praised of his mother, one beloved of all his siblings.

iw rdi.n.(i) t n ḥkr ḥbs n ḥꜣy smꜣ n tꜣ m iwt mḫnt.f i ꜥnḫw tpw tꜣ swꜣt.sn ḥr is pn m ḫd m ḫsfwt ḏdt.sn 2 ḫꜣ t ḥnḳt n nb n is pn iw.(i) r sbt ḥr.sn m ḫrt-nṯr = I gave bread to the hungry, clothes to the naked, passage to the one without his ferry boat. O living ones upon the earth, may they pass by this tomb in traveling north and in traveling south; may they say 2000 bread and beer to the lord of this tomb, I will watch over them from the necropolis.

ink ꜣḫ iḳr ꜥpr ḫry-ḥbt rḫ r.f ir nb ꜥḳt.f r is pn m ꜥb.f iw.(i) r iṯt ṯst.f mi ꜣpd iwf (for *iw.f*) *r wḏꜥ ḥr.s in nṯr ꜥꜣ* = I was/am an excellent, equipped spirit, a lector priest who knows his mouth (speech). As for anyone who may enter this tomb in his impurity, I will wring his neck like a bird; He will be judged on account of it by the great god.

Exercise 50: The Autobiography of Harkhuf III

m iw(t) r.k m ḫdt r ḫnw ḥr-ꜥw ḥꜣꜥ in n.k dng pn m-ꜥ.k in.n.k m tꜣ ꜣḫtiw ꜥnḫ wḏꜣ snb r ibꜣw nṯr r sḫmḫ-ib r snḫꜣḫꜣ-ib n nswt bity nfr-kꜣ-rꜥ ꜥnḫ ḏt = In coming yourself, in traveling north to the Residence at once, descend, bring you this pygmy with you (in your charge) which you have brought from the land of the Akhtiu, life, prosperity, health, in order to be a divine dancer [or in order to do the dance of the god], in order to gladden the heart, in order to soothe the heart of the king of Upper and Lower Egypt, Neferkare (Pepi II), living forever.

ir hꜣ.f m-ꜥ.k r dpt ir rmṯ iḳrw wnnw ḥꜣ.f ḥr gswy dpt sꜣw ḫr.f m mw ir sḏr.f m grḥ ir rmṯ iḳrw sḏrw ḥꜣ.f m ḫn.f sp sp 10 n grḥ mr ḥm mꜣꜣ dng pw r inw biꜣw pwnt = As for his descending (when he descends) with you (in your charge) to the boat, make (choose) excellent people who will be behind him upon the two sides of the boat, guard [*or* who will guard] his falling in the water. If he sleeps [As for his sleeping] in the night, make (choose) excellent people who will sleep behind him in his tent. Inspect ten times in the night. His Majesty wishes to see this pygmy more than the tribute of the mines and of Punt.

Exercise 51: The Battle of Qadesh

ḥsbt 5 ꜣbd 3 n šmw sw 9 ḫr ḥm n ḥr kꜣ-nḫt mry-mꜣꜥt nswt bỉty wsr-mꜣꜥt-rꜥ stp-n-rꜥ sꜣ rꜥ rꜥ-ms.s mry-ỉmn = Year 5, 3rd month of Shemu, 9th day under the majesty of the victorious bull, beloved of Maat, king of Upper and Lower Egypt Usermaatre, chosen of Re, son of Re Ramesses, beloved of Amen.

ỉst ḥm.f ḥr ḏꜣhy m wḏyt.f 2nwt nt nḫt rs nfr m ꜥnḫ wḏꜣ snb m ỉmꜣw n ḥm.f ḥr ṯst rsy n ḳdš
Lo, his Majesty was in Djahy in his second campaign of victory. A good awakening in life, prosperity, health in the tent of his majesty upon the southern mountain of Qadesh.

ḫꜥ ḥm.f mỉ rꜥ wbn šsp.n.f ḫḳrw nw ỉt.(f) mnṯw wḏꜣ nb m-ḫd spr ḥm.f r rsy dmỉ n šꜣbwtn
His majesty appeared, like Re rising. He received the adornments of his father, Montu. The Lord proceeded northward, (and) His Majesty arrived at the south of the town of Shabuten.

ỉỉt ỉn šꜣsw r ḏd n ḥm.f m nꜣy.n snw nty m ꜥꜣw m-ꜥ hwt m-dỉ ḫr n ḫtꜣ dỉ ỉwt.n n ḥm.f r ḏd
A coming by Shasu in order to say to his majesty in these (thus): The brothers who are as great ones among the kindred with the fallen one of Kheta (the Hittites) caused [this is one of those constructions you have not learned, where the verb comes second] that we come to his majesty in order to say:

ỉw.n r ỉrt bꜣkw n prwy-ꜥꜣ ꜥnḫ wḏꜣ snb m.tw.n r wỉ n m-ꜥ pꜣ wr ḫtꜣ ḫr pꜣ ḫr n ḫtꜣ m pꜣ tꜣ n ḫyrbꜣ ḥr mḥt twnp snḏrw.f n prwy ꜥꜣ ꜥnḫ wḏꜣ snb r ỉỉt m-ḫntyw = We will make (become) servants of the pharaoh, life, prosperity, health. Behold, we will separate us (ourselves) from the charge of the great one of Kheta. Indeed the fallen one of Kheta is in the land of Herbai (Aleppo) upon the north of Tunip, he fearing (because) of the pharaoh, life, prosperity, health, in order to come southward.

ỉst ḏd nꜣ šꜣsw nꜣ mdwt ḏd.sn n ḥm.f m-ꜥḏꜣ ỉw m pꜣ ḫr n ḫtꜣ dỉ ỉwt.sn r ptr pꜣ nty ḥm.f ỉm n-ỉb-n tm dỉ.(tw) ḥr sw pꜣ mšꜥ n ḥm.f r ꜥḥꜣ ḥnꜥ pꜣ ḫr n ḫtꜣ = Lo, these Shasu spoke these words which they said to his Majesty falsely. As (It was) the fallen one of Kheta who caused that they come in order to see the place where his Majesty was therein, in order to prevent that one make ready to fight and that the army of his Majesty would fight with the fallen one of Kheta.

APPENDIX B
PRONOUN CHARTS

SUFFIX PRONOUNS

	*ỉ*	I, my		*s*	she, hers, it, its
	*k*	you, your (m.)		*n*	we, our
	*ṯ, t*	you, your (f.)	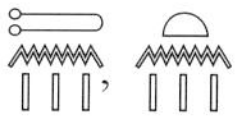	*ṯn, tn*	you, yours
	*f*	he, his, it, its	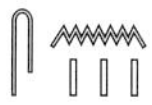	*sn*	they, theirs

DEPENDENT PRONOUNS

	*wỉ*	I		*n*	we
	*ṯw, tw*	you (m.)	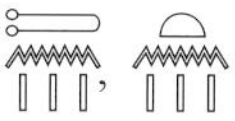	*ṯn, tn*	you (plural)
	*ṯn, tn*	you (f.)	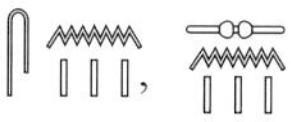	*sn*	they
	*sw*	he; it		*st*	they; it
	*sy*	she; it			

INDEPENDENT PRONOUNS

	*ỉnk*	I	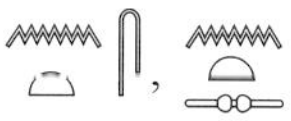	*nts*	she; it
	*ntk*	you (masculine)		*ỉnn*	we
	*ntṯ, ntt*	you (feminine)	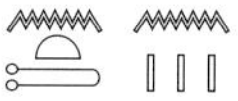	*ntṯn, nttn*	you (pl.)
	*ntf*	he; it	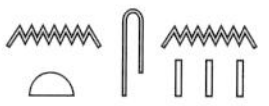	*ntsn*	they

Appendix C: Key to Sign List

The following list will help you to find signs that you don't recognize. They are grouped by category; if you recognize that it is, for example, human, or something to do with land or sky, you will be able to find it easily here. If you aren't sure what it is, you can skim the sections that seem likely. Once you have identified it by letter and number, you can go to the following sign list to get more information. The primary sources for this list are Alan Gardiner's Egyptian Grammar, James P. Allen's Middle Egyptian and Rainer Hannig's Grosses Handworterbuch, all excellent references (any errors are my own).

A. Human Beings, Male

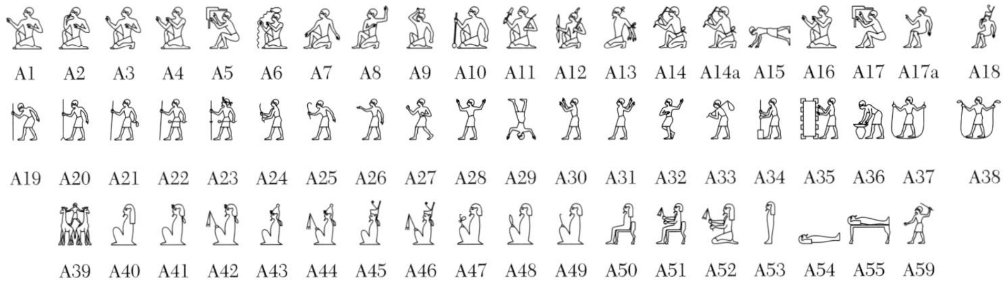

B. Humans, Female

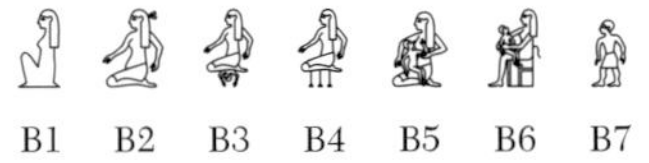

C. Anthropomorphic deities

D. Parts of Humans

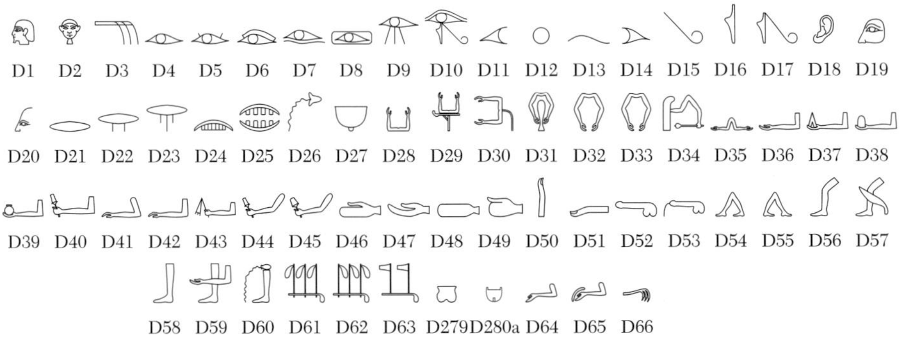

E. Mammals

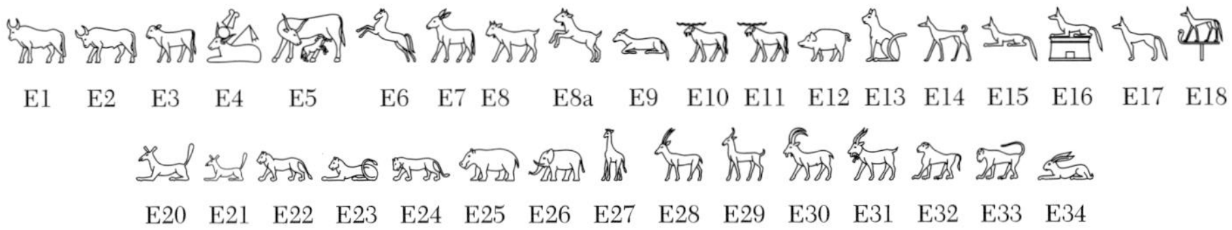

F. Parts of Mammals

F1 F2 F3 F4 F5 F6 F7 F8 F9 F19 F11 F12 F13 F14 F15 F16 F17 F18 F19

F20 F21 F22 F23 F24 F25 F26 F27 F28 F29 F30 F31 F32 F33 F34 F35 F36 F37 F38

F39 F49 F41 F42 F43 F44 F45 F46 F47 F48 F49 F50 F51 F52

G. Birds

G1 G2 G3 G4 G5 G6 G7 G7b G8 G9 G10 G11 G12 G13 G14 G15 G16 G17 G18

G19 G20 G21 G22 G23 G24 G25 G26 G26a G27 G28 G29 G30 G31 G32 G33 G34 G36 G37

G38 G39 G40 G41 G42 G43 G44 G45 G46 G47 G48 G49 G50 G51 G52 G53 G54

H. Parts of Birds

H1 H2 H3 H4 H5 H6 H6a H7 H8

I. Reptiles and Amphibians

I1 I2 I3 I4 I5 I5a I6 I7 I8 I9 I10 I11 I12 I13 I14 I15

K. Fish

K1 K2 K3 K4 K6 K7 K8

L. Insects and Invertebrates

L1 L2 L3 L4 L6 L7

M. Vegetation

M1 M2 M3 M4 M5 M6 M7 M8 M9 M10 M11 M12 M13 M14 M15 M16 M17 M18 M19

M20 M21 M22 M23 M24 M25 M26 M27 M28 M29 M30 M31 M32 M33 M34 M35 M36 M37 M38

M39 M40 M41 M42 M43 M44

N. Sky, Earth, Water

N1 N2 N3 N4 N5 N6 N7 N8 N9 N10 N11 N12 N13 N14 N15 N16 N17 N18 N19

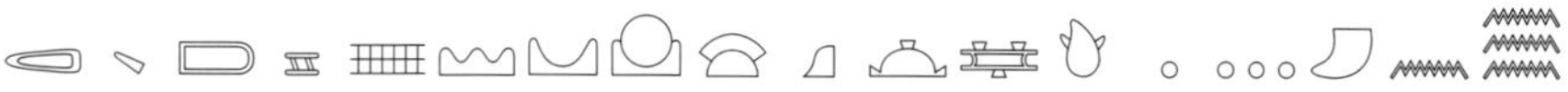

N20 N21 N22 N23 N24 N25 N26 N27 N28 N29 N30 N31 N32 N33 N33a N34 N35 N35a

N36 N37 N38 N39 N40 N41 N42

O. Structures and Parts of Structures

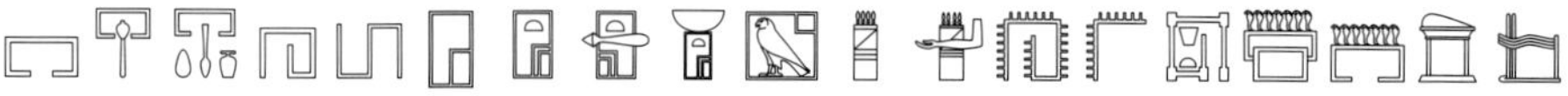

O1 O2 O3 O4 O5 O6 O7 O8 O9 O10 O11 O12 O13 O14 O15 O16 O17 O18 O19

O20 O21 O22 O23 O24 O25 O26 O27 O28 O29 O30 O31 O32 O33 O34 O35 O36 O37 O38

O39 O40 O41 O42 O43 O44 O45 O46 O47 O48 O49 O50 O51

P. Ships

P1 P2 P3 P4 P5 P6 P7 P8 P9 P10 P11

Q. Domestic and Funerary Furniture

Q1 Q2 Q3 Q4 Q5 Q6 Q7

R. Temple Furniture and Sacred Emblems

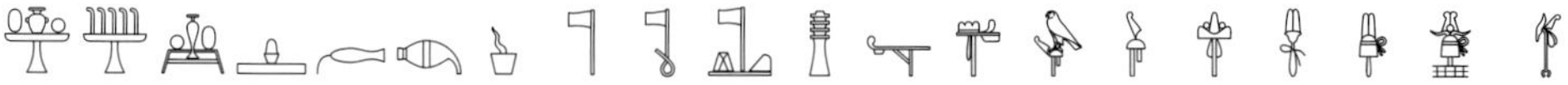

R1 R2 R3 R4 R5 R6 R7 R8 R9 R10 R11 R12 R12a R13 R14 R15 R16 R17 R18 R19

R20 R22 R23 R24 R25

S. Regalia and Clothing

S1 S3 S4 S5 S6 S7 S8 S9 S10 S11 S12 S13 S14 S14a S15 S16 S17 S18 S19

S20 S21 S22 S23 S24 S25 S26 S27 S28 S29 S30 S31 S32 S33 S34 S35 S36 S37 D38

S39 S40 S41 S42 S43 S44 S45 S46

T. Warfare, Hunting, and Slaughter

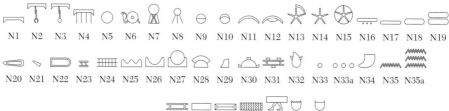

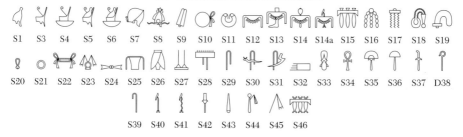

T1 T2 T3 T4 T5 T6 T7 T7a T8 T8a T9 T9a T10 T11 T12 T13 T14 T15 T16

T17 T18 T19 T20 A21 T22 T23 T24 T25 T26 T27 T28 T29 T30 T31 T32 T33 T34 T35

U. Agriculture, Crafts, and Professions

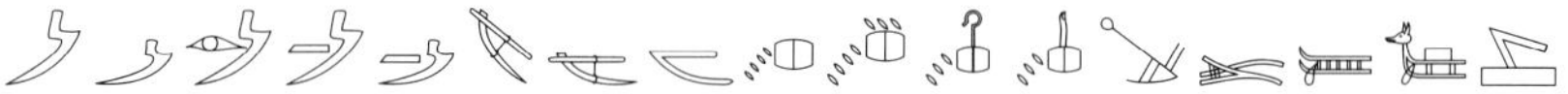

U1 U2 U3 U4 U5 U6 U7 U8 U9 U10 U11 U12 U13 U14 U15 U16 U17

U18 U19 U20 U21 U22 U23 U24 U25 U26 U27 U28 U29 U30 U31 U32 U33 U34 U35 U36

U37 U38 U39 U40 U41

V. Rope, Baskets, and Cloth

V1 V2 V3 V4 V5 V6 V7 V8 V9 V10 V11 V12 V13 V14 V15 V16 V17 V18 V19 V20

V21 V22 V23 V24 V25 V26 V27 V28 V29 V30 V31 V32 V33 V34 V35 V36 V37 V38

W. Stone and Ceramic Vessels

W1 W2 W3 W4 W5 W6 W7 W8 W9 W10 W10a W11 W12 W13 W14 W15 W16 W17 W18 W19

W20 W21 W22 W23 W24 W25

X. Bread

X1 X2 X3 X4 X5 X6 X7 X8

Y. Writing, Games, Music

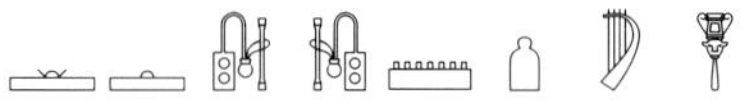

Y1 Y2 Y3 Y4 Y5 Y6 Y7 Y8

Z. Strokes and Figures

Z1 Z2 Z3 Z4 Z5 Z6 Z7 Z8 Z9 Z10 Z11

Aa. Unclassified

Aa1 Aa2 Aa3 Aa4 Aa5 Aa6 Aa7 Aa8 Aa9 Aa10 Aa11 Aa12 Aa13 Aa14 Aa15 Aa16 Aa17 Aa18 Aa19 Aa20

Aa21 Aa22 Aa24 Aa25 Aa26 Aa27 Aa28 Aa29 Aa30 Aa31 Aa32 Aa33

Appendix D
Sign List

Key

Column 1: Sign number
Column 2: Sign
Column 3: Identification.
Column 4: Phonetic values, if any, are given first, followed by ideographic uses, and then by uses as a determinative.

A. Human Figures, Male

A1		seated man	*s* (man); *rḫw* (companion); *ỉ* (I – suffix pronoun)/det. man
A2		man w/hand to mouth	det. actions having to do with the mouth; some emotions
A3		man sitting on heel	det. sit *(ḥms)*
A4		man with hands raised	det. worship *(dwꜣ)*; hide *(ỉmn)*
A5		man behind wall	det. hide *(ỉmn)*
A6		man w/libation over head	*wꜥb* (pure)
A7		tired man	det. weary *(wrd)*; weak; soft
A8		man making ritual gesture	*hnw* (jubilation)
A9		man w/basket on head	*ꜣtp* (load); *fꜣỉ* (carry, lift); *kꜣt* (work)
A10		man with oar	det. sail *(sḳdw)*; row
A11		man w/crook and scepter	det. friend *(ḫnms)*
A12		man w/bow	*mšꜥ* (army, expeditionary force)/ det. soldier *(mnfyt)*
A13		man w/hands tied	det. enemy *(sbỉ)*
A14		wounded man	det. die *(mwt)*; enemy *(ḫvtỉ)*. Also A14a
A15		falling man	*ḫr* (fall)/ det. fall *(ḫr)*; die *(nwt)*
A16		man bowing	det. bow *(ksỉ)*
A17		child	*nnỉ*; *ẖrd* (child)/det. child *(šrỉ)*; young. Also 17a
A18		child in red crown	det. child-king *(ỉnp)*
A19		old man	*ỉk*; *ỉꜣw* (old); *smsw* (eldest); *wr* (great)/det. old. Also A20
A21		man w/staff	*srỉ* (official)/det. dignitary *(smr)*
A22		statue	det. statue *(ḫntỉ, twt)*
A23		king	det. king *(ỉty)*
A24		man w/stick	*nḫt* (victory)/det. force *(ḥwỉ)*; strong *(nḫt)*
A25		man w/stick	*ḥwỉ* (hit)
A59		man w/stick	det. drive away *(sḥr)*
A26		man beckoning	*ỉ* (oh!); *ꜥš* (call)/det. call *(nis)*
A27		man running	*ỉn* (messenger)
A28		man gesturing	det. high *(ḳꜣỉ)*; joy *(ḥꜥỉ)*; mourn *(ḥꜣỉ)*; frustration *(ỉꜣs)*
A29		man upside-down	det. invert *(sḫd)*
A30		man praying	det. worship *(dwꜣ)*; respect *(tr)*
A31		man w/hands behind head	det. turn away *(ꜥnw)*
A32		man dancing	det. dance *(ḫbỉ)*
A33		man with bundle	*mniw* (herdsman)/det. wander; stranger *(šmꜣw)*
A34		man pounding	det. pound; construst *(ḫwsỉ)*
A35		man w/wall	*ḳd* (build)

A36	man w/vat	*ꜥfti* (brewer). Also A37
A38	man w/two animals	*ḳis/ḳsi* (Qus – a town). Also A39
A40	seated god	*ỉ* (I – suffix pronoun)/det. god; king
A41	seated king in nemes	*ỉ* (I – suffix pronoun)/det. king. Also A42
A43	seated king w/white crown	*nswt* (king); *wsỉr* (Osiris). Also A44
A45	seated king w/red crown	*bỉty* (king of Lower Egypt). Also A46
A47	seated shepherd	*sꜣw* (guard); *mniw* (herdsman). Variant of A48
A48	man w/knife	*ỉry* (pertaining to)
A49	foreigner w/stick	det. foreigner *(ꜥꜣmw)*
A50	seated noble	*ỉ* (I); *špss* (noble)/det. dignitary *(smr)*. Also A51; A52
A53	upright mummy	*twṯ* (statue)/det. mummy *(wỉ)*; statue *(twt)*; likeness; form *(ḳỉ)*
A54	mummy	det. dead *(mnỉ)*
A55	mummy on bier	*sḏr* (lie down)/det. lie down

B. Human Females

B1	seated woman	*ỉ* (I – suffix pronoun when female)/det. female
B2	pregnant woman	det. pregnant *(ỉwr; bkꜣ)*
B3	woman giving birth	*msỉ* (give birth). Also B4
B5	woman nursing child	det. nurse *(mnꜥt)*
B6	nurse w/child on lap	det. rear; foster *(rnn)*
B7	seated queen	det. for queen's names

C. Antrhopomorphic gods

C1	god w/sun-disk	*rꜥ* (Re – the sun god)/det. Re. Also C2
C3	god w/ibis head	*ḏḥwty* (Thoth – god of wisdom)/det. Thoth
C4	god w/ram head	*ẖnmw* (Khnum – potter god)/det. Khnum. Also C5
C6	god w/jackal head	*ỉnpw* (Anubis – god of embalming); *wp-wꜣwt* (Wepwawet)
C7	god w/canine head	*stẖ/stš* (Seth – god of chaos)/det. Seth
C8	ithyphallic god	*mnw* (Min – god of fertility)/det. Min
C9	goddess w/horned sun	*ḥwt-ḥr* (Hathor – goddess of music and love)/det. Hathor
C10	goddess w/feather	*mꜣꜥt* (Ma'at – goddess of truth)/ det. Ma'at
C11	god w/arms raised	*ḥḥ* (million; Heh – god who holds up sky)
C12	god w/plumes	*ỉmn* (Amen – god of Thebes)/det. Amen
C17	god w/hawk head	*mnṯw* (Montu – god of war)/det. Montu
C18	god w/horned plumes	*tꜣ-ṯnnỉ* (Tatanen – primitive god)/det. Tatanen
C19	standing god	*ptḥ* (Ptah – god of craftsmen)/det. Ptah. Also C20

D. Parts of the Human Body

D1	head	*tp, ḏꜣḏꜣ* (head)/det. head
D2	face	*ḥr* (face)
D3	hair	*wš* (missing)/det. hair *(šnỉ)*; color *(ỉwn)*; widow; mourn *(ỉꜣkb)*
D4	eye	*ỉr; ỉrt* (eye)/det. see *(mꜣꜣ)*
D5	eye w/makeup	det. actions associated with the eye. Also D6
D7	eye w/makeup	det. adorn *(msdmt)*, beautiful *(ꜥn)*; Tura *(ꜥnw)*. Also D8
D9	eye w/tears	*rmỉ* (weep)
D10	eye w/falcon markings	*wḏꜣt* (healthy eye of Horus)

D11	part of eye	(1/2 heqat)
D12	pupil of eye	(1/4 heqat)/det. pupil (ḏfḏ)/det. see *(mꜣꜣ)*
D13	eyebrow	(1/8 heqat)/det. eyebrow *(smd)*
D14	part of eye	(1/16 heqat)
D15	part of falcon markings	(1/32 heqat)
D16	part of falcon markings	(1/64 heqat)
D17	falcon markings	*tỉt* (image)/det. image
D18	ear	*msḏr* (ear)
D19	face	*ḫnt; fnḏ* (nose)/det. nose *(šrt)*; face *(ḫnt)*. Also D20
D21	mouth	*r; r* (mouth)
D22	mouth w/strokes	*rwỉ* (2/3)
D23	mouth w/strokes	*ḥmt-rw* (3/4)
D24	upper lip	*spt* (lip)/det. lip
D25	lips	*sptỉ* (lips)/det. lips
D26	mouth spitting	det. spit *(psg)*; vomit *(bšỉ)*; blood *(snf)*
D27	breast	*mnḏ* (breast)/det. breast *(mnḏ)*
D28	two arms in an embrace	*kꜣ*; *kꜣ* (ka – an aspect of the soul). Also D29
D30	two arms with tail	det. the god 'assigner of kas '*(nḥb-kꜣw)*
D31	two arms w/club	*ḥm-kꜣ* (hem-ka – mortuary priest)
D32	two arms	det. embrace *(ḥpt)*; open the arms *(pgꜣ)*
D33	two arms w/oar	*ẖn*
D34	two arms w/shield	*ꜥḥꜣ* (fight). Also D34a
D35	two arms outstretched	*nỉ, n; nỉ* (not); *ỉwtỉ* (who/what not)
D36	arm and hand	ꜥ; ꜥ (arm, hand)
D37	arm w/bread mold	*dỉ*
D38	arm w/bread	*mỉ, m*/det. give! *(ỉmỉ)*
D39	arm w/jar	det. offer *(ḥnk)*; intimate *(mḥnk)*. Also Variant of D37 or D38.
D40	arm w/stick	*ḫꜣỉ* (measure; evaluate)/det. strong *(nḫt)*; effort
D41	arm w/palm down	*nỉ; rmn* (shoulder)/det. arm *(gbꜣ)*; sing *(ḥsỉ)*; bow *(ḫms)*
D42	arm w/palm down	*mḥ* (cubit)/det. cubit
D43	arm w/flail	*ḫw*
D44	arm w/scepter	*ḫrp* (manage)
D45	arm w/brush	*ḏsr* (sacred; clear the way; raise the arm)
D46	hand	*d; ḏrt* (hand)
D46a	hand dripping water	*ỉdt* (fragrance)
D47	cupped hand	det. hand *(ḏrt)*
D48	hand w/no thumb	*šsp* (palm)
D49	fist	det. grasp *(ꜣmm)*
D50	finger	*ḏbꜥ* (finger; 10,000)/when doubled, det. accurate *(mtỉ)*
D51	finger	*dḳrw* (fruit); *ḳꜣw; ꜥnt* fingernail; measure *(ḫꜣỉ)*
D52	penis	*mt*/det. male *(ṯꜣy)*; donkey *(ꜥꜣ)*; bull *(kꜣ)*
D53	dripping penis	*bꜣḥ*/det. penis *(ḥnn)*; urinate *(wsš)*; husband *(hy)*
D279	testicles	*ḫrwỉ* (testicles)
D280a	pelvis and vulva	*ḥm; ỉdt* (vulva; cow)

D54		walking legs	*ỉw*; *nmtt* (step)/det. motion
D55		walking legs	det. reverse *(ꜥnn)*
D56		leg	*pds*; *rd* (foot); *wꜥrt* (district); *sbḳ* (excellent); *gḥs* (gazelle)/det. foot and associated actions
D57		leg w/knife	*ỉꜣṯw* (place of execution); *siꜣtỉ* (fruit)/det. mutilate
D58		lower leg and foot	*b*; *bw* (place; thing)
D59		leg and arm	*ꜥb*
D60		leg w/water jar	*wꜥb* (clean; pure)
D61		toes(?)	*sꜣḥ* (toe; kick; touch with the foot)

E. Mammals

E1		bull	*kꜣ* (bull, ox); *ỉḥw* (cattle)/det. cattle *(mnmnt)*
E2		charging bull	*kꜣ* (bull)/det. fighting bull *(smꜣ)*
E3		calf	det. calf *(bḥs)*; short-horned cattle
E4		divine cow	det. sacred cow *(ḥsꜣt)*
E5		cow nursing calf	det. solicitous *(ꜣms)*
E6		prancing horse	*ssmt* (horse)/det. horse
E7		donkey	*ꜥꜣ* (donkey)/det. donkey
E8		kid	*ỉb*/det. goat. Also E8a 
E9		newborn antelope	*ỉw*
E10		ram	*bꜣ* (ram); *ẖnmw* (Khnum)/det. sheep. Also E11 
E12		pig	det. pig *(rrỉ)*
E13		cat	det. cat *(mỉw)*
E14		dog	det. dog *(ỉw; ṯsm)*
E15		recumbent jackal	*ỉnpw* (Anubis); *ḥry-sštꜣ* (one over the secrets)/det. Anubis. Also E16 
E17		jackal	*sꜣb* (jackal; dignitary; judge)/det. jackal; dignitary; judge
E18		jackal on standard	*wp-wꜣwt* (Wepwawet)/det. Wepwawet
E20		inidentified canine	*stẖ/stš* (Seth)/det. turmoil; chaos. Also E21 
E22		lion	*mꜣi* (lion)/det. lion
E23		recumbent lion	*l; rw*; *rw* (lion)
E24		panther	*ꜣby* (panther; leopard)/det. panther; leopard
E25		hippopotamus	det. hippopotamus *(db)*
E26		elephant	*ꜣbw* (Elephatine)/det. elephant
E27		giraffe	*mmỉ* (giraffe)/det. foretell *(sr)*; giraffe
E28		oryx	det. oryx *(mꜣ-ḥḏ)*
E29		gazelle	det. gazelle *(gḥs)*
E30		ibex	det. ibex *(miꜣw)*
E31		goat w/collar	*šꜣḥ* (privilege)/det. privilege
E32		baboon	det. baboon *(iꜥn)*; monkey *(ky)*; furious *(ḳnd)*
E33		monkey	det. monkey *(gỉf)*
E34		hare	*wn*

F. Parts of Mammals

F1		head of ox	*kꜣ; ỉḥ* (cattle)

F2	head of charging bull	det. rage *(ḏnd)*
F3	head of hippopotamus	*ꜣt* (moment)/det. power; might
F4	forepart of lion	*ḥꜣt* (front)
F5	head of antelope	*sšꜣ* (skilled)/det. prayer; pylon. Also F6
F7	head of ram	*šft* (ram's head)*; šfyt* (worth)/det. worth. Also F8
F9	head of panther	*ꜣt;* doubled *sp̣ḥty* (strength)
F10	head and neck of animal	det. neck *(ḫḫ)*; throat. Also F11
F12	head and neck of jackal	*wsr*
F13	horns	*wp*; *wpt* (brow)
F14	horns w/year sign	*wp-rnpt* ("Opening of the Year" – New Year's*)*. Also F15
F16	horn	*ꜥb*; *ꜥb* (horn)
F17	horn w/water jar	*ꜥbw* (purificatin)
F18	tusk	*bḥ, ḥw*/det. tooth *(i͗bḥ; nḥḏt)*
F19	jaw	det. jaw *(ꜥrt)*
F20	tongue	*ns*; *ns* (tongue); *i͗mi͗-r* (overseer)
F21	cow's ear	*sḏm, i͗dn*; *msḏr* (ear); *ḏrḏ* (leaf)/det. ear
F22	lion's hindquarters	*pḥ*; *pḥwi͗* (end); *kfꜣ* (discreet)/det. end; bottom
F23	foreleg of ox	foreleg (*ḫpš)*/det. ursa major *(msḫti͗w)*. Also F24
F25	hoof	*wḥm*; *wḥm*/*wḥmt* (hoof)
F26	animal skin	*ẖn*; *ẖnt* (hide, skin)
F27	cowskin	det. hide; leather *(dḥr)*; mouse *(pnw)*
F28	cowskin	*ꜣb; sꜣb*; *sꜣb* (dappled). See also U32
F29	skin w/tail and arrow	*st; sti͗* (shoot)/det. shoot
F30	waterskin	*šd*
F31	three foxtails	*ms*
F32	udder	*ẖ*; *ẖt* (belly, body)
F33	tail	*sd* (tail)
F34	animal heart	*i͗b* (heart)/det. heart *(ḥꜣti͗)*
F35	heart and windpipe	*nfr*
F36	lungs and windpipe	*smꜣ*/unite *(smꜣ)*
F37	spine and ribs	*i͗ꜣt* (back). Also F38. Sometimes variant of M21
F39	spine and spinal cord	*i͗mꜣḫ* (honor); *i͗mꜣḫ* (spinal cord)
F40	spine and spinal cord	*ꜣw*
F41	vertebrae	det. back *(psḏ);* Slaughter *(šꜥt)*. Variant of Y10
F42	rib	*spr*; *spr* (rib)
F43	ribs	det. rib *(spḥt)*
F44	joint of meat	*i͗sw*; *i͗wꜥ* (inherit, etc.)/det. femur *(i͗wꜥ);* tibia *(swt)*
F45	cow uterus	*i͗dt* (vulva; cow)
F46	intestine	*pḫr; dbn; ḳꜣb*; midst; turn; intestine; shore. Also F47 , F48 , and F49 .
F50	intestine and cloth	*spḫr*
F51	piece of flesh	*i͗s, ꜣs; ws*; *kns* (vagina); *ꜥt* (body); *ḥꜥw* (flesh - when tripled)
F52	spoor	excrement *(ḥs)*

G. Birds

G1	Egyptian vulture	*ꜣ*
G2	two vultures	*ꜣꜣ*
G3	vulture w/sickle	*mꜣ*
G4	buzzard	*tw; ti͗w*
G5	falcon	*ḥr* (Horus)
G6	falcon w/flail	det. falcon *(bi͗k)*
G7	falcon on standard	*i͗* (I, when speaker is divine)/det. divine
G7b	falcon on stand	*nmti͗* (Nemti – a god)
G8	falcon on gold sign	*bi͗k nbw* (Golden Horus)
G9	falcon w/sun disk	*rꜥ-ḥr-ꜣḫty* (Re-Horakhty)
G10	falcon on divine barque	*skr* (Sokar)/det. Sokar-boat *(ḥnw)*
G11	mummified falcon	det. idol *(ꜥḫm/ꜥšm/ꜥḫm)*; breast *(šnbt)*. Also G12
G13	falcon w/plumes	*ḥrw nḫni͗* (Horus of Edfu/Hierakonpolis)/det. Sopdu *(spdw)*
G14	vulture	*mwt, mi͗t, mi͗wt, mt*; mother *(mwt)*/det. vulture *(nrt)*
G15	vulture w/flail	*mwt* (Mut – goddess)
G16	vulture and cobra	*nbty* (Two Ladies)
G17	owl	*m*
G18	two owls	*mm*
G19	owl w/arm and jar	*mi͗, m*. Also G20
G21	guinea-fowl	*nḥ*; *nḥ* (guinea-fowl)
G22	hoopoe	*ḏb, db*
G23	lapwing	*rḫwt/rḫyt* (subjects). Also G24
G25	crested ibis	*ꜣḫ*
G26	ibis	*ḏḥwty* (Thoth)/det. ibis *(hbi͗)*. Also G26a
G27	flamingo	*dšr*/det. flamingo *(dšr)*
G28	black ibis	*gm*
G29	jabiru	*bꜣ*
G30	three jabirus	*bꜣw* (impressiveness)
G31	heron	det. heron *(bnw)*
G32	heron on standard	*bꜥḥi͗* (inundate)
G33	egret	det. tremble *(sdꜣ/sdꜣdꜣ)*
G34	ostrich	*ni͗w* (ostrich)
G35	cormorant	*ꜥḳ*
G36	swallow	*wr*/det. swallow *(mnt)*
G37	sparrow	det. small *(nḏs)*; bad, evil *(bi͗n)*
G38	goose	*gb, sꜣ*/det. bird; insect; discuss *(wfꜣ)*; idle *(wsf)*; delay *(wdfi͗)*; perish; destroy *(ḥtm)*
G39	duck	*sꜣ*/det. pintail duck *(sr/srt/si͗/si͗t)*
G40	duck flying	*pꜣ*
G41	duck landing	*pꜣ*/det. land, alight *(ḫni͗)*; gather *(sḥwi͗)*; gum *(ḳmyt)*; etc.
G42	fattened bird	*wšꜣ* (fatten)/food *(ḏfꜣw)*
G43	quail chick	*w*; *w* (chick)
G44	two quail chicks	*ww*
G45	chick w/ arm	*wꜥ*

G46	chick w/chisel	*mꜣw*
G47	duckling	*ṯꜣ*; duckling *(ṯꜣ)*
G48	ducklings in a nest	*sš* (nest). Also G49
G50	two plovers	*rḫtỉ* (washerman)
G51	bird eating fish	det. catch fish *(ḥꜣm/ḥỉm)*
G52	bird eating grain	det. feed *(smn)*
G53	human-headed bird	*bꜣ* (ba)
G54	plucked bird	*snḏ;snd*/det. wring the neck *(wšn)*

H. Part of Birds

H1	head of duck	*ꜣpd* (bird); *r* (goose)/det. wring the neck *(wšn)*. Also for H2
H2	head of crested bird	*pꜣḳ, wšm*/det. temple of forehead *(mꜣꜥ)*; real *(mꜣꜥ)*
H3	head of spoonbill	*pꜣḳ*
H4	head of vulture	*rmṯ* (people). Also used for G14
H5	wing	det. wing *(ḏnḥ)*; fly *(pꜣỉ)*
H6	feather	*šw*; *šwt* (feather); *(mꜣꜥt)*/det. Ma'at *(mꜣꜥt)*
H7	claw	*šꜣ*/det. claw *(ỉꜣft)*
H8	egg	*sꜣ* (son)/det. egg *(swḥt)*; the elite *(pꜥt)*

I. Reptiles, Amphibians, and their Parts

I1	lizard	*ꜥšꜣ*/det. lizard
I2	turtle	*štỉw* (turtle)/det. turtle
I3	crocodile	*ỉty* (sovereign – when doubled)/det. crocodile; aggression
I4	crocodile on shrine	*sbkw* (Sobek)/det. Sobek
I5	crocodile	*sꜣḳ* (collect)/det. collect
I6	crocodile scale	*km*
I7	frog	*wḥm ꜥnḫ* (repeating life)/det. frog *(ḳrr)*; Heqat *(ḥḳt)*
I8	tadpole	*sꜣḳ* (collect)/det. collect
I9	horned viper	*f*/det. father *(ỉt)*
I10	cobra	*ḏ*
I11	two cobras	*ḏḏ*
I12	hooding cobra	det. uraeus *(ỉꜥrt)*; names of goddesses
I13	hooding cobra on basket	det. Wadjet *(wꜣḏt)*; names of goddesses
I14	snake	det. snake *(ḥfꜣw)*; worm. Also I15

K. Fish and Parts of Fish

K1	bulti-fish	*ỉn*/det. bulti- fish *(ỉnt)*
K2	barbel	det. abomination *(bwt)*
K3	mullet	*ꜥḏ*/det. mullet *(ꜥḏw)*
K4	oxyrhynchus fish	*ḫꜣ*; *ḫꜣt* (oxyrhynchus - a fish)
K6	fish scale	*nšmt* (fish scale)
K7	blowfish	det. angry *(špt)*
K8	catfish	*nꜥr* (catfish)

L. Insects and Invertebrates

L1	scarab beetle	*ḫpr*; *ḫpr* (scarab beetle)

L2	bee	*bỉt* (bee; honey); *bỉty* (He of the Bee; King of Lower Egypt)
L3	fly	det. fly (*ꜥff*)
L4	locust	det. locust *(snḥm)*
L6	shell	*ḫꜣ*
L7	scorpion	*srḳt* (Selket – protective goddess)

M. Vegetation

M1	tree	*ỉm; ỉmꜣ; ỉꜣm*/det. fortunate *(mꜥr)*; wing *(ngt; nbs)*
M2	plant	*ḥn*/det. light *(ỉsỉ)*; tomb *(ỉs)*; old *(ỉs)*; plant. See also A1; T24.
M3	stick	*ḫt*; *ḫt* (wood, stick, tree, mast)/det. seek *(ḏꜥr)*
M4	palm rib	*rnpt* (year); *ḥsbt* (regnal year); *snf* (last year – doubled)/det. young *(rnpỉ)*; time, season *(tr)*
M5	palm rib w/bread	*tr* (time, season). Also M6
M7	palm rib w/stool	*rnpỉ* (young)
M8	pool with lilies	*šꜣ*; *ꜣḫt* (Inundation - season); *šꜣ* (pool, marsh)
M9	lily orl otus	*sssnỉ* (lily, lotus)
M10	lily bud	det. lily; lotus bud *(nḥbt)*
M11	flower on stem	*wdn* (dedicate; offer). Variant of F47
M12	lotus bud	*ḫꜣ*; *ḫꜣ* (1,000; lily or lotus)
M13	papyrus plant	*wꜣḏ/wꜣd; wḏ/wd*; *wꜣḏ* (papyrus column)
M14	cobra and papyrus	*wꜣḏ/wꜣd; wḏ/wd*
M15	clump of papyrus	*ꜣḫ*; *wꜣḫ; mḥw* (north; delta)/det. papyrus *(ḏyt)*
M16	clump of papyrus	*ḫꜣ*; *mḥw* (north; delta)
M17	read leaf	*ỉ*; *ỉ* (reed). See also A1
M17	two reed leaves	*y*
M18	reed leaf on legs	*ỉ*; *ỉỉ* (come)
M19	leaf and club	*ꜥꜣbt* (offer)/det. offer
M20	field of reeds	*sm; sḫt* (field); *sḫtỉ* (peasant)
M21	field of reeds w/root	det. grass *(sm)*; help *(sm)*
M22	sedge plant	*nḫb*
M22	two sedge plants	*nn*
M23	sedge plant	*sw*; *swt* (sedge); *nswt* (king). See also M24, M26.
M24	sedge w/mouth	*rsw* (south). Also M25
M26	flowering sedge	*šmꜥ*; *šmꜥw* (Upper Egypt). Also M27
M28	sedge w/hobble	*10 (mḏw)-šmꜥw* (tens of Upper Egypt)
M29	seed pod	*nḏm*; *nḏm* (pleasant)
M30	root	*bnr* (sweet)
M31	rhizome	det. grow *(rd)*; firm *(rwḏ)*. Also M32
M33	grain	*ỉtỉ* (grain)
M34	emmer wheat	*bdt/btỉ* (emmer)
M35	pile of grain	det. heap *(ꜥḥꜥw)*
M36	bundle of flax	*ḏr*/det. bundle *(dmꜣ)*. Also M37
M40	bundle of reeds	*ỉs*
M41	piece of wood	det. wood *(wꜥn)*
M42	rosette	*wn*

M43	grapes on trellis	*ỉrp* (wine); *kꜣny* (gardener)/det. fruit *(dꜣb)*
M44	thorn	*spd* (sharp)/det. thorn *(srt)*; white-bread *(t-ḥḏ)*

N. Sky, Earth, Water

N1	sky	*ḥrỉ* (upper); *hꜣyt* (ceiling; portal)/det. sky *(pt)*; above; gate *(rwt)*
N2	sky w/scepter	*grḥ* (night). Also N3
N4	sky w/rain	*ỉꜣdt* (dew)/det. rain *(šnyt)*
N5	disk of sun	*rꜥ* (sun; Re); *hrw* (day); *sw* (day)/det. time *(wnwt)*
N6	sun disk w/cobra	*rꜥ* (Re – the sun god)/det. Re
N7	sun on a butcher's block	*ḫrt-hrw* (daytime)
N8	sun w/rays streaming down	*wbn*; *ḥnmmt* (human beings)
N9	moon	*psḏ, psḏntỉw*. Also N10; variant of X6.
N11	crescent moon	*ỉꜥḥ* (moon); *ꜣbd* (month); *wꜥḥ* (carob bean); *šsp* (palm). Also N12. Variant of F42
N13	star w/quarter moon	*mḏdỉwnt/smdt* (half-month festival)
N14	star	*sbꜣ, dwꜣ*; *wnwt* (hour)/det. star *(sbꜣ)*
N15	star inside circle	*dwꜣt* (Duat – the Netherworld)
N16	land w/sand beneath it	*tꜣ*; *tꜣ* (land, earth, world)/det. eternity *(ḏt)*. Also N17
N18	strip of land	*ỉw* (island); *sṯꜣt* (aroura)/det. desert; foreign land.
N19	two strips of land	*ꜣḫtỉ* (Akhet)
N20	tongue of land	*wḏb/wdb*/det. land; short *(wḏb)*/det. Sed festival *(ḥb-sd)*. Also N22.
N21	tongue of land	*ỉdb* (bank); *ỉdbwỉ*
N23	canal	*gbb/gbw* (Geb – earth god)/det. land
N24	system of canals	*spꜣt* (nome); *ḏꜣtt* (estate; farm)/det. garden *(ḥsp)*
N25	mountain range	*ḫꜣst* (foreign land; desert)
N26	two mountains or hills	*ḏw*; *ḏw* (mountain)
N27	sun between two hills	*ꜣḫt* (Akhet)
N28	rays of sun behind hill	*ḫꜥ*
N29	hill	*ḳ*
N30	hill w/shrubs	*ỉꜣt* (mound)
N31	road bordered by shrubs	*wꜣt* (road); *wꜣỉ* (tend, start)
N32	lump of clay	Variant of Aa2 and F52
N33	grain of sand	det. sand; mineral. Tripled, in place of plural strokes.
N34	metal ingot	*ḥmt* (copper; bronze)
N35	wave of water	*n; nt*
N35a	three waves	*mw*; *mw* (water)
N36	canal	*mr, mỉ*; *mr* (canal)/det. body of water
N37	pool of water	*š*; *šỉ* (basin, pool, lake); *sṯꜣt* (aroura); Also N38; N39
N40	feet and pool	*šm*
N41	well	*ḥm; bỉꜣ; pḥww* (outer limits – tripled)/det. well *(ḥnmt)*; copper.

O. Structures and Parts of Structures

O1	house plan	*pr*; *pr* (house)/det. building; place
O2	house plan w/mace	*pr-ḥḏ* (treasury)

O3	house plan w/oar & bread	*prt-ḫrw* (invocation offerings)
O4	courtyard	*h*; *h* (courtyard)
O5	wall	*nm, mr*/det. street *(mrrt)*
O6	enclosure	*ḥwt* (enclosure). Also O7
O8	enclosure w/column	*ḥwt-ꜥꜣ* (Great Enclosure – temple of On)
O9	enclosure w/basket	*nbt-ḥwt* (Nephthys – goddess; sister of Osiris)
O10	enclosure w/falcon	*ḥwt-ḥr* (Hathor – goddess of love and music)
O11	palace w/battlements	*ꜥḥ* (palace). Also O12
O13	crenellated enclosure	det. wall in *(sbḫ)*. Also O14
O15	enclosure w/pot	*wsḫt* (broad hall)
O16	cornice w/uraei	*tꜣyt* (curtain); *tꜣỉtỉ* (he of the curtain). Also O17
O18	Upper Egyptian shrine	*kꜣr* (shrine)
O19	shrine w/flagpoles	*pr-wr* (Great House – original shrine of Upper Egypt at Hierakonpolis); *ỉtrt šmꜥt* (Nile Valley shrine)
O20	Lower Egyptian shrine	det. shrine *(ỉtrt; pr-nw)*
O21	façade of shrine	*sḥ* (booth)
O22	booth	*ḥꜣb; sḥ* (tent; booth)/det. counsel, advice *(sḥ)*
O23	double throne platform	*ḥb-sd* (Heb-Sed, Sed Festival)
O24	pyramid	det. pyramid *(mr)*
O25	obelisk	*tḫn* (obelisk)
O26	stela	*wḏ* (stela)
O27	columned hall	*ḫꜣwỉ* (dusk)/det. hall
O28	column	*ỉwn*; *ỉwn* (column)
O29	wooden column	*ꜥꜣ*
O30	crutch	*sḫnt* (support)
O31	door leaf	*ꜥꜣ* (door)/det. open
O32	doorway	*sbꜣ* (doorway)
O33	niched façade	det. serekh *(srḫ)*—rectangle enclosing the name of the king
O34	doorbolt	*s*; *s* (doorbolt). See also R22.
O35	doorbolt on legs	*s*
O36	wall	*ỉnb* (wall)/det. enclosure wall *(sbtỉ)*
O37	falling wall	det. topple *(wḥn)*; tilt *(gsꜣ)*
O38	corner	*tm; ḳnbt* (kenbet—council)/det. corner *(ḳnbt)*
O39	stone block	det. stone *(ỉnr)*; brick
O40	staircase	*rwd* (stairs); *ḫtỉw* (terrace)
O41	double staircase	det. stairway; ascend
O42	fence	*šsp, sšp*. Also O43
O44	emblem of Min	*ỉꜣt* (office)
O45	part of a dome	*ipꜣt* (private quarters). Also O46
O47	enclosed mound	*nḫn* (Hierakonpolis); *mḫnt* (jasper). Also O48
O49	crossroads	*nwt/nỉwt* (town)
O50	threshing floor	*sp*; *sp* (time; occasion; event)/det. threshing floor *(spt)*
O51	pile of grain in granary	*šnwt* (granary)

P. Ships and Parts of Ships

P1	boat	*dpt/ḥꜥw/ỉmw/ḳꜣḳꜣw* (boat)
P2	boat under sail	det. sail/travel upstream *(ḫntỉ)*
P3	divine barque	*wỉꜣ* (sacred barque)
P4	boat w/net	*wẖꜥ*
P5	sail and mast	*ṯꜣw* (air); *nfw* (sailor)
P6	mast	*ꜥḥꜥ*
P7	mast and arm	*ꜥḥꜥ*
P8	oar	*ḫrw*; *ḫrw* (voice); *ḥipt* (oar)
P9	oar and snake	*ḥr.fi* (says; said)
P10	steering oar	det. rudder *(ḥmw)*
P11	mooring post	det. moor; die *(mnỉt)*

Q. Domestic and Funerary Furniture

Q1	throne	*st, ws, ḥtm*; *st* (seat, place)
Q2	carrying chair	*ws*; *st* (seat)
Q3	stool	*p*
Q4	headrest	det. headrest *(wrs)*
Q5	chest	det. chest; box *(hn)*
Q6	coffin	*ḳrs* (bury)
Q7	brazier	*srf* (temperature); *nsrsr* (Island of Flame)/det. cook *(fsỉ)*

R. Temple Furniture

R1	offering table	*ḫꜣwt/ḫꜣyt* (altar). Also R2
R3	low offering table	*wḏḥw* (offering table)
R4	mat w/bread loaf	*ḥtp*; *ḥtp* (offering table)
R5	censer	*k(ꜣ)p*; *kꜣp* (fumigate). Also R6
R7	bowl w/smoke	*snṯr* (incense)
R8	flagpole w/flag	*nṯr*; *nṯr* (god)
R9	flagpole on bag	*bd* (incense)
R10	flag w/butcher's block	*ẖrỉ-nṯr/ẖrt-nṯr* (necropolis)
R11	reed column	*ḏd*; *ḏd* (djed-column/amulet)
R12	carrying standard	det. standard *(iꜣt)*
R12a	standard w/land sign	det. Ha (a god) *(hꜣ)*
R14	feather on standard	*ỉmnt* (West); *wnmỉ* (right). Also R13
R15	standard	*ỉꜣb* (East; left); Variant of U23
R16	scepter w/feathers	*wẖ* (emblem of Qus)
R17	wig and feathers on pole	*tꜣ-wr* (This – nome in Middle Egypt). Also R18
R19	scepter w/feather	*wꜣst* (Thebes)
R20	Seshat emblem	*sšꜣt* (Seshat – goddess of writing and measurement)
R22	Min emblem	*ḫm*; *mnw* (Min - a god). Also R23
R24	two bows bound together	*nit/nrt* (Neith – goddes of warfare). Also R24

S. Regalia and Clothing

S1	white crown	*ḥḏt* (white crown).
S3	red crown	*n*/det. red crown *(nt)*. Also S4. See also L2.

S5	double crown	*sḫmtỉ* (double crown). Also S5
S7	blue war helmet	*ḫprš* (blue crown)
S8	Atef crown	*ꜣtf* (Atef Crown)
S9	double plumes of Amen	*šwtỉ* (double plumes)
S10	fillet	*mḏḥ*; *mḏḥ* (fillet; headband); *wꜣḥw* (wreath)
S11	broad collar	*wsḫ*; *wsḫ* (broad collar)
S12	beaded collar	*nbw* (gold)/det. precious metal
S13	collar and leg	*nb*
S14	collar and mace	*ḥḏ* (silver)
S14s	collar and scepter	*ḏꜥm* (electrum)
S15	pectoral	*ṯḥn* (sparkle); *šsmt* (malachite). Also S16 and S17.
S18	necklace w/counterwieght	*mnỉt* (bead necklace; counterweight)
S19	necklace w/seal	*ḫtm* (seal); *š(n)tỉ* (ring)
S20	necklace w/seal	*ḫtm* (seal); *š(n)tỉ* (ring)
S21	ring	det. ring *(ỉwꜥw)*
S22	shoulder knot	*sṯ; st*; *tꜣ-wr* (port)
S23	knotted cloth	*dmḏ/dmd*; *dmḏ/dmd* (total)
S24	belt w/knot	*ṯꜣs*; *ṯꜣs, ṯs* (knot); *ṯꜣs* (vertebra)
S25	apron	*ỉꜥꜣw* (guide; interpreter; dragoman)
S26	kilt	*šndyt/šnḏwt* (kilt)
S27	fringe	*mnḫt* (cloth)
S28	cloth w/fringe	*mnḫt* (cloth)
S29	folded bolt of cloth	*s*; *snb* (abbreviation for health)
S30	cloth w/viper	*sf*
S31	cloth w/sickle	*smꜣ*
S32	cloth w/fringed edge	*sỉꜣ*; *sỉꜣ* (fringed cloth)
S33	sandal	*ṯbt* (sandal); *ṯbw* (sandalmaker)
S34	sandal strap	*ꜥnḫ*; *ꜥnḫ* (sandal strap); *ꜥnḫ* (mirror)
S35	fan	*šwt* (shadow, shade); *sryt* (fan)
S36	fan	Variant of S35. Doubled, *ḥỉpwỉ* (Hepwi – a god)
S37	fan	*ḫw* (fan)
S38	shepherd's crook	*hkꜣ*; *ḥkꜣ* (ruler); *ḥḳꜣt* (scepter)
S39	shepherd's crook	*ꜥwt*
S40	staff w/animal head	*wꜣs*; *wꜣs* (staff); *ỉꜣtt* (Iatet - goddess of milk); *ỉꜣtt* (milk, cream). See also S41 and R19.
S41	staff w/animal head	*ḏꜥm*; *ḏꜥm* (staff)
S42	scepter	*sḫm, ꜥbꜣ*; *sḫm* (sistrum); *ꜥbꜣ* (scepter, stela); *ḫrp* (manage)
S43	staff	*md*; *mdw* (staff)
S44	staff w/flail	*ꜣms* (Ames scepter)
S45	flail	*nḫꜣḫꜣw* (flail)

T. Warfare, Hunting, and Butchery

T1	mace w/flat head	*mn*
T2	mace w/round head	det. smite *(sḳr)*
T3	mace w/round head	*ḥḏ*; *ḥḏ* (mace). Also T5 and T6.

T6	mace w/cobras	*ḥḏḏ*
T7	axe	det. carpenter (*mḏḥ*); axe (*mỉbt*)
T7a	axe	det. axe (*ꜣkḥw*)
T8	dagger	*tp*/det. dagger (*mtpnt*)
T8a	dagger	det. dagger (*bꜣgsw*)
T9	bow	*pḏ*/*pd*; *pḏt* (bow). Also T9a and T10 .
T11	arrow	*sỉn; swn; sšr; sẖr*/det. arrow
T12	bowstring	*rwḏ*/*rwd*; *rwḏ* (bowstring); *dꜣr* (subdue)
T13	pices of wood tied together	*rs*
T14	throwstick	*ꜥꜣm* (Asiatic); *ṯḥnw* (Libyan); *ḥḳꜣt* (heqat – unit of measurement); *ḳmꜣ* (throw); *ḳmꜣỉ* (create)/det. foreign. Variant of D50; M3; P11; S39; T13; Aa6. Also T15 .
T16	scimitar	det. scimitar (*ḫpš*)
T17	chariot	*wrrt* (chariot)
T18	crook w/package	*šms*
T19	harpoon head	*ḳs*; *gnwt* (annals); *gnwty* (sculptor)/det. bury (*ḳrs*); pure (*twr*); bone (*ḳs*). Also T20 .
T21	harpoon	*wꜥ*
T22	arrowhead	*sn*. Also T22 .
T24	net	*ꜥḥ*/*ỉb*
T25	reed float	*ḏbꜣ*/*dbꜣ*
T26	bird trap	*sẖt* (trap). Also T27 .
T28	butcher's block	*ẖr*
T29	block w/knife	*nmt* (slaughtering place)
T30	knife	*dmt* (knife)/det. sharp
T31	knife sharpener	*šm*. Also T32 and T33 .
T34	butcher's knife	*nm*/det. butcher's knife (*nm*). Also T35 .

U. Agriculture, Crafts, and Professions

U1	sickle	*mꜣ*/det. reap; crooked. Also U2 , U3 , U4 , U5 .
U6	hoe	*mr*/det. hack. Also U7 .
U8	hoe	*ḥn*
U9	sack of grain	*ḥḳꜥt* (heqat); *ỉpt* (oipe)/det. grain (*bdt*). Also U10 .
U11	sack w/crook	*ḥḳꜣt* (heqat). Also U12 .
U13	plow	*šnꜥ; hb*; *prt* (seed)/det. plow (*skꜣ*). Also U14 .
U15	sledge	*tm*
U16	sledge w/jackal head	*bỉꜣ* (wonder)/det. sledge (*wnš*)
U17	pick and basin	*grg*. Also U 18 .
U19	adze	*nw*. Also U20 .
U21	adze w/wood	*stp*/*sṯp*
U22	chisel	det. functional (*mnḫ*); carve (*mnḫ*)
U23	chisel	*ꜣb, mr*
U24	drill for stone	*ḥmwt* (craft). Also U25 .
U26	drill for beads	*wbꜣ* (open). Variant of U24. Also U27 .
U28	fire-drill	*ḏꜣ; wḏꜣ* (abbreviation for prosperity). Also U 29 .

U30		kiln	*tꜣ*
U31		baker's rake	*ẖnr* (restrain); *rḥtỉ* (baker). Variant of D19-20
U32		pestle and mortar	*ḥsmn* (natron; bronze)/det. set; fix *(smn)*; pound; heavy *(dns)*
U33		pestle	*tỉ/t*
U34		spindle	*ḫsf*/det. spin *(ḫsf)*. Also U35 .
U36		launderer's club	*ḥm*
U37		razor	det. shave *(ẖꜥḳ)*
U38		scale	*mḫꜣt* (scale, balance)/det. scale
U39		part of scale	det. hold up; carry; wear *(wṯs)*; pick up *(ṯsỉ)*. Also U40 .
U41		plumb bob	det. plumb bob *(tḫ)*

V. Rope, Baskets, and Cloth

V1		coil of rope	*šn*; *št* (100)/det. rope; tie; coil
V2		coil of rope w/door bolt	*sṯꜣt* (aroura)/det. pull *(sṯꜣ)*; hasten *(ꜣš)*
V3		three coils of rope	*sṯꜣw* (in *r-sṯꜣw* – the Giza necropolis)
V4		lasso	*wꜣ*
V5		loop of rope	*snṯ* (lay out)
V6		loop of rope	*sš*, *sšr*; *šsrw/šs* (linen)
V7		loop of rope	*šn*. Also V8 .
V9		rope in round shape	*šnw* (circuit of the sun)
V10		rope in oval shape	det. cartouche *(šnw)*; name *(rn)*
V11		part of cartouche	*pḫꜣ* (kind of grain); *ḏỉwt/dyt* (shriek)/det. dam *(dnỉ)*; split *(pḫꜣ)*
V12		string	*ꜥrḳy* (last day of the month); *fḫ* (loosen)/Phoenicians *(fnḫw)*; loosen *(fḫ)*; bine *(ꜥrḳ)*; papyrus scroll *(šfdw)*; string, swear *(ꜥrḳ)*
V13		hobble	*ṯ/t*. Also V14
V15		hobble w/legs	*ỉṯ*
V16		hobble for cattle	*sꜣ*
V17		rolled-up tent	*sꜣ*; Also V18 .
V19		hobble	*tmꜣ*; *mḏt* (stable; stall); *ẖꜣr* (sack)/det. shrine*(kꜣr)*; palanquin *(ḳnỉ)*; sheaf *(ḳnỉ)*; mat *(tmꜣ)*
V20		hobble	*mḏ* (ten)
V21		hobble w/cobra	*mḏ*
V22		whip	*mḥ*; Also A23 .
V24		string wound on stick	*wḏ/wd* Also V25 .
V26		spool w/thread	*ꜥḏ/ꜥd*; *ꜥḏ* (reel). Also V27 .
V28		wick	*ḥ*
V29		swab	*wꜣḥ/sk*/det. ward off *(ḫsr)*. See also M1.
V30		basket	*nb*
V31		basket w/handle	*k*
V32		wicker satchel	*msn*/det. bundle *(gꜣwt)*; lack *(gꜣw)*; need *(ḏꜣrw)*
V33		bag	*g*; *šrw* (grain)/det. envelop *(ꜥrf)*; perfume *(stỉ)*; fine linen *(šs(r))*. Also V34 and V35 .
V36		cloth bag	*ḥn*
V37		bandage	*ỉdr* (herd)/det. bandage *(ỉdr)*
V38		bandage	det. wrapping *(wt)*

W. Stone and Ceramic Vessels

W1	oil jar	*mrḥt* (oil)
W2	oil jar	*bȝs*/det. oil jar *(bȝs)*. See also W1.
W3	alabaster basin	*ḥb* (feast). Also W4 .
W5	basin and butcher's block	*ẖri-ḥbt* (lector priest)
W6	metal vessel	det. cauldron *(wḥȝt)*
W7	granite bowl	*ȝbw* (Elephantine)/det. granite, proclaim *(mȝṯ)*. Also W8 .
W9	stone jug	*ẖnm*
W10	cup	*ḥnw*; *wsḫ* (wide)/det. cup. See also N41.
W10a	jar	with E10 or G29, *bȝ*
W11	jar stand	*g*; *nst* (seat). Also W12 .
W13	pot	*dšrt* (red-ware)
W14	water jar	*ḥs*/*ḥs*; *ḥst* (water jar)/det. jar *(snbt)*
W15	jar pouring water	*ḳbḥ* (cool water)/det. cool *(ḳbb)*; cool water. Also W16 .
W17	rack of water jars	*ḫnt*; *ḫntw* (jar-rack). Also W18 .
W19	milk jug w/handle	*mi*/det. milk jug *(mḥr)*
W20	milk-jug w/cover	det. milk *(ỉrṯt)*
W21	wine jars	det. wine *(ỉrp)*
W22	beer jugs	*ḥnḳt* (beer); *wdpw* (butler). Also W23 .
W24	pot	*nw, ỉn*/det. council *(ḏȝḏȝt)*; Nekhbet - a goddess *(nḫbt)*. See also W22 and W23.
W25	pot on legs	*ỉn*

X. Bread

X1	*t*	*t* (bread)
X2	*t*	*t* (bread); *ḏḥwtỉ* (Thoth)/det. bread; food. See also X3 . X4 . and X5 .
X6	round loaf of bread	det. origin *(pȝt)*; loaf *(pȝt)*
X7	half a loaf of bread	*wnm* (eat – doubled)/det. bread
X8	bread mold	*dỉ*/*d*/*ḏỉ*

Y. Writing, Games, and Music

Y1	book roll	*dmḏ* (total); *mḏȝt* (scroll; chisel)/det. for words connected with writing and abstract concepts. Also Y2 .
Y3	scribal equipment	*sẖȝ* (write; scribe; etc.)/det smooth *(nꜥꜥ)*; ruddy *(ṯms)*; scribe's kit *(mnhd)*. Also Y4 .
Y5	gameboard and pieces	*mn*
Y6	gamepiece	*ỉbȝ* (game piece; dance)
Y7	harp	det. harp *(bỉnt)*
Y8	sistrum	det. sistrum *(sššt)*
Y10	bundle of stems	det. murderousness *(šꜥt)*

Z. Strokes and Figures

Z1	stroke	Indicates that word is to be read as an ideogram. *wꜥ* (one). Multiple strokes used for numbers from 1 to 9.

Z2	three strokes	Used as ending for plurals, collective nouns, and false plurals. det. think *(ḫmtw)*. Also Z3.
Z4	two strokes	*y* as ending/det. dual
Z5	diagonal stroke	Used as a substitute for complex or dangerous signs
Z6	hieratic prisoner	det. die; enemy
Z7	hieratic quail chick	*w*
Z8	oval	det. round *(šnw)*; oval
Z9	crossed sticks	*swꜣ/swꜣ, sḏ, šbn, ḫbs, wp, wr*/det. break; cross; number. Also Z10.
Z11	crossed planks	*im*. Variant of M42

AA. UNCLASSIFIED

Aa1	placenta?	*ḫ*
Aa2	pustule	det. swelling; unhealthy. Variant in specific words of: F52; N32; M41; V32; V38; W6; W7; Z10. Also Aa3.
Aa4	pot	Variant of W10a
Aa5	part of a ship	*ḥ(i)p*; *ḥipt* (oar)
Aa6	unknown	*ṯmꜣ;* mat *(tmꜣ)*
Aa7	unknown	det. smash *(sḳr)*
Aa8	irrigation channel?	*ḳn, s, ꜥḏ*; *spꜣt* (estate, farm, nome)/det. council *(ḏꜣḏꜣt)*
Aa9	unknown	det. rich *(ḫwd)*
Aa10	unknown	det. writing *(drf)*
Aa11	throne platform	*mꜣꜥ*/det. platform *(ṯntꜣt)*. Also Aa12.
Aa13	unknown	*im, m*. Also Aa14, Aa 15.
Aa16	unknown	*gs*; *gs* (half, side)
Aa17	lid of pot?	*sꜣ*; *sꜣ* (back). Also Aa18.
Aa19	unknown	10 *(mḏw)*/det. prepare *(ḥr);* terrified *(ḥri);* secure *(ṯꜣr)*
Aa20	bag for clothing	*ꜥpr*
Aa21	unknown	*wḏꜥ*; *wḏꜥw* (judged one - Seth). Also Aa22.
Aa24	warp between stakes	*mdd* (puncture; press; adhere)
Aa25	unknown	*smꜣ* (stolist—priest)
Aa26	unknown	det. rebel *(sbi)*
Aa27	spindle	*nḏ*
Aa28	builder's level	*ḳd*. Also Aa29.
Aa30	top of reed bundle	*ḫkr* (adorn)/det. adorn. Also Aa31.

Appendix E: Word List

? cult image?

2nwt (snwt) second

ꜣ

ꜣw ỉb.f happiness (lit. may he be happy)

ꜣbd month

ꜣbḏw Abdju (Abydos)

ꜣpd bird; fowl

ꜣms *ames* scepter

ꜣḫ effective spirit

ꜣḫt horizon

ꜣḫt Akhet (season of the inundation)

ꜣst Isis (sister of Osiris)

ꜣtp carry

ỉ

ỉ my (masculine)

ỉ my (feminine)

ỉ O!

ỉꜣỉ adore

ỉꜣbty eastern

ỉꜣbtt East

ỉꜣtt milk

ỉỉ come

ỉꜥ ascend (with *n*, ascend to)

ỉꜥꜣw foreign worker, interpreter

ỉꜥw tools for ritual washing

ỉwf flesh

ỉw come

ỉwnw Iunu (Heliopolis)

ỉwty who/which is/has not

ỉb heart

ỉbꜣw do a dance

ỉbḥ tooth; dentist

ỉp count; inspect

ỉm give

ỉmꜣw tent

ỉmꜣḫỉ revere (verb); reverence

ỉmy who, which is in

ỉmy-ỉs councillor

ỉmy-wrt starboard

ỉmyt will (last testament)

ỉmn Amen (a god)

ỉmn-rꜥ Amen-Re

ỉmnty western

ỉmntt West, western

ỉmntỉyw Westerners

ỉn by (as agent)

ỉnỉ bring

ỉnw produce

ỉnb wall

ỉnpw Anubis

ỉnn we

ỉnk I

ỉr as for; if

ỉrỉ make; do (verb)

or *ỉry* guardian

ỉry ꜥnt manicurist

ỉry-nḫn guardian of Nekhen

ỉrw census

ỉrp wine

ỉs tomb; council chamber

ỉst crew; gang

ỉst lo!

ỉšd persea fruit

ỉḳr excellent

ỉt father

ỉtn Aten (divine sun disk)

ỉt nṯr god's father

ỉṯỉ take; conquer; wring

ỉdmy idemy cloth

ꜥ

ꜥ arm

ꜥꜣ great

ꜥꜣ Aa linen

ꜥꜣ donkey

ꜥꜣ door

ꜥb impurity; impure

ꜥpr crew; equip

ꜥnḫ life, live (verb)

ꜥnḳt Anuket (goddess)

ꜥnt nail

ꜥḥ palace

ꜥḥꜥw lifetime

ꜥḫnwty audience-chamber

ꜥšꜣ many; much

ꜥšꜣt often

ꜥḳ enter (with *r*, into) (verb)

ꜥg(w)t grain

ꜥḏꜣ wrongly; *m-ꜥḏꜣ*=falsely

ꜥḏ-mr administrator

w

wꜣs dominion

wꜣst Waset (Thebes)

wꜣt path, road

wꜣḏ green, fresh

wꜣḏw green eye paint

wi̓ me

wi̓ separate

wi̓ꜣ sacred barque

wꜥ one, sole, unique

wꜥb pure; purify; cleanse

wꜥb wab priest (literally "purifier")

wꜥḥ carob bean

wꜥty sole, unique

wbn rise

wpi̓ open

wp-wꜣwt Wepwawet

wnn be, exist (verb)

wnn-nfr Wenennefer

wr great, good; great one

wr mꜣꜣ great seer

wḥm repeat (verb); repeater

wḥmw herald

wsi̓r/ꜣsi̓r Osiris (god of dead)

wšꜣ fatten

wt bandages; place of embalming

wḏꜣ prosperity

wḏꜣ proceed; go; set out

wḏyt campaign; expedition

wḏꜥ-mdw judge

b

bꜣ soul

bꜣk servant

bꜣstt Bastet

bi̓ꜣw mine

bi̓n evil, bad

bnw benu-bird; phoenix

bnr sweet

bnrt date wine

bḥdty the Behdetite

bs Bes (household god)

p

pꜣ the; this; that (m.)

pw this

pn this (m.)

pr house

pri̓ go forth

pr ḥḏ treasury

prt Peret (season of emergence)

prt-ḫrw voice (spoken) offerings

psḏ back; spine

psḏt Ennead (group of nine gods)

pt sky

ptḥ Ptah (patron god of Memphis)

pḏt bow; foreigner

f

f he, his, it, its

fsỉ cook, heat

m

m in, from, as

m take

mꜣꜣ see

mꜣꜥ ḫrw true of voice; justified

mꜣꜥt Maat (goddess)

mꜣꜥty Maaty (a place-name)

mꜣ-ḥḏ oryx

mỉ Come!

mỉ like (similar to)

mỉn today

mỉ rꜥ ḏt Like Re, forever

m-ꜥ in the hand/possession/charge of

mw water

mwt mother

mwt Mut (consort of Amen)

mwt nswt mother of the king

mnỉ mooring (metaphor for death)

mnỉw herdsman

mnw Min (god of fertility)

mnw monument

mnmnt animals

mnḫt linen

mnṯw Mentu/Montu (god of war)

mrỉ love

mry beloved

mry fighting bull

mrḥt oil for (anointing)

mḥyt Mehyt

mḥnk intimate

mḥt north

mḥty northern

m-ḫnt southwards

m-ḥd northwards

mḫnt ferry-boat

m ḫrt ḥrw nt rꜥ nb daily

ms bring, carry

msỉ give birth, bear

mswt birth

msn Mesen

msdmt black eye paint

mšꜥ army, expeditionary force

mk Behold!; Look!

mky protect; one who protects

mtw Behold!; Look!

or *mḏꜣt* document

mḏḥ carpenter; craftsman; overseer

mḏḏỉwnt the half-monthly festival

mḏdnỉ Medjedny (a place name)

n

n of (m.), to

n us; we; our

nꜣy n the; these; those (pl.)

nw of (plural)

nwt Nut (goddess of the sky)

nwḏw antelope

nb lord, master

nb each, every, all

nb ỉrt ḫt lord of ritual

nbw gold

nbwty He of Ombos (the god Seth)

nbs zizyphus fruit

nb tꜣwy Lord of the Two Lands

nbty The Two Ladies

nbt-ḥwt Nebthys (goddess)

npt Nepet (a town)

nht sycomore

nḥḥ eternity

nḫn Nekhen (a town)

nḫt strong; victorious; victory

nswt bỉty King of U. and L. Egypt

nfr beautiful; good

ngꜣw long-horned cattle

nst seat, throne

nswt king; king of Upper Egypt

nt of (f.), to

nt Neith (a goddess)

nty who are, which are

ntk you (masculine)

ntṯ, ntt you (feminine)

ntf he; it

nts she; it

ntsn they

ntṯn, nttn you (plural)

nṯr god

ỉt nṯr god's father

nṯr nfr good god/perfect god

nḏm sweet

r

r to, toward; in order to; more than

rꜥ Re (the sun god)

rꜥ sun, day; daylight

r-pꜥ hereditary prince

rmṯ people

rn name; young

rnpt year

rḫ know; one who knows, acquaintance

rḫ nswt king's acquaintance

rs awaken; awakening

rsy south; southern

rdỉ give, put, cause (verb)

h

hꜣỉ descend; tackle (verb)

hꜣỉ naked

hꜣw kindred

hy husband

hn head

hnỉ praise; honor (verb); praise

hrw day

hkꜣ Heka priest

ḥ

ḥꜣ behind

ḥꜣ Ha (a god of the desert)

ḥꜣw wealth

ḥꜣty-ꜥ high official

ḥꜣtt the best

ḥwꜥ (wḥꜥ) carob beans

ḥwt mansion

ḥwt-ḥr Hathor (goddess of love)

ḥwt-nṯr temple

ḥb festival

ḥbs clothe

ḥr upon

ḥr Horus (royal god)

ḥr-ꜥw at once

ḥry sštꜣ one over the secrets

ḥry-tp chief

ḥr nbw Falcon of Gold/Horus of Gold

ḥry-ỉb who dwells in

ḥm servant; Majesty

ḥm nṯr god's servant

ḥm kꜣ ka servant (mortuary priest)

ḥmwt craft

ḥmwwt craftsmen

ḥmt woman; wife

ḥmt nswt wife of the king

ḥmt nswt wrt great wife of the king

ḥnꜥ together with

ḥnk-m offer

ḥnkt beer (the *n* is not written)

ḥsỉ praise

ḥsb counter

ḥsbt (ḥꜣt-sp) year (for regnal dates)

ḥḳꜣ ruler

ꜣ, ỉ, ꜥ, w, b, p, f, m, n, r, h, ḥ, ḫ, ẖ, s, š, ḳ, k, g, t, ṯ, d, ḏ

ḥḳr hungry

ḥḳt Heqat

ḥtp offering

ḥtpw peace

ḥtpt offerings

ḥṯt hyena

ḥḏ white; silver

ḫ

ḫꜣꜥ abandon; despatch (messages)

ḫꜣst foreign land

ḫꜥỉ rise, appear in glory (verb)

ḫꜥ appearance

ḫws slaughter; cut (verb)

ḫpỉ travel; encounter (verb)

ḫpš foreleg of ox

ḫpr form, shape

ḫpr happen; occur (with *m*, become); create

ḫfty enemy

ḫnsw Khonsu (son of Amen)

ḫnt before; in front of

ḫnty who is in front of; foremost

ḫnty-š land official; palace attendent

ḫr before, in front of; with

ḫr fall (verb); fallen one

ḫrw voice

ḫrp, sḫm staff

ḫsfw travel upstream (south)

ḫt wood

ḫt thing

ḫt attendant

ḫt ḥr attendant of Horus

ḫtmw-bỉty sealer of the King of Lower Egypt

ḫdỉ travel downstream (north)

ẖ

ẖꜣt corpse; body

ẖnw interior

ẖnm Khnum (ram-headed god)

ẖr under, carrying

ẖry ḥbt lector priest

ẖrt-nṯr necropolis

ẖkr ornament

ẖkrt wrt great royal ornament

ẖt body

s

s she, hers, it, its

s man

sꜣ son

sꜣ protect, protection; phyle

sꜣw Saw (Sais)

sꜣb many-colored of plumage

sꜣb legal

sꜣb judge

sꜣ nswt king's son

sꜣ nswt n ẖt.f king's son of his bod

sꜣ nswt smsw eldest king's son

sꜣ rꜥ Son of Re

sꜣw guard; protect

sꜣt daughter

sy, s her; it

sꜥḥ noble

sꜥḥꜥ raise up; erect; install

sw him; it

swꜣ cut; break

swꜣỉ pass (*swꜣỉ ḥr*, pass by)

swnw doctor

swt wheat

sbỉ travel; send; watch over (with *ḥr*)

sbk Sobek (crocodile god)

sp inspect

sp time; occasion

spr rib

spr arrive (with *r*, arrive at)

spḥ lasso

sfḫ separate; part (verb)

sm sem priest (funerary priest)

smꜣꜥ justifier

smꜣ n tꜣ ferry

smr companion

smr wꜥty unique companion

smrt ḥr companion of Horus

sḫmḫ-ỉb gladden the heart

smswv elder, eldest

.sn they, theirs

sn them

sn brother, companion

snb health

snmỉ feed

snḥꜣḥꜣ-ỉb soothe the heart

snt sister

snṯr incense

snḏ fear

srd plant

sḥ booth

sḫp bring

sḫpr create; bring into being

sḫm scepter

sḫmt Sekhmet (lion-headed goddess)

sš scribe

sšꜣt Seshat (goddess)

sšr sesher linen

sšḫt (sḫt) cake

sštꜣ secret

skr Sokar (a god)

st them; it

st woman

st (smyt) desert, necropolis

stt Satet/Satis (goddess)

srḳt Selqet (goddess)

stp chosen

st seat; throne

stḫ, stḥ Seth (god of chaos)

sṯt transport worker(s)

sḏm hear

sḏr sleep; spend the night (verb)

š

šꜣd dig

šw empty, free

šw Shu (god of air)

špntỉw the Shepentiu

špss noble; courtier

šmꜥy musucian; singer

šmꜥw Upper Egypt

10 šmꜥw 10 of Upper Egypt

šmꜥt-nfrt fine linen

šmw Shemu (season of summer)

šms follow

šnwt granary

šs alabaster

šsp recieve, accept

ḳ

ḳbḥ container of cool water

ḳrs bury

ḳrst burial

ḳd build

k

(m.) *.k (m.)* you, your

kꜣ ka (the soul)

kꜣ bull

kꜣ meat

kꜣt work

ky another (m.)

kt another (f.)

ꜣ, ỉ, ꜥ, w, b, p, f, m, n, r, h, ḥ, ḫ, ẖ, s, š, ḳ, k, g, t, ṯ, d, ḏ

g

gb Geb (god of earth)

grḥ night

gḥs gazelle

gs side

t

t you, your (f.)

t bread

tꜣ earth

tꜣ the; this; that (f.)

tꜣitỉ he of the curtain

tꜣwrt Taweret (goddess)

tỉst intimate

tỉst ḥr intimate of Horus

tw you (masculine); one (impersonal)

tn you (feminine)

tn you (plural)

twt image; statue

tp, tpy upon, who is upon

tpy head; chief

tm Atum (creator god)

tmꜣ bowmen

tn this (f.)

tn you, your (pl.)

tr season

ṯ

ṯ you, your (f.)

ṯꜣw breath; air

ṯꜣw nḏm sweet breath (of life)

ṯꜣty vizier

ṯw you (masculine)

ṯn you (feminine)

ṯn you; your (plural)

ṯs troop

ṯs neck

d

dꜣbw figs

dỉ give, put, cause

dỉ ꜥnḫ ḏt given life, forever

dwꜣ praise; worship

dwꜣ nṯr divine adorer

dwꜣt Duat (Netherworld)

dbḥ funerary requirements

dbḥt-ḥtp funerary meal

dpwt boat

dmỉ town

dng pygmy

dr expel, drive out

ḏ

ḏꜣt crane

ḏꜣtt estate; farm

ḏw mountain

ḏw evil, sad

ḏf(ꜣw) provisions

ḏḥwty Thoth (god of writing)

ḏḥwtt the festival of Thoth

ḏs self

ḏs.f himself

ḏsrt ale

ḏt forever

ḏd speak

ḏd stability

ḏdw Djedu (Busiris)